MARKETS NEVER FORGET (BUT PEOPLE DO)

FISHER INVESTMENTS PRESS

Fisher Investments Press brings the research, analysis and market intelligence of Fisher Investments' research team, headed by CEO and *New York Times* best-selling author Ken Fisher, to all investors. The Press covers a range of investing and market-related topics for a wide audience—from novices to enthusiasts to professionals.

Books by Ken Fisher

Debunkery
How to Smell a Rat
The Ten Roads to Riches
The Only Three Questions That Count
100 Minds That Made the Market
The Wall Street Waltz
Super Stocks
Markets Never Forget (But People Do)

Fisher Investments Series

Own the World by
Aaron Anderson

20/20 Money by
Michael Hanson

Fisher Investments On Series

Fisher Investments on Energy
Fisher Investments on Materials
Fisher Investments on Consumer Staples
Fisher Investments on Industrials
Fisher Investments on Emerging Markets
Fisher Investments on Technology
Fisher Investments on Consumer Discretionary
Fisher Investments on Utilities
Fisher Investments on Health Care

FISHER
INVESTMENTS
PRESS

MARKETS NEVER FORGET (BUT PEOPLE DO)

HOW YOUR MEMORY IS COSTING YOU MONEY—AND WHY THIS TIME ISN'T DIFFERENT

Ken Fisher

with
Lara Hoffmans

WILEY

John Wiley & Sons, Inc.

Published by John Wiley & Sons, Inc., Hoboken, New Jersey.

Published simultaneously in Canada.

Important Disclaimers: This book reflects personal opinions, viewpoints and analyses of the authors and should not be regarded as a description of advisory services provided by Fisher Investments or performance returns of any Fisher Investments client. Fisher Investments manages its clients' accounts using a variety of investment techniques and strategies not necessarily discussed in this book. Nothing in this book constitutes investment advice or any recommendation with respect to a particular country, sector, industry, security or portfolio of securities. All information is impersonal and not tailored to the circumstances or investment needs of any specific person.

Limit of Liability/Disclaimer of Warranty: While the publisher and author have used their best efforts in preparing this book, they make no representations or warranties with respect to the accuracy or completeness of the contents of this book and specifically disclaim any implied warranties of merchantability or fitness for a particular purpose. No warranty may be created or extended by sales representatives or written sales materials. The advice and strategies contained herein may not be suitable for your situation. You should consult with a professional where appropriate. Neither the publisher nor author shall be liable for any loss of profit or any other commercial damages, including but not limited to special, incidental, consequential, or other damages.

For general information on our other products and services or for technical support, please contact our Customer Care Department within the United States at (800) 762–2974, outside the United States at (317) 572–3993 or fax (317) 572–4002.

Wiley also publishes its books in a variety of electronic formats. Some content that appears in print may not be available in electronic books. For more information about Wiley products, visit our web site at www.wiley.com.

Library of Congress Cataloging-in-Publication Data:

Fisher, Kenneth L.
    Markets never forget (but people do) : how your memory is costing you money and why this time isn't different / Ken Fisher with Lara Hoffmans. —1st ed.
      p. cm.
    Includes index.
    ISBN 978-1-118-09154-8 (hardback); ISBN 978-1-118-16760-1 (ebk);
    ISBN 978-1-118-16761-8 (ebk); ISBN 978-1-118-16762-5 (ebk)
      1. Investments.   2. Portfolio management.   3. Finance, Personal.   I. Hoffmans, Lara.
  II. Title.
  HG4521.F5848   2011
  332.6—dc23   2011037193

Printed in the United States of America
10 9 8 7 6 5 4 3 2 1

To Bob Hope—Thanks for the memory.

Contents

Preface

Hope Springs Eternal

Bob Hope (1903–2003) was huge when I was young. Funny, funny, funny! Whether in the *Road to . . .* movies with Bing Crosby (Hope was in 52 major flicks), with the US armed forces overseas wherever conflict occurred at his own personal danger, on TV, doing stand-up, etc., Hope was everywhere. And every performance since 1938 included his anthem, *Thanks for the Memory* (words by Leo Robin, music by Ralph Rainger and first recorded by Hope and Shirley Ross). Hope was huge and beyond great. And hope springs eternal. Then and now! But sadly, our memories aren't so functional. Fact is, our memories are beyond terrible when it comes to economic and market realities.

People forget. So much! So often! So fast! Stuff that happened not long ago—and more often than not. And it causes investing errors—pretty commonly humongous ones. Maybe Hope should have been singing, *Pranks for My Memory.* Because for a fact, our memories play pranks on us in markets, and always have and we never learn.

We forget facts, events, causes, outcomes, even *feelings.* And because we forget, we tend to be hyper-focused on the here-and-now and immediate past—behavioralists call it *myopia.* We tend to think what we see is new and different—and significant—when pretty often, we've seen the exact same thing before or something very close to it and history is littered with similar examples.

This species-wide tendency to myopia isn't accidental—it's evolutionary. Humans evolved over millennia to forget pain fast. If we didn't, we wouldn't do crazy things like hunt giant beasts with sticks and stones or plow our fields again after drought, hail, fire, what-have-you destroyed our crops. And for sure no female would ever have more than one kid. But we do forget, and fast.

Forgetting pain is a survival instinct, but unfortunately, that means we also forget the lessons. Then, too, though people individually forget, markets don't. History does not, in fact, repeat—not exactly. Every bear market has a distinct set of drivers, as does every bull market. But human behavior doesn't change—not enough and not very fast to matter. Investors may not remember how panicked or euphoric they were over past events. They may not remember they had the exact same repeating fears over debt, deficits, stupid politicians, high oil, low oil, consumers spending too much, consumers not spending enough, etc., etc., etc. But markets remember very well that details may change but behavior generally doesn't.

For decades, I've heard otherwise intelligent business folks express (as fact) opinions about current phenomena being extreme, when history shows they're not extreme or even unusual. Examples are plentiful and throughout this book. But if you point out to someone that his opinion-stated-as-fact is actually false, you will run into a brick wall because he simply won't believe it. They *know*. They read it in the media or online. Their friends agree. It's a fact to them. It may also be a false fact and one easily known if we didn't simply forget so easily. But because we forget as individuals, we do so as a society, too.

This is why investors, as a group, make the same mistakes repeatedly. Don't think investors are error-prone? CXO Advisory Group measures so-called gurus—folks who make public market forecasts in a variety of forums. Some also manage money professionally (as I do—they include me in their guru rankings); some don't and instead do newsletters, write columns, etc. But everyone on the list is a professional in some way at making public market proclamations.

And the average accuracy of this group, as measured by CXO? As I write, it's 47%.[1] (See Chapter 1 for how they rate me.) I can't ever recall seeing that average over 50%. And these are pros! This group of well-known, professional market prognosticators is, on average, right *less than half the time!* If that's the case, you know non-professional do-it-yourselfers can't have a much better record. (In fact, the average non-pro investor likely does much, much worse. See Chapter 2.)

We Can't Remember That We Forget

Why do investors fail to be right even half of the time? A huge single reason: We forget! And hence, we don't really learn from past mistakes. Investors get overwhelmed by greed or fear but also forget that being greedy or fearful didn't work out for them in the past. But they *also* forget they were wrongly greedy or fearful because feelings *now* seem so much stronger (even though they're probably not).

They get head-faked by what later turns out to be normal volatility—because they forget they've lived through volatility many times before. They overreact—either too bearish or too bullish— based on some widely dispersed media report that later turns out to be highly overstated or just plain wrong and often backward. Why? They forget the media is often and repeatedly wrong for the exact same reason—it's made up of humans.

They get terrified, for example, by huge market volatility in 2008 that's fairly consistent with the bottoming period of any bear market, though they lived through something similar in 2003 and more so in 1974. And they missed the huge boom off the bottom in 2009—never could imagine stocks could move up so fast— though we saw something similar (to a lesser degree) in 2003. (And 1975–1976—and again and again and again in past bear markets and new bull markets—but 2002 and 2003 were just a few years ago and investors should at least remember that!)

Yes, 2008 was volatile relative to recent history, but not compared with a bit longer history—but investors forget to check history, too. Learning from history is scant in our world. First, history is usually boring to most. And second, most folks can't quite believe in their myopic minds that what happened a few too many decades ago has any bearing on today. In reality, markets don't change much in the basics of how they function because the people whose interactions make them work don't change much over time. One of the most basic lessons of behavioral psychology is that humans are slow to change and learn.

More examples: Investors believe *their* favorite politician from *their* political party is just better for stocks, even though very recent history should teach that no one party is better or worse overall for stocks (Chapter 7). They think their favorite asset class is just better over time, forgetting the not-so-distant past when they were proven wrong (Chapter 6). And they forget that they forgot the last time because it is too painful to do otherwise! And the time before that! Repeatedly making the same errors based on the same misunderstandings and misperceptions.

Fortunately, you needn't be right 100% of the time to do well at investing. Such a thing is impossible. And if you're banking your financial future on being 100% right, you'll be sorely disappointed—for a fact—because no one is ever right all the time. Rather, you want to aim to be right more than wrong. The all-time best investors were wrong an awful lot. In investing, if you're right 60% of the time, you're a legend—and 70% of the time you're a god. Just being right slightly more than 50% of the time means you likely do better than most investors—including the overwhelming bulk of investment professionals.

In my view, a good way to improve your results is aiming to reduce your error rate. If you see the world more clearly and don't fall prey to the same misperceptions that plague most other investors, you can start making fewer mistakes. This is, in essence, what most of my books, *Forbes* columns and other writings are about and have always been about—looking at the world and trying to see it differently but more correctly (in my view) and then determining how to act or not act—all largely centered on error-rate reduction. And you'll still make lots of errors, but that's ok.

And one great tool for seeing the world more clearly and reducing your error rate is simply improving your memory by a steady and regular application of even just a bit of market history. This book shows you how.

History as a (Powerful) Lab

If you go to work tomorrow wearing a green shirt and say, "I'm going to win a million dollars today because everyone knows when you wear a green shirt on Tuesdays, you win a million dollars," your colleagues will grab a giant butterfly net. You're predicting an outcome that 1) has no historical precedent and 2) lacks any rooting in reality. You see that clearly.

Yet every time I talk about history's role as a powerful tool in capital markets forecasting, inevitably some say, "Past performance is no indication of the future!" Well, that's not why you should look at history. Use history as a laboratory—to understand the range of reasonable expectations. For example, when event X happens, the outcomes are usually B, C or D, but can be anywhere from A to F. So I know that anything could happen, but odds are greater something like A through F happens, with odds still higher on B, C and D. And the odds of something outside that range happening is very, very low, so it would take exceptional extra knowledge to bet on something like that happening.

Then, too, you should consider other factors that might affect the outcome—the world of economic, political and sentiment drivers. Maybe Event Y is happening simultaneously, which likely reduces the odds of D happening and increases B. Heck, maybe Event Z is likely to happen soon, which usually near-guarantees a Q, so even though it's an outlier, I know to throw that into my bucket of probabilities. That's how I would have you think—in terms of the probabilities. At its basics, investing is a probabilities game; it's not a certainties game.

But what's interesting is the same people who huff that history isn't a useful guide will still say, with absolute certainty, things like: "This high debt will ruin the economy and drag down stocks." Or, "The economy can't recover with high unemployment." Really? And what's the basis for that?

Presumably, if you say with certainty some condition leads to some other condition, that's because you've *observed that in the past* or can otherwise measure it historically. Either that, or sound economic fundamentals says it must be so. Fair enough? And if a lot of people say Event X must cause Outcome Y, there's no harm in checking to see if that's what happened historically most of the time. Because if it hasn't happened before, it's unlikely to happen now whether most folks think it will or not.

Yet most people in the media, blogosphere or social circuit go nuts when I say there's absolutely no historical precedent—zero—for this particular thing causing that particular outcome once it has become socially accepted that it will. I'll not cite facts and history here—because we will later in the book. But more often than not, things people think of as new, bigger-than-ever, worse-than-ever and certainly causal of predictable outcome are things we've seen many, many times before and can document don't cause the outcomes that are widely and socially expected.

Critics love to criticize the use of market history to debunk widely held views. Yet when people claim things like the economy can't expand because unemployment is too high, *they too are trying to make a historical claim.* Just so happens theirs doesn't hold up since we have a long history of levels of unemployment here and around the world to measure the claim against. In effect, saying high unemployment causes economies to slow or stocks to tank is identical to the magic green shirt claim. It provably isn't so. It's not observable in a lab (i.e., history), and it makes no economic sense for a firm to start aggressively hiring if its sales haven't recovered.

Sometimes, weird stuff happens. You wear your magic green shirt and you *do* win the lottery! Hooray! But no one in their right mind would bet on you winning the lottery again, even if you wore your green shirt and bought 1,000 lottery tickets. Winning the lottery is a *possible* outcome—the odds are just near-immeasurably low. And there's not good evidence the green shirt was a material driver in the previous win. And that you may feel good in green (my favorite color) doesn't change the odds one iota.

That's why history is powerful. Investing, as said earlier, is a probabilities game, not a certainties game. No one can ever say with any certainty what will happen. (Anyone claiming otherwise is probably trying to sell you something very bad for you—or just rob you blind.) Just so, while investing is a *probabilities* game, it's not a *possibilities* game. It's possible you wear a green shirt and win a million dollars! It's possible an asteroid hits Earth and obliterates life as we know it. It's possible you buy a penny stock that turns out to be the next Microsoft. There are endless, almost infinite possibilities. But you can't bet on things just because they are possible. You can't build an investment portfolio around endless possibilities—whether good or bad. (You probably wouldn't get out of bed in the morning if you dwelt on every possibility.) You must instead consider the range of likely outcomes and then form forward-looking expectations based on probabilities. You will be wrong—a lot. Expect it. But if you can craft reasonable probabilities, you likely start getting better results over time (while still being wrong an awful lot).

If you suffer memory loss, that gets very tough to do. But if you remember that you have a lousy memory and can train yourself to use history to understand probabilities, you can better understand what's likelier (or not at all likely) going forward. And you can begin reducing your error rate.

A Walk Down Memory Lane

Throughout the book, I use quotes from old news stories. They're meant to be illustrative, not comprehensive. For example, if I want to show that people frequently fear a double-dip recession early in a new recession—and this isn't a new phenomenon indicative of uniquely new trouble—I show a selection of historic quotes from older news stories. They're meant to show the sentiment existed. Could I have found quotes saying, "No way! Double dippers are crazy! There'll be no double dip," to counter every instance? Sure! But I don't think that's useful to you.

Typically, people tend to seek things reconfirming what they already believe and ignore or discount things not supporting their worldview. This is a known cognitive error people who study all forms of behavioralism (including behavioral finance) call *confirmation bias*. We find evidence to confirm our biases and make ourselves blind to evidence contradicting them. Behavioralists have documented why this is basic to the human condition of successful evolution. It makes us more confident and willing to try harder repeatedly in the face of the brutishly difficult conditions we've faced in normal human evolution. But it hurts in markets.

Further, more investors are prone to be naturally skeptical—bearish—than are prone to be naturally optimistic. Not always and everywhere, and even the most dug-in bears can have times when they're euphorically bullish (though it's usually a bad sign when dug-in bears become bullish). But overwhelmingly, since stocks rise much more than fall (over two-thirds of history), folks counterintuitively tend to be bearish more than bullish. That concept—that people overwhelmingly tend to be fearful when they shouldn't—is at the very core of why so many fail to get the long-term results they want. It's behind the quote Warren Buffett is famous for (though it's not his—he just made it broadly popular): You should be greedy when others are fearful and fearful when others are greedy.

I'm not advocating contrarianism. That doesn't work, either. Just because people mostly think one thing doesn't necessarily mean the opposite will occur, which is the pure definition of contrarianism. Instead, I advocate not blindly following the herd.

The fact is, most people, if already bullish or bearish, usually seek out and believe news stories and pundits supporting their existing view. So yes, you can find plenty of news stories that rationally say at any given time, for example:

- A recession isn't likely.
- This is likely just a correction.
- Global growth is fine.
- Corporate profits are healthy; don't panic.
- And so on.

But if you fail to remember history and are misguidedly bearish more often than not, you likely discount the non-alarmist stories and seek out those who bolster the views you want to have anyway. Ditto if you're misguidedly bullish. Which is why I decided to highlight just a smattering of quotes instead of turning this into an 800-page academic tome. (Plus, it's just fun to see how in history, people have the same exact fears we have now and will have 1, 3, 7, 23 and 189 years into the future.)

So feel free to quibble with the quotes I pulled. I don't expect to change most readers' views because I know most readers are hard-wired to find evidence that confirms their prior biases and make themselves blind to evidence that contradicts them.

But you should feel free to have fun with your own hunt for past stories, headlines, quotes—Google's timeline feature is simultaneously useful and insanely fun. The *New York Times* also has a huge archive of past issues you can access online. And any decent-sized library will have tons of back publications on microfiche—a bit less high-tech than Google but will surely bring back memories of study carrels in the college library (if that's your thing). My point is, none of the sentiments or behaviors I write about here are anything new. And you can use that to your advantage if you can start using history as a tool to counteract what can sometimes be a faulty memory.

Also, this is my eighth book—which I can hardly believe. Though my outlook from year to year changes based on my expectations for the next 12 months or so, my overriding worldview changes much less. I'm a firm believer in capitalism and the power of the capital markets pricing mechanism. As such, I believe supply and demand are the two primary determinants for stock prices—though there are myriad factors impacting both supply and demand.

Therefore, if you've read my past books, you may notice some charts are repeated in some books (though updated with the most recent data). And that's intentional—if there's a powerful way to illustrate some concept, I don't mind re-using that. However, I may describe the chart in a new way or use it in an entirely new context. In fact, in this book I use quite a few charts from my 1987 book *The Wall Street Waltz*—many of them were too good to not use again. After all, in a book about the usefulness of history, I think it's only fair I use a bit of my own history. So I hope you'll forgive me if you've seen some images before—some market truths endure not just the decades of my 40-year professional career but much, much longer.

So let's get to it!

And thanks for the memory.

Acknowledgments

I'm a history buff. I'm a maniac over nineteenth-century steam-era redwood lumbering history—which links to my love of tall trees, particularly redwoods. But I'm also a fan of market and economic history. The redwoods are a hobby, whereas the latter is a hobby that is also a profession I love dearly. So the idea of writing a book (another hobby) about using history seemed like an idea whose time had come. I've written two before (*The Wall Street Waltz* in 1987 and *100 Minds That Made the Market* in 1993), but not for a long, long time and not one like this.

Not only that, but as I write this in 2011, we've just been through a period many called *historic* and *unprecedented*—the 2008 credit crisis, recession and the big 2007–2009 bear market. In many ways, it was historic—a big bear market and an above-average recession. But in many other ways, it was just another bear market. The differences tend to be over-accentuated in our social psyche and the similarities downplayed. The causes were different—they almost always are. But investor behavior into and out of the bear market was pretty standard. In 2010 and even 2011—after the recession was long over—investors were still saying, "This time it's different," and fearing all the same events that had triggered the recession three years prior—though the market had a historically huge surge from its low and global GDP was at all-time highs. But investors almost always disbelieve the recovery and routinely believe the world is irrevocably and fundamentally changed—though it almost never is.

So I decided now was as good a time as ever for a primer on how to use history—not as a silver bullet for forecasting the future (such a thing doesn't exist) but as one additional tool investors can add in the non-stop query session that is capital markets forecasting.

A book is never the work of one person. And a book written by the CEO of an investment firm with tens of billions in assets under management by definition requires a strong supporting cast. Books are a leisure time activity for me, and as the years pass, I find I have ever more demands on my non-working hours. So I must thank Lara Hoffmans—who not only writes endlessly for me and my firm, but manages a group of writers and is managing editor of my firm's daily webzine, *MarketMinder*. For this, my eighth book and our fifth book together, she once again did the grunt work in drafting outlines from my specifications and guidelines for my approval, then providing very polished drafts. She does the hard work, and I have all the fun of conceiving it and then stylizing it—an ideal situation. Not as good as grandchildren—nothing better than that—but pretty darned fun, nonetheless.

Lara has a day job, too—and it seems each year I yank her from it. So I must thank her team for backstopping her while she works on my book. That includes Dave Eckerly, Group Vice President of Corporate Communications, who helped Lara's team load balance, and also Todd Bliman and Amanda Williams—also firm writers who shouldered some of Lara's non-book writing responsibilities with aplomb (and very fine writers in their own rights). Thanks also to Naj Srinivas, Elisabeth Dellinger, Ashley Muth and Evelyn Chea— also members of Lara's team who took on many more of her offloaded tasks. Jake Gamble assisted Lara in running down many of the quotes in the book. My sincere thanks also go to Aaron, Lara's husband, who must deal with her being preoccupied at night and on weekends during what's become annual book season.

Leading the team that provided all the graphs, tables and every datapoint you see in the book was Matt Schrader, Team Leader of our Research Analysis and Production team. Handling most of many day-to-day requests was Danielle Lynch. It's no easy feat providing data for one of my books—we (mostly Lara) double check, triple check, question, challenge and demand duplicate and triplicate confirmation. Theory is fine but doesn't hold water if you can't somehow prove it—and for that we want our data to be sound. Danielle gamely handled it all and never broke a sweat in what is inherently a very sweaty process.

Leila Amiri, a graphic designer at my firm, designed what I think is a very cool cover. Molly Lienesch, Vice President of Branding, always provides excellent advice on positioning the book. And Fab Ornani, Vice President of Marketing Content and resident web guru and Jim Smolinski, Group Vice President of Marketing, assist in our marketing efforts—which my publisher, John Wiley & Sons, likes very much.

As always, many thanks to Jeff Herman, my excellent agent, who led me to John Wiley & Sons. Speaking of Wiley, I must thank Laura Walsh, who is our very patient editor there. She and the rest of the Wiley team, Judy Howarth, Sharon Polese, Nancy Rothschild, Jocelyn Cordova-Wagner and Tula Batanchiev, quite literally make the book what it is. Putting up with me isn't always so easy, and they make it seem very easy, indeed!

I must also thank Jeff Silk and Andrew Teufel, both Vice Chairmen at my firm, and Aaron Anderson and William Glaser. Although they didn't contribute to the book, those four fine gentlemen assist me in guiding portfolios at my firm. They also help me think. Running the business of the firm day to day are Co-Presidents Steve Triplett and Damian Ornani. My firm couldn't be the success it continues to be without those six, and if my firm weren't a success, I doubt anyone would want to read so much as a haiku if I'd written it. I also don't think I'd be able to take the time to create such a work today.

I've saved the most important for last. Sherrilyn, my wife of 41 years. Time on the book is time away from her and my family. I'm eternally grateful for her patience and eternally grateful for her.

KEN FISHER
Woodside, CA

MARKETS NEVER FORGET (BUT PEOPLE DO)

The Plain-Old Normal

Yes Sir, Sir John

"The four most expensive words in the English language are, 'This time it's different.'" So saith Sir John Templeton (1912–2008), forever and ever, amen. Of course, he was only talking about investing. Or maybe spirituality—or maybe both.

To say Sir John is legendary is an injustice to the word *legendary*. He was a mutual fund pioneer—founded and built one of the first big firms. He was a global investing pioneer, too—doing global for clients before anyone did. Sir John had ice water in his veins and really lived the idea: Don't follow the herd. He knew to be greedy when others were fearful and vice versa before Buffett made that his. He never believed in chart voodoo, no matter how trendy it was. He was firmly grounded in fundamentals. He believed in what he called *bargains*.

I was fortunate to meet Sir John several times, and always paid him a lot of attention (not just because I realized we shared the same birthday almost a half century apart). To me, he was personal. He was also humble, understated, unflappable, soft-spoken, courtly, civil and gentlemanly in all circumstances. He was and is an ideal role model for almost anyone—I don't care who you are.

Sir John was simply an all-around great guy. He gave heavily to charitable foundations (many he established himself), among other things the world's largest financial prize, the Templeton Prize in Religion. He was thrifty—preferred driving junky used cars instead of being chauffeured in a limousine. He flew coach. He was knighted (through no fault of his own) but down-to-earth. He played a mean game of poker—put himself through Yale on his winnings. He, like me, thought the US government was a lousy steward of his, yours and his employees' money, so he bolted for the Bahamas. He also built an ongoing business interest, which itself helped launched many thousands of good careers in a well-paying industry—lots of smart folks learned the business at Sir John's knee—not to mention the countless numbers of investors who got wealthier investing with him. It was his success that first made me envision building a big investment firm.

He was a stunning spiritual thinker. If you can ever get your hands on a copy of his long-out-of-print spiritual book, *The Humble Approach*, I assure you, whatever your spiritual views, it will impact them somehow. Sir John was a deep, deep thinker.

But to my mind, one of his greatest contributions was that admirably short admonition. That if you think, "This time it's different," you're in all likelihood dead wrong and almost surely about to cost yourself dearly.

This isn't to say history repeats perfectly. It doesn't—not exactly. That's not what Sir John meant. But a recession is a recession. Some are worse than others—but we've lived through them before. Credit crises aren't new, nor are bear markets—or bull markets. Geopolitical tension is as old as mankind, as are war and even terror attacks. Natural disasters aren't new! And this idea that natural disasters are bigger, badder and more frequent now simply isn't true. Only human arrogance allows us to believe we're living in some new, unique age. Sure, we are—just like every previous generation did. And in that sense, Sir John understood the great value of studying and remembering history. Without that history anchor, you have no context to understand the here-and-now or any way to determine what's reasonable to expect in the future. Sir John was a historian in a world in which most market practitioners' sense of history is largely limited to their career span.

Sir John also knew then what every good investor should know now (but they don't because they forget): Humans don't evolve fast. We don't! The same things that freaked us out during the early Mesopotamian market days are the types of things freaking us out in the twenty-first century. And because human nature is a slowly evolving beast, the scenery can change, but we still have the same basic reactions to things.

We have the same reactions because *we don't remember* very well at all. My line on this subject is that societally, we're like chittering chimpanzees with no memories. We chitter about whatever without any sense of history, data or analysis. Sir John was exquisite with all three and knew we falsely believe every recession that hits is more agonizingly painful than the last. Every credit crisis we live through we think beats all the rest. (Anyone who thinks the 2008 credit crisis was history's worst knows zero about nineteenth-century history. Zippo!) Behaviorally, this is evolution's gift to humanity so we don't give up in despair.

And that's why Sir John's admonition that *it's never different this time* is so eternally useful. No matter how big and scary something seems, we've almost always been through something similar before. And if you can remember that and find those times and learn the lessons from them, you can know better how to react—or not react. You can know that it's never as bad or as great or as lasting as your Swiss-cheese monkey's memory makes you think.

What's also not different this time is how resilient economies and capital markets are—particularly in more developed countries. People forget that. Sir John never would. There's this nonsense notion about secular bear markets lurking around every corner (Chapter 4). But if that's true and if capital markets aren't remarkably resilient, how can it be the value of all publicly traded stocks globally keeps rising over time—currently $54 trillion?[1] Global economic output is now at $63 trillion![2] It was $31 trillion in 2000.[3] (For all the 2000s being frequently referred to as a "lost decade," somehow the global economy doubled.) It was $19 trillion in 1990.[4] It will be higher still in 2020 and 2050 and 2083 and 3754. Exactly how much? I don't have a clue. Neither would Sir John, were he still alive. But I only heard him say about 40 times over the decades it would be much higher and at about the same growth rates as we've seen before—maybe a little more or a little less. Almost no one ever believed him on that—particularly not when he said it in the midst of a bear market or recession. Yet he was always right.

Side note: One reason folks fall prey to the notion of long-term stagnancy now, I believe, is the death of journalism. Once upon a time, journalism was a serious pursuit. To be a journalist, you went to school, you interned, you learned your five W's and your H—who, what, when, where, why and how. You put all the pertinent information in the first paragraph: Man bites dog in Tulsa suburb because dog stole his rib-eye steak. Then you elaborate. Editors knew they could "trim from the bottom." Don't need the details about the dog's breed or creed (purple Pekinese with three legs and no tail) in paragraph seven? Trim that. Don't need to know it was the man's birthday party from paragraph five? Trim that.

On magazine and newspapers' mastheads, there used to be a roster of staff writers. Some new, but many older and grizzled. They were the best and the core of the organ. They'd seen things. So when the young pups would say, "Golly gee! This Tech bubble is the biggest thing ever! The world is ending!" the Grizzled Veterans would say, "You don't know anything. The Energy bubble in 1980 was just as bad or worse!" They'd been around the block—lots of times.

Now, traditional journalism is dying. Blame the Internet, blame cable, blame whatever you want. Doesn't much matter! Traditional media is bleeding money. Pick up any newspaper or magazine. The masthead has been obliterated. Maybe there are just a few staff writers. Maybe those staff writers weren't there five years ago. They let all the grizzled guys go a long time ago to hire cheap guys and often kids who write for pennies. Or maybe for free! Online blog sites get tons of free contributors—they'll print any nonsense folks write. Or maybe they print just wire stuff and have a few go-to editorialists for some spice.

But most of the folks writing news today haven't been around the block. Maybe 2007 to 2009 really *was* the biggest thing they'd ever seen. Maybe they were in college during the last recession and bear market or (eek!) high school. Maybe they weren't even born for the one before that! They have no context. To them, the world really is ending and they can't fathom how we get past this bad time (whenever it is) because they've never seen that happen before—not as an adult.

I'm not saying that's it 100%. And there are still a very few old grizzled journalists around, but precious few. As a whole, we don't remember even very recent events. But it doesn't help when media confirms our worst nonsensical monkey memory fears.

Compounded by no-memory no-context journalism, it's harder to pause, take a deep breath and ask, "What am I forgetting? Has this happened before? Have I seen this or something like this before?" Because, except for the truly young pups reading this, you probably have.

Believing "this time it's different"—when it isn't—is more than just seeing the world wrong. It can lead to serious investing errors. In my world, people make bets—bets with their own or frequently with other people's money—based on their world views. The idea isn't to be perfect. No one is. To do well at money management—whether for yourself or others—means being right more than wrong over long periods. That means you will still be wrong a lot and frequently in clumpy patches of wrongness. But being right more than wrong is easier if you see the world more correctly.

It matters because seeing the world right and remembering it's never truly different this time could have saved people from making huge errors in 2009 and 2010. And it could save you big when the next big panic, super bull market or gotta-have-it investing fad hits.

The good news is that it's easy to spot the "this time it's different" mentality. It often masquerades as:

- The "new normal" or "a new era" or sometimes a "new economy." Just because people think, "This time it's different," doesn't mean they think all is terrible! Sometimes they are overly, dangerously bullish. Sometimes bearish.
- The "jobless recovery." Except every recovery is jobless—until it isn't anymore. No one remembers this.
- Fears about a "double dip"—which is always talked about but rarely seen.

There are other iterations, but these are the ones you likely run into most. So let's examine them.

The Normal Normal

Starting early 2009, the term *new normal* (a same-but-different way of saying, "This time it's different") started ping-ponging through the media. The new normal was specifically the idea that the bad problems newly emerged or envisioned in the recent recession were insurmountable—resulting in a new era of below-average economic growth, poor market returns, maybe even a double dip.

The basis for the new normal was a litany of ills—some real, some vastly overstated: A housing crash that hadn't recovered, too much US federal debt, too much consumer debt. Many believed greedy bankers had pushed our financial system beyond the brink and it was irrevocably broken. The economy couldn't recover because banks wouldn't lend. And tapped-out consumers couldn't spend!

(Now, a rational person might pause to think you can't simultaneously and logically fear banks *not* lending while fearing everyone being overindebted. If you fear people are overindebted, then banks not lending would be good! And you can't simultaneously complain consumers are all recklessly and irresponsibly tapped out and also complain they don't spend enough. But never mind—this is all part of the irrational psychosis that accompanies most every recession and bear market.)

Politicians got on the bandwagon, too, claiming the new normal supported whatever it was they wanted to do anyway—hike taxes, cut taxes, socialize medicine, whatever. Pundits and journalists jumped on *new normal* like they'd never heard it before. Novel! Except there's nothing so new about the new normal. We get some concept like it every cycle. Following are just a few historic examples from the media (*with my comments in italics*):

- September 2009—"The applicable word in **New Normal** is, of course, 'new.'"[5] *This was from the latest round of new-normaling.*
- December 13, 2003—"The Industry is starting to settle on a **new normal** where growth is more muted but sustainable."[6]
- April 30, 2003—A *F@stCompany* headline said, "Welcome to the **New Normal**"—calling it a "slightly awkward, slightly odd place" where corporate profitability is more challenging.[7] *Except when this was published, a recession had ended about a year and a half earlier, and a massive bull market run-up from the recent bear had started a month before.*
- November 2, 1987—A *Time* magazine cover said, "After a wild week on Wall Street, the world is different."[8] *Not the new normal, but a variation of "this time it's different." (And no, it wasn't different. The world recovered from the October 1987 crash and subsequent bear to finish the decade strongly.)*
- January 7, 1978—"The **'new normal'** is here and now."[9] *Same new normal, different country—from a Canadian newspaper.*

- June 15, 1959—"We could expect the country to return to the **New Normal** of the depressed Nineteen Thirties."[10] *You could expect it, but it didn't happen. Annual GDP growth was 7.2% in 1959, 2.5% in 1960, 2.1% in 1961 and 4.4% in 1963.[11] Normal, fine economic growth. A bit volatile, but normal normal, not new normal.*
- October 20, 1939—"Present conditions must be regarded as 'normal'—a '**new normal**.'"[12] *Sure, if new normal meant GDP annualized 8.1%, 8.8%, 17.1%, 18.5% then 16.4% as it did in 1939, 1940, 1941, 1942 and 1943.[13]*

This isn't to say every period following widespread use of *new normal* had fine (sometimes great) GDP growth. It's just the phrase tends to pop up most around the end of recessions and in the few years of recovery thereafter—when people are bleakest but the actual future is brightest. Regardless, it's never a very novel concept—or very prescient.

2009 and the New Normal

The latest new normal round doesn't appear to be very different at all. The latest cycle kicked into high gear in May 2009 when Bloomberg, Reuters, MarketWatch and *BusinessWeek* all featured new normal headlines or stories or both.[14] From there, it exploded. Check Google News for search results on *new normal* for any month in 2009 and 2010—you get thousands of hits.

Suppose in 2009 and 2010, while the media was almost uniformly handwringing a new era of economic lousiness, you decided stocks couldn't rise? First, you'd be wrong about the economic lousiness. The National Bureau of Economic Research (NBER) dated the recession's end as June 2009—but that announcement wasn't released until September 2010, which is normal. NBER always dates recession start- and end-dates at a big lag.

Even without the NBER's official pronouncement, GDP growth signaled the recession was likely over. US GDP was just flattish in Q2 2009—a first sign. Then, Q3 2009 1.7% GDP growth was followed by 3.8% growth in Q4 2009 and 3.9% in Q1 2010 (all annualized figures).[15] Positive GDP isn't the only factor NBER looks at to date a recession's end, but it's a major component. Put another way, I can't find two positive quarters together that NBER has ever called a recession.

More damaging if you'd acted on new normal fears: The stock market bottomed in March 2009, before the economy. Then stocks boomed—world stocks were up 44.1% three months off the bottom, and US stocks 40.2%.[16] Twelve months later, world stocks were up 74.3%, US stocks 72.3%[17]—the biggest initial 3- and 12-month bounce since 1932. From the market bottom through year-end 2010, world stocks surged 93.3% and US stocks 93.1%.[18]

If you believed this time was different—an era of eternal stagnation rather than the normal normal that follows every bear market—you missed that market surge. A surge that, for those who remained invested and well diversified, likely quickly erased a major chunk of previous bear market losses much faster than most everyone then thought possible.

This isn't unusual, either. It's normal—normal normal—how it almost always happens. Stocks typically fall before a recession officially begins, pricing in glum times ahead. Then when most folks envision only the worst possible outcomes, the market knows (we forget, the market doesn't) that things aren't ridiculously rosy, but it isn't Armageddon. Stocks start moving sharply higher on that disconnect between reality and perception, bottoming before the economy does.

Table 1.1 shows this phenomenon. Bear markets and recessions don't always overlap, but they usually do. Stocks at the major bull and bear market magnitudes are a leading indicator. Stocks fall into a bear market before the economy falls into recession and start rallying gangbusters before the economy turns up into recovery. For those common bear markets that do overlap recessions in the traditional way, stocks almost always rise first—and by a lot. It is the normal normal.

Missing from this list is the 2001–2003 bear market. The 2001 recession was short and shallow, and the bear market outlasted it. The 1987 bear market wasn't accompanied by a recession, nor were the 1966 or the 1961–1962 bear markets. (A recession ended earlier in 1961—in February. The subsequent bear market had nothing to do with it.) The big bear market of 1937 to 1942 also outlasted the relatively more minor second contraction of the period known as the Great Depression, from May 1937 to June 1938.

But when bear markets and recessions do coincide, history is clear—you want to be invested before the recession ends. Stock

Table 1.1   Recession Ends and Stock Returns

Start of Bear	Start of Bull	Recession End Date	Return From Bull Market Start to Recession's End	Total Bull Market Return
09/07/1929	06/01/1932	03/31/1933	32.57%	323.71%
05/29/1946	06/13/1949	10/31/1949	18.36%	267.10%
08/02/1956	10/22/1957	04/30/1958	11.44%	86.35%
11/29/1968	05/26/1970	11/30/1970	25.85%	73.53%
01/11/1973	10/03/1974	03/31/1975	33.85%	125.63%
11/28/1980	08/12/1982	11/30/1982	35.27%	228.81%
07/16/1990	10/11/1990	03/31/1991	27.00%	416.98%
10/09/2007	03/09/2009	06/30/2009	35.89%	???
		Average return	*27.5%*	
		Median return	*29.8%*	

Sources: Global Financial Data, Inc., S&P 500 price level returns, Thomson Reuters, National Bureau of Economic Research.

returns average 27.5% from the date a bull begins and a recession officially ends—because stocks start pricing in the coming recovery before growth is even thought of.

And even long after a new bull begins, and then a new recovery begins and rolls into expansion, people keep saying, "This time it's different"—believing with their souls the recovery *that is already under way* will never appear. That's normal normal.

A New *New Normal*

Another normal normal occurrence: As it becomes clear things aren't so bad, folks who heralded a new normal don't wave white flags and say, "Oops, we were wrong." Instead, the definition can just morph! This was on full display in 2009 into 2011. First, it was the new normal of low corporate profits. That didn't last long—corporate profit growth was historically huge (thanks to easy comparisons since profits tanked in the recession). *Then* it was a new normal of high profits or strong economic growth, but with high unemployment (e.g., "Obama Fears 'New Normal' of High Profits Without Job Growth"[19] and "Higher Jobless Rate Could Be New Normal"[20] or "Strong Growth Could Come With High Unemployment").[21] Then a new normal of lower consumer spending. ("Is Inflation Causing Americans to Stop Spending?")[22] This morphing is normal.

(Another side note: Another example of faulty memory is believing the economy can't recover if consumer spending doesn't bounce back hard. People forget: US consumer spending never falls much in recessions and doesn't need to bounce back much—and rarely does. Consumer spending is amazingly resilient because the largest chunk is staples—and even in tough times, we don't stop buying toothpaste and heart medicine. I show this in my 2010 book *Debunkery*.)

This is what I call the "pessimism of disbelief." Throughout 2009, good fundamentals started cropping up. They weren't outrageously great, just better—and much better than expected. Corporate profits were hugely above too-dour expectations—which is good! But people said, "Yeah, but that's because they fell so much." Fair enough! GDP was better than expected. "Yeah, but it's going to crater again." Everyone had a "Yeah, but." They refused to see anything positive. If they did see it, it was wrong or soon to morph to bad. This, too, you see after every recession and bear market I can find. And if you start seeing it in droves, as you did in 2009, a bear market bottom is likely either immediately ahead, or you may have just missed it. Either way, bad days can't last forever (they never do). And as Sir John and Mr. Buffett know, when the world is as gloomy as can be, that might be a great time to be greedy.

Same Old, Same Old

I knew the pessimism in 2009 and 2010 was wrong—not just because stocks had rebounded so strongly (though stocks are the ultimate leading economic indicator). But because I'd seen it all before. By November 2010—a full year and a half since the global stock market bottomed and over a year since the world returned to growth—headlines still warned of impending doom. That month, I included the following in my monthly *Forbes* column ("Don't Be Distracted by Monkey Business," *Forbes*, November 4, 2010):

> Supporting most bears right now is a bunch of bull: namely, the notion that too much debt will bite us in the butt. Since last fall the guts underlying gloom-and-doom market forecasts

have been disproven one by one. Excessive debt is the main argument the bears still hug.

Which is one reason the bull market has a long way to run—the bears are basing their case on a wrong argument. Debt doomers come in varying styles. There is the banking-crisis style and the real estate implosion style— often linked, as in "falling real estate prices will bankrupt the banks, which will cause chaos." Then, too, are those noting the "tapped-out consumer" who can't or won't borrow, thereby causing an anemic recovery or no recovery, or finally, the pseudo-sophisticate's favorite—the double-dip recession.[23]

Except, I didn't write those words in November 2010. I lifted that passage straight from my August 5, 1991, *Forbes* column "Dumb Bears." But they read like I wrote them that November morning, almost 20 years later!

People were still fretting the same things—debt, a credit crisis, housing weakness, bad banks, tapped-out consumers—they fretted in 1991! All over again! Chittering chimpanzees with no memories or historical sense! And what didn't happen after I first wrote those words in 1991?

- Armageddon, though it was widely expected.
- A US implosion.
- The end of the world.
- The S&P 500 falling to zero.

What did happen?

- A nearly uninterrupted decade of global economic vibrance.
- A historically massive bull market.
- Both led by the US, mostly.

I wrote those words in 1991 because being in this business myself since 1974 in varying degrees and witnessing my father in the business for decades before that, I had seen the same darn things happen repeatedly. And being a fan and scholar of market and economic history, I knew there was no new phenomenon here: When all the world thinks things can only be bleak going forward, that doesn't make it so. In fact, that probably (but not certainly) means the reverse is (soon or already) true.

So no, I didn't necessarily know the 1990s would be historically tremendous. But I did know what everyone was fearing was unlikely to happen—and almost certainly already priced into markets. That is, after all, what markets are supposed to do—price in now all widely known and discussed fears and hopes so only the unexpected has power to move markets big in the future.

People in 2009 and 2010 forgot we'd been through recession, credit crises and periods of big debt before. Many times! Forever, since the dawn of time, recession comes. People feel bad. They think the world can never get better. Yet it does—and growth surpasses previous peaks and keeps going. Then, at some point in the future, recession again. Repeat, repeat, repeat, with periods of expansions frequently longer than people predict, and always hitting fresh output highs at irregular intervals.

A simple fact that received no media attention at all in 2011 was that GDP hit all-time highs globally by mid-year. As I write, almost no one knows that or believes it. Two years later and GDP being at all-time highs is a normal normal story—and one the media hasn't covered and won't. That's normal.

People who believe "this time" is truly different must have a dim view of humanity I don't share. For this time to be different, on a global scale, it means humanity is no longer motivated by profits. Profit motive is a good and wonderful thing. It leads to fabulous things like life-saving medicine and medical devices but also increasingly tiny and ever more powerful computers, must-have tech toys like smartphones and tablets, better housing, safer cars, even mundane stuff like increasingly better yet cheaper sneakers. Profit motive is what drives financial innovations that let more people buy homes, borrow money to go to college, buy cars and so on. I don't think that ever stops—human ingenuity is nearly boundless. Sir John talked about that nearly endlessly for decades. When we run into barriers (slow growth, regulation, disease, dumb legislation), eventually we innovate a way around it. But people who think this time is different evidently have decided it's time to pack it in and expect a dismal future.

But despite the endless headlines over time that "this time it's different" and we're in a new normal, all we get is the plain old normal of a return to growth—growth that is variable but typically stronger than what anyone was predicting.

If folks stopped forgetting, they wouldn't be so surprised. And if they remembered, they might make fewer costly errors—like sitting on the market's sidelines during a historic market surge.

Some may read this and misunderstand, thinking I'm a knee-jerk Pollyanna who doesn't believe recessions are bad or bear markets happen. Wrong conclusion. They do. Most assuredly! But they're normal, not a new normal. Just a part of life. They hurt. But for some reason, people can't get in their bones that expansions and bull markets happen, too. They follow those recessions and are part of the normal ebb and flow. The expansionary periods are almost always longer and stronger than the downturns. If you go through life seeing only the bad times and cowering in fear, you likely miss out on the vastly more frequent, longer and stronger times when economies cook along and capital markets hit new highs and keep going.

I don't know when the next recession will be. I can't predict that with certainty. But I can near-guarantee that after it hits—when the stock market is maybe already bottoming and bouncing back strongly, and the recession is almost over (or maybe already over but people don't know it, see it, feel it or believe it yet)—you will hear some variation of the new normal concept again. And that likely goes on for another one to three years, even well past the point at which the recession is officially acknowledged to be over. That's the way it works—almost always.

The Not-So-New Economy

People have a tendency to forget that every recession is followed by expansion. But people are chittering chimpanzees with no memory or historical sense on the upside, too. Remember the *New Economy*? This buzz phrase was huge late in 1998 and 1999 and throughout 2000 even into 2001 and immortalized in a January 2000 *BusinessWeek* cover story titled, "The New Economy: It Works in America. Will It Go Global?"[24]

For those who don't remember, the new economy was the polar opposite of new normal—but driven by the same inability for humans to remember even recent history. It was the idea that the super-fast growth in Tech-industry market capitalization was eternally sustainable—and possible in other industries. Profits didn't matter—which was good because a lot of those high-flying Tech firms didn't have any. New Economy adherents thought profits would come around eventually. Or maybe not! If you have an endless stream of investors willing to throw money at you, who needs profits?

Turns out, we all do, eventually. The new economy was an almost exact replay of the energy boom in the late 1970s. But people forgot about that, too. (I wrote about the eerie similarities I saw between tech in 2000 and the 1980 energy bubble in a March 6, 2000, *Forbes* column titled, "1980 Revisited." I suspected we were at or near a top, but my timing, mere days before the actual global tech peak, was pure happenstance.)

Whether positive or negative, if all the world is hectoring about a new economy or a new normal, it probably just means there's a society-wide case of very contagious amnesia—which is the normal normal.

Figure 1.1 is a good chart to revisit occasionally. It's old, but it shows business activity cycles back to 1790. Your takeaway should be: Sometimes contractions are bigger or smaller, and expansions can vary greatly. But the economy is cyclical—in America and elsewhere. Economies have never just gone down forever. I doubt they do in the future.

The Jobless Recovery

Even well after every rational person acknowledges a recession is over, you get headlines and news stories saying something like, "It may not be a recession, but it sure feels like one!"

But what does a recession feel like? A recession isn't a *feeling*—according to NBER:

> A recession is a significant decline in economic activity spread across the economy, lasting more than a few months, normally visible in real GDP, real income, employment, industrial production, and wholesale-retail sales.

They don't say anything about feelings. Granted, when economic activity is slow, that can make you feel pretty crummy. But then, when economic activity is provably picking up, why do people still feel like it's a recession?

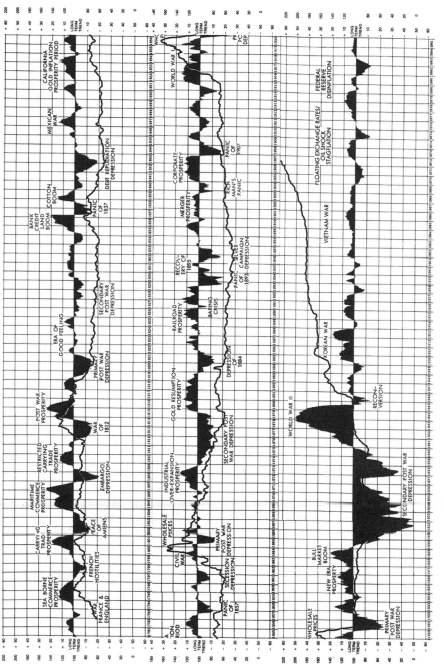

Figure 1.1 American Business Activity, 1790 to 1986

Source: Ameritrust Corporation, January 1986.

My guess? A big part is unemployment. Unemployment rises in every recession—and keeps rising after recessions end. True fact. Being unemployed can be agonizing. The uncertainty about the future is possibly worse. So when more people are unemployed, you have larger sets of people feeling bad all at once. What's more, when unemployment is elevated, more people fear they may be unemployed soon, too—and they feel bad.

Interestingly, in dating recessions, NBER does cite employment but not unemployment, which statistically are two extremely different things—far from the mirror images that many commonly think. Unemployment is and has always been a long-late-lagging indicator and isn't directly linked to employment because of the bizarre way the official stats are calculated. *Employment* stats aim to measure how many folks have jobs, and the employment rate is the number of folks having jobs relative to the total labor force. But official *unemployment* stats don't measure the number of people who don't have jobs. The way the government calculates it, it's the number of people who are looking for jobs at a point in time.

Early in a recovery, as some folks get jobs, others see that, get more optimistic and start looking, too—which also helps keep unemployment high long into an economic expansion. This is why payrolls can increase and the unemployment rate can also rise—always the case in every expansion. (The media particularly never seems to remember this.)

But people can be truly jobless during even very robust growth periods. And for those people, that still feels awful to them. So feelings aren't necessarily the best economic indicators.

Still, this idea, that it's not a recession but it sure feels like one, pops up in media, usually, as the *jobless recovery*. Fact is, every recovery is relatively low on job growth, some more and some less so . . . until it isn't anymore. This is nothing new—yet investors, pundits, politicians, everyone, routinely forgets. If you've lived through more than one recession, you've heard this. (But maybe you've forgotten.) By the third time you hear "jobless recovery," you should start remembering, "Oh yeah! That's what they always say. And *they*, whoever they are, are pretty much always wrong."

Google has a fun tool letting you run a timeline—back to the Magna Carta, practically—of search terms. You can see where certain terms spike in popularity and usage. Granted, sometimes the terms show up and are utter nonsense. But something like "jobless recovery" is a pretty targeted search. Look for it and, lo and behold, you see it spiking in popularity at the end of every recession as far back as you care to search.

For example, after the recession that ended June 2009:

- February 5, 2010: Headline—"Analyst: This Is What We Call a **Jobless Recovery**."[25]
- June 10, 2010: "The hope of a robust labor market recovery is fading. We may be in for another **jobless recovery**."[26] *The journalist writing this article may not have realized there has never been a truly jobless recovery, so having "another" one is rather tough.*

After the 2001 recession:

- July 6, 2002: Headline—"Higher Jobless Rate Reflects Slow Recovery." The article also said: "With the government reporting yesterday that the unemployment rate rose slightly to 5.9% last month, the economy appears to have fallen into a *jobless recovery* that resembles the slow growth of the early 1990s. . . . In a sense, the recession is over, but the recovery has not begun."[27] *This one is a double whammy because most reading this should automatically know the 1990s was overall a terrific decade!*
- November 2, 2002: "Some Fed bank presidents have worried that businesses are not expanding as quickly as hoped—and that the nation is locked in what is essentially a **jobless recovery**."[28]
- October 2003: "We're sensing from our members that the 'new normal' may well be economic growth with **only small gains in employment**."[29] *New normal* **and** *a jobless recovery.*

But we weren't in a jobless recovery. The unemployment rate fell eventually, at a lag—as it always does. People just forget—even Fed bank presidents.

After the recession ending in 1991:

- January 19, 1993: "If you take the two months together, it confirms what we already knew, that this has been a **jobless recovery**."[30] *Of course, the 1990s weren't jobless.*
- May 8, 1993: "Labor Secretary Robert Reich said Friday that the April employment data is 'clear evidence' that the economy remains stuck in a **'jobless recovery.**'"[31]

Labor secretaries are particularly prone to forget. Politicians of all stripes are just about the worst offenders. I think they intentionally forget.

Then, this sometimes happens: The jobs come back, but they aren't the *right* ones.

- September 7, 1993: Headline—"More Jobs, But Not Good Ones." The article said, "First there was the jobless recovery. Now there's the '**joyless recovery**.' That's the name of a new report out by the Economic Policy Institute that finds little reason to celebrate the kinds of jobs being created in the 1990s."[32]

Some follow-up questions: Who is the Economic Policy Institute to decide whether jobs are the right kind of jobs or not? Do they think *your* job is the right kind of job? Do you even care? And do you think they get razzed by other think tanks for taking exception to the kinds of jobs being created in the early part of the 1990s, at the beginning of a historic period of global economic expansion? My guess is they, too, forgot they said anything about it. Think tanks forget, too! Pretty often, think tanks think too little and tank too much.

Jobs came back in the 1990s, though. In case you forgot, unemployment fell throughout the 1990s to a low of 3.9% in September 2000[33]—and the decade overall was a terrific one for stocks and the economy. (Recall, again, employment and unemployment aren't directly linked, but sometimes they appear to be, and it's usually late in an economic expansion—shortly before the next recession.)

It keeps going. After the two recessions early in the 1980s:

- June 4, 1983: In reference to then-Tennessee Congressman Jim Cooper, "The Congressman called the current recovery a weak one. 'You can almost call it a **jobless recovery**.'" *Almost, but not quite, Jim. As I said, politicians have particularly bad memories.*[34]

You can find endless examples. There's this *New York Times* quote from 1938, "Observers wonder if we're experiencing a '**jobless recovery**.'"[35]

In every single recession—as far back as we have good data on both economic cycles and unemployment—improvements in unemployment lagged the recovery. Again, this is normal and healthy, not weird and worrisome. Journalists probably wouldn't write so many alarming headlines—and investors wouldn't get so alarmed—if they simply remembered how it all happened the last time (and the time before, and the time before that).

When Do You Hire? But forget about unemployment for a second and think about employment, which is more important and something NBER does consider in deciding when we have a recession and when we don't. Pretend you're a CEO. Sales of your widgets are slowing. Maybe a recession is coming or already here—you may not know it yet for sure because, of course, recessions are officially dated at a lag.

Sales are plummeting. You don't want to cut staff—no one does. So you hunker down. You cut costs. No more air travel, everyone has to do conference calls. You find ways to make your widgets cheaper. Sales keep falling. You pull out all the cost-saving stops. But after a quarter or two, you know: You must cut staff. If you don't, your entire firm could implode. To preserve your firm, keep your customers and keep some staff, you cut.

Things keep getting bad for a while, but you have a bare-bones staff and they keep innovating ways to be more productive. And you barely get by. Then, one day, sales level off. Maybe you're through the worst, maybe not. Maybe you fear that double dip everyone talks about (but rarely happens—we'll cover that in a bit). Do you hire then?

No. That would be insane. Your board would fire you. Your staff has learned to make do with less—you don't need to hire, so you don't. Then, sales start increasing. You're cautiously optimistic about the future, but you still don't hire. Because of productivity gains, your staff can handle the sales increase. You get a bump in earnings too because those increased sales with low costs are highly profitable. But you still don't hire because profits fell so much in the contraction, you want to refill your coffers first.

Sales really start cooking. Your team is looking a little stressed. But you still aren't convinced. Is the recession really over? Finally, after a few quarters, you're convinced things are solidly better. You find out the recession ended three quarters ago, but you pretty much knew that based on your sales. Your sales manager comes to you and says, "Listen, we're leaving money on the table here.

We don't have enough staff to fulfill all our orders, and our sales guys can't get to all the sales calls." Fine! Now, you hire.

But even that doesn't happen overnight! Maybe you start with temp or contract workers because even though things look great, it could all go kablooey fast—and contract workers are easier and cheaper to hire. And you can let them go more easily if things head south again—and you're still being rationally cautious. Maybe you wait a few quarters to start committing to long-term permanent workers, who are harder and more expensive to hire. And it still takes time to recruit, interview, hire and train new workers.

This is, pretty much, how most CEOs approach hiring. They don't think, "Gee whiz. My sales are way down. The economy is terrible. But I'll do my civic duty and hire a bunch because the president wants me to so he can look good, even though it might put me out of business." Only politicians think that's how businesses should be run because most of them have never had a real job. No, this is not how the real world works.

And that's what Figures 1.2 and 1.3 show—recessions (shaded bars) and the unemployment rate (the line) since December 1928 (since that's as far back as we have monthly data). I use this graph a lot and usually put all the data in one graph. But to show how long the lag can be, I broke it up here.

Note, unemployment starts rising a little before, maybe a little after the recession starts. But without fail, throughout history, recessions end and unemployment keeps rising. Sometimes for many months; sometimes for over a year or more! But unemployment never peaks until after the recession ends, and it can then stay high for a long time. But it falls—sometimes faster, sometimes slower, but it falls.

People also frequently complain—in and after a recession—that the official unemployment rate is a fake number, and people are really underemployed, or they have the wrong jobs. But that's always the case, too! People are underemployed even in the best of times, and official unemployment numbers, being produced by governments, are always wonky. You can either accept that or go shake your fist at the sky. The result will be the same, for a fact.

For darn sure the next time we have a recession, unemployment will still rise for some time after it ends. And headlines will complain that it's a jobless recovery. Count on it.

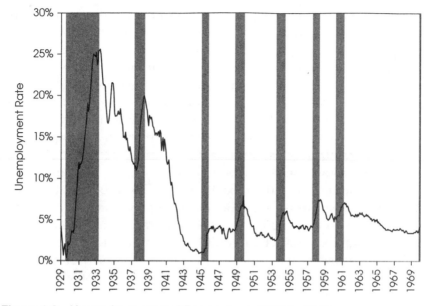

Figure 1.2   Unemployment and Recessions, 1929 to 1970

Sources: US Bureau of Labor Statistics, National Bureau of Economic Research, from 12/31/1928 to 12/31/1969.

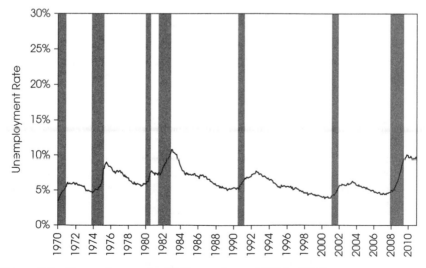

Figure 1.3   Unemployment and Recessions, 1970 to 2010

Sources: US Bureau of Labor Statistics, National Bureau of Economic Research, from 12/31/1969 to 12/31/2010.

The reason this is an important lesson to remember is folks tend to think, wrongly (as you now know), the economy can't grow on high unemployment. It seems so logical to think that, but it has never been true for all the reasons we've covered. And they think stocks can't rise until the economy kicks into gear. And that, too, seems logical and also has never been true. This is all backward and wrong (as this chapter showed earlier). But it's also costly. If you wait for confirmation from unemployment all is well, you miss out. Confirmation in general is expensive in capital markets. Especially so here!

Table 1.2 shows the return you got in US stocks (because of the longer data history) over the next 12 months if you bought at historical unemployment peaks—just before unemployment started falling. (Mind you, to do this, you'd have to *know* it was a peak—and you can only know that in retrospect. I don't know anyone who's ever successfully and repeatedly called unemployment peaks. Nor do I know any reason why you'd want to.) The table also shows how stocks do over the next 12 months if you buy 6 months *before* the peak, i.e., while

Table 1.2   Unemployment and S&P 500 Returns—Stocks Lead, Jobs Lag

Unemployment Peak	S&P 500 Forward 12-Month Returns	6 Months Before Unemployment Peak	S&P 500 Forward 12-Month Returns
05/31/1933	3.0%	11/30/1932	57.7%
06/30/1938	−1.7%	12/31/1937	33.2%
02/28/1947	−4.3%	08/30/1946	−3.4%
10/31/1949	30.5%	04/30/1949	31.3%
09/30/1954	40.9%	03/31/1954	42.3%
07/31/1958	32.4%	01/31/1958	37.9%
05/31/1961	−7.7%	11/30/1960	32.3%
08/31/1971	15.5%	02/26/1971	13.6%
05/30/1975	14.4%	11/29/1974	36.2%
07/31/1980	13.0%	01/31/1980	19.5%
12/31/1982	22.6%	06/30/1982	61.2%
06/30/1992	13.6%	12/31/1991	7.6%
06/30/2003	19.1%	12/31/2002	28.7%
10/31/2009	16.5%	04/30/2009	38.8%
Average	**14.8%**		**31.2%**

Sources: Bureau of Labor Statistics; Global Financial Data Inc., S&P 500 total return, as of 05/01/2011.

everyone's calling it a jobless recovery and it still "feels" like a recession. Overwhelmingly, returns are better if you buy before the unemployment peak and by a huge margin. Forward 12-month returns average 14.8% from historic unemployment peaks, compared to a big 31.2% if you buy six months before the peak—a return twice as high.

If you knew this history, you'd know not to panic if unemployment fails to fall early in a recovery. You'd know waiting to invest until unemployment fell could be very costly. But the fact is the overwhelming bulk of investors don't know this—because they've forgotten what they've been through many times before. But if you did know, you would also know unemployment being elevated shouldn't halt the recovery or ding stocks. There's no precedent for that. Pundits and politicians, however, will say it's true because they just can't remember it's never been like that.

The Always Feared, Rarely Seen Double Dip

Few things cause a sudden and myopic loss of memory like the fear of that near-mythical creature, the double-dip recession. All 2010, headlines were relentless—I needn't repeat them. They reappeared in 2011, too. A sizable global stock market correction kicked off mid-year 2010, partly on fears of a debt contagion from peripheral Eurozone countries, and partly on fears the US (and the world) would double dip.

Needless to say, there was no double dip. Not even in Europe (overall), where Portugal, Italy, Ireland, Greece and Spain (the PIIGS) did their darnedest to drag the entire EU down. Despite two good-sized corrections, US and world stocks ended 2010 up 15.1% and 11.8%, respectively, and the US and the world logged positive economic growth every quarter.[36] Investors moving heavily away from stocks based on double-dip fears in 2010 made a costly mistake—both in absolute and relative terms. Counteracting short-term memories with a little study of history could have prevented that.

Like the new normal, people readily forget double-dip fears aren't new. They pop up regularly after recessions. After the short and shallow 2001 recession, the US economy grew uninterrupted until December 2007, i.e., no double dip. But still, you got headlines like the following:

- July 13, 2002: "Stock Market's Nose Dive Fuels Fears of **'Double-Dip'** Recession."[37]

- August 1, 2002: "Anemic Showing Stirs Worries of **Double-Dip** Recession."[38]
- August 2, 2002: "Markets Spooked by Possibility of **Double-Dip** Recession."[39]

In December 2001, a *New York Times* headline warned, "Recession, Then a Boom? Maybe Not This Time," The story said, "But the rules for recoveries *may well be different today*—not because of Sept. 11, but *because of fundamental changes in the economy*."[40] (I added the emphasis to the "this time it's different" sentiment.)

But what were the fundamental changes? According to the article, in recent decades, expansions had gotten longer and downturns were less frequent and less severe. So that was supposed to mean the economy, without a big downturn, lacked juice for a sustained recovery.[41] Which confuses me and should confuse you.

It's true, downturns over recent decades have been less frequent than they were in the first half of the twentieth century. First, that may be just a quirk of statistics. Sometimes things are longer than average, sometimes shorter. That's what an average means. But the increasing expansions also speak to technology's increasing role in business management. Firms can use technology and computers to react faster now when they suspect trouble—by ratcheting down on inventories, for example—and ramp back up fast once they gain confidence. That's a fundamental change for good, not one that makes our economy inherently more anemic going forward.

Then after the recession that ended in March 1991, a July 1991 headline warned, "Double-Dip Recession Is Feared."[42] The article said, "Even if that scenario does not develop, analysts believe that the variety of problems facing the United States, from strains on the banking system to an overload of consumer debt, will make this expansion the weakest in US history."[43] It included (new normalish) predictions of a modest annual rate "of around 2%."[44] Yes, this, in the middle of 1991, before one of the longest, strongest US expansions on record and a massive bull market!

Other headlines from that period:

- August 11, 1991: "Fed Fears **Double-Dip** Recession."[45]
- August 13, 1991: "Retail Sales Bounce Back. Economists Watch for '**Double Dip**.'"[46] *This was from the UK (which did*

not fall into a double dip) and a great example of what I call the pessimism of disbelief. Good news (e.g., rebounding retail sales) is just ignored.

- December 4, 1991: "National Economy Stalled on Brink of **Double-Dip** Recession."[47]

Oddly, I found very few double-dip headlines between July 1980 and July 1981—the short 12-month interval between the two early 1980s recessions, which legitimately could be seen as a double dip. I did find a February 1981 headline saying a double dip *wasn't* coming—"Economists Backing Off on Recession Predictions."[48] Then, in March 1981, Louis Rukeyser wrote:

> It's beginning to look as if the so-called **double-dip** recession has gone to that great never-never land in the sky. . . . The latest consensus forecast of 44 top business economists is that the first 3 months of 1981 will show solid real growth (exceeding 2%), that the second quarter will be no worse than flat, and that the second half of the year will bring a strong resumption of economic expansion—culminating in a 4% pace at year-end that would be well above the over-all growth rate of recent years.[49]

Except the US economy did sink back into recession July 1981 until November 1982.[50] I'm not picking on Rukeyser—not at all. Economic forecasting is devilishly tough. There's that joke about economists having predicted 11 of the past 2 recessions. Also, when you put yourself out there regularly—writing and appearing on TV and making regular pronouncements—you're going to be wrong. Sometimes a lot!

I know that—I've written a monthly column in *Forbes* for over 27 years. Each month, I usually pick some stocks (except for those periods when I've been fully bearish). I make or reiterate a market forecast or otherwise muse on some sector or industry's direction. I've been wrong. A lot! And when I am, I'm hammered for it regularly in the blogosphere or by other pundits. I don't mind it—I expect it.

Anyone who makes any public predictions on anything—stocks, the economy, football games, wheat harvests—knows people (and particularly snarky people) will endlessly hammer them when they're wrong and utterly ignore them when they're right. If your ego requires that people congratulate you for being right, don't write, don't go into money management and certainly don't do both. I don't much need congratulations (never been that way) so I've managed to have both a long writing and money management career.

I am, however, fortunate and grateful in my long career to have been right more than wrong. Third-party research firm CXO ranks market "gurus" (their term) who make public proclamations. For years now, I've been among the most accurate forecasters of those they measure—based on my stock picks in *Forbes*, which by and large reflect the same outlook I have for my firm's private client portfolios. My stock picks in *Forbes*, since they started measuring in 1996, have lagged the S&P 500 only three times in 15 years. We tied once, and my picks beat 11 times. Not too shabby. As of year-end 2010, my picks annualized 10.5% to the S&P 500's 5.2%.[51] (Forbes measures by taking equal-sized investments in the S&P 500 the day my column publishes, giving a 1% haircut to my picks for transactions costs but no such haircut to the S&P 500 and comparing year-end performance.) And my firm has a long-term history of beating both the S&P 500 and the MSCI World Index in all-equity portfolios.* That's pretty good for a career as long as mine, and I'm satisfied that, though I've been wrong and expect to be wrong again quite often (and often for periods that at the time feel like they go on forever), overall, in the long term, I've done well for my clients and readers.

So I'm not slamming Rukeyser. He was a fine gentleman and in very many ways a pioneer in TV financial journalism. He had me on his show, back when I was an utter nobody. He was that kind of guy.

But ironically in mid-1981, there were precious few mentions of a coming double dip—just at the one ultra-rare time when one would actually happen. And Rukeyser, who was about as big a name as you'd find in those days, was actively pooh-poohing a double dip,

---

*The Fisher Investments Private Client Group (FI PCG) Global Total Return (GTR) strategy was incepted on January 1, 1995, and is managed against the Morgan Stanley Capital International (MSCI) World Index. For the period from inception through December 31, 2010, performance returns (net of advisory fees, commissions and other expenses, and reflecting the reinvestment of dividends and other earnings) of the FI PCG GTR composite exceeded total returns of the MSCI World Index as well as the S&P 500 Index. Past performance is no guarantee of future returns. Investing in stock markets involves the risk of loss.

though another recession was on the way. Life in capital markets and punditry is very, very quirky and ironic.

But after most every other recession, when new recessions don't appear so quickly, it's easy to find endless blather about double dips that don't, in fact, occur. Like in February 1975, when a member of the Ford administration said, "What is now likely is a 'double dip recession.'"[52] Then the recession ended a month later, and the economy expanded until January 1980.[53] On and on and on and on again.

What Exactly Is a Double Dip?

Instead of asking, "When have there been double-dip recessions?" a better question might be, "What exactly is a double dip?"

NBER defines a *double dip* as . . . just kidding, they don't define it, nor identify one. Not at all. A double dip is rather like *stagflation*—a term without an official definition that a lot of people fear and think is frequently just around the corner but doesn't show up as often as media headlines imply. Still, you'd think we'd know a double dip in some official way when we see one.

When (most) people say double dip, they mean we were in recession, grew a bit and then shrank back into recession because we couldn't outgrow all the problems from the beginning of the recession. But since double dip isn't officially defined, what time period should we use as the intervening growth period? Some people say 12 months. But when that doesn't materialize, the double-dip interval gets mysteriously pushed out to 18 or 24 months. Heck, why not use three or four years? By that kind of logic, 2007 to 2009 could be the fourteenth dip of the 1930s Great Depression—a decaquadruple dip! Geesh!

Twelve months or less seems fair—and the two recessions starting January 1980 and July 1981 qualify with 12 months between the two. (See Table 1.3, which shows economic cycles as dated by NBER.) Still, that first recession lasted just 7 months, and the second one lasted 14 months. An average recession (since 1854—as far back as NBER has data) lasts 16 months. Add the two 1980s recessions together and you get one recession that lasted a bit longer than average with a growth break in between. Note it came at the start of an awesome, near decade-long bull run for stocks and a huge economic expansion, and then a near repeat in the 1990s, so the double dip didn't doom stocks long term.

Table 1.3   US Economic Cycles Since 1854

Business Cycle		Duration in Months	
Peak	Trough	Contraction (peak to trough)	Expansion (previous trough to this peak)
	December 1854	—	—
June 1857	December 1858	18	30
October 1860	June 1861	8	22
April 1865	December 1867	32	46
June 1869	December 1870	18	18
October 1873	March 1879	65	34
March 1882	May 1885	38	36
March 1887	April 1888	13	22
July 1890	May 1891	10	27
January 1893	June 1894	17	20
December 1895	June 1897	18	18
June 1899	December 1900	18	24
September 1902	August 1904	23	21
May 1907	June 1908	13	33
January 1910	January 1912	24	19
January 1913	December 1914	23	12
August 1918	March 1919	7	44
January 1920	July 1921	18	10
May 1923	July 1924	14	22
October 1926	November 1927	13	27
August 1929	March 1933	43	21
May 1937	June 1938	13	50
February 1945	October 1945	8	80
November 1948	October 1949	11	37
July 1953	May 1954	10	45
August 1957	April 1958	8	39
April 1960	February 1961	10	24
December 1969	November 1970	11	106
November 1973	March 1975	16	36
January 1980	July 1980	6	58
July 1981	November 1982	16	12
July 1990	March 1991	8	92

(*continued*)

Table 1.3 *Continued*

Business Cycle		Duration in Months	
Peak	Trough	Contraction (peak to trough)	Expansion (previous trough to this peak)
March 2001	November 2001	8	120
December 2007	June 2009	18	73
Average (all cycles)			
1854–2009 (33 cycles)		16	42
1854–1919 (16 cycles)		22	27
1919–1945 (6 cycles)		18	35
1945–2009 (11 cycles)		11	59

Source: The National Bureau of Economic Research, as of 05/31/2011.

Before 1980, the most recent US double dip was . . . *not* the Great Depression. The Great Depression was two distinct recessions (and two distinct bear markets, by the way). The first recession was brutal—43 months starting in August 1929—way above average (and skewing the average higher, mind you). Then we got over four years of uninterrupted growth—50 months. The average growth cycle lasts 38 months (which is skewed down by some shorter cycles in the nineteenth and early twentieth centuries), so that mid-1930s growth cycle was markedly above average in duration! Not a double dip. Overall and on average a miserable period—but not one long period of uniform stagnation.

Before 1980, you must go back to 1918 for a 12-month-or-less-interval double dip. A recession started August 1918 and lasted seven months (short). Ten months later, a new one started January 1920 and lasted 18 months. Considering the first recession was so short and the growth interval short, maybe—and I'm not criticizing NBER here—but just maybe, data back then weren't as precise as more modern data and that was really a longish recession, not a double dip. Don't really know. But never mind!

Before that, starting in 1910 you get a 24-month recession, 12 months of growth and another 23 months of recession starting

January 1913. Regardless of what you think of the Federal Reserve System, monetary policy was just miserable, or rather, nonexistent, before the Fed was created in 1914, hence we had more recessions before (bank panics, too). And before that, you get . . . none. No double dips that I can find in the US, the world's largest single economy.

Let's review. Since 1854, we've had three double dips. Two came fast on the heels of one another pre- and early-Fed. (And one of those is a touch debatable in my view, though the NBER folks can feel free to send me a strongly worded letter.) One started in 1980. Three double dips in 33 cycles—a 10% occurrence.

Maybe you think an 18-month interval qualifies. Fine—add two more double dips. The last started in 1893. The one before that was 1865. Both pre-Fed.

Next time you hear someone predicting a double dip, ask if he would make a big bet on something that occurs 10% of the time? And most of those times were before we had a central bank. That's not to say low-probability events can't happen. They do! But if you're banking on a double dip, you better have a good reason— one that explains away the vast majority of cycles that aren't double dips. Otherwise, your faulty memory is letting you just bet on black 25 in Vegas.

To summarize: People tend to remember and expect things that never or rarely occurred. They forget things that happen regularly. They look for a concept like the new normal at the same stage of every cycle. They always fear unemployment in every new economic expansion. They regularly fear double-dip recessions that rarely seem to happen. There is much more, but the central problem is: Our memories are faulty. There is a lot more we fail to remember correctly, and all of it leads to the truth of Sir John Templeton's utterance, "The four most expensive words in the English language are, 'This time it's different.'"

CHAPTER 2

Fooled by Averages

Bull markets aren't average. (Nor are bear markets.) *Average* returns are, in actuality, very, very unusual. You'd think that would be easy to remember—but this is something investors routinely forget fast. Stock market returns are widely varied, and returns close to the average occur in a small percentage of years.

Instead of wildly volatile years (read more in Chapter 3), folks often think bull market years should steadily rise—conveniently signaling, "Hey! Bull market on the run here! Time to get all in!" Conversely, we'd all love it if bear markets politely fell in an orderly fashion—just a bit a day, letting us develop conviction a bear market is under way without too much harm and giving us ample time to exit.

People may say, "That's silly! Everyone knows markets are volatile." Then why does return variability freak people out so much? Big down days happen regularly in the course of a bull market, yet even just one or a few consecutive big down days freak people out. Never mind full-fledged corrections—fast drops of 10% to 20% or more that rebound equally fast—that convince folks a bull market is over (when it's not). And in bear markets, countertrend rallies also fool investors into complacency.

This is The Great Humiliator (TGH—the proper name for the stock market) at work. What's worse, no matter how many investing years people log, many still seemingly forget, even during the course of an overall bull market, returns are wildly variable—day to day, month to month and year to year. Forget that, and you can fool yourself into missing serious upside.

Market averages are useful tools, but individual weeks, months and years are anything but average—in both bull *and* bear markets. In this chapter, we look at how investors forget:

- Bull markets are inherently above average.
- Early bull markets are *really* above average.
- Normal returns are extremely extreme.
- Even within bull markets, annual returns can be wildly variable—including up a little and, yes, down a little.
- Because annual returns aren't average, achieving average returns is tactically easy, but mentally very, very difficult.

Bull Markets Are Inherently Above Average

One common way market-average amnesia manifests: Almost uniformly for the first stage of a new bull market—the first year or even two—headlines claim, "No Bull!" or something similar. Many (maybe most) pundits don't want to look silly by being too optimistic. It's not a new bull, they say, but a countertrend in a longer bear. "It's just a bear market rally!" cries occur most often during the first, initial, massive bounce off a bear market bottom—though such booms are perfectly normal (people just forget). And they can go on long after we get confirmation from the economy (which almost always lags).

But fears normal bull market upward volatility (and yes, volatility can go up, too) is really a bear market rally can occur at any point—and have through history. For example:

- March 26, 2009: In this article, a financial services CEO warned, "This is a **bear market rally**, not something more."[1] *Oops—it was something more. Globally, the bear market bottomed 17 days earlier, and the bull market runs still as I write.*
- May 8, 2003: "Hochberg of Elliot Wave also says this is just another **bear market rally**."[2] *But it wasn't. The global bear market double-bottomed just two months earlier, and another bear market didn't materialize for another four-plus years.*
- August 3, 1996: "My feeling is this is simply a **bear market rally**."[3] *This one's strange—it was smack in the middle of the decade-long bull market. No bear in sight. Stocks had pulled back a bit in July—not even enough to be a correction—and then*

rebounded strongly. Normal bull market volatility and not a bear market.

- December 28, 1990: "The market has generally adhered to our **bear-market rally** forecast since the September-October bottom."[4] *Actually, the 1990s mega-bull market started in October—two months before this quote.*
- May 6, 1985: "I still think the recession lurks . . . but continually falling interest rates could ease recession fears enough to cause a healthy **bear market rally**."[5] *The bull market that started in August 1982 would run through August 1987, pause for that short 1987 bear, then run to July 1990.*
- November 1, 1962: ". . . the simple fact that sudden violent advances of this type represent typical **bear market rally** action."[6] *Or rather, new bull market action. The bull market that started in June 1962 ran through February 1966.*
- And so on . . .

Interestingly, people frequently think being cautious about a new bull market is prudent. They believe it's better to be wrong and too bearish rather than wrong and too bullish, even though history shows being wrongly bearish can be more harmful to long-term returns if you're growth oriented. (Read more in Chapter 7.)

Big bull market returns at any stage shouldn't surprise or frighten you. Why? Bull markets are inherently above average. I hope that seems beyond basic to you—tautology to the *n*th ridiculous degree.

Yet, amazingly, when I say that, many guffaw and call me a perma-bull with blinders on. I'm not! I'm more bullish than not over time because stocks rise more often than not and historically deliver superior returns to similarly liquid alternatives. I've been bearish on the entire market at times—most notably in 1987, 1999 and much of the 2001–2002 bear market. I've been bearish on certain investing categories while bullish on others. I've also been bullish sometimes and wrong. But I'm not a perma-bull.

Still, people can't remember that bull markets do deliver above-average returns. Most people remember over the very long term stocks return about 10% a year, on average. Give or take a bit. Some people will grump that's not right, and only true if you include dividends. (Why wouldn't you include dividends?) Or you must account for inflation. (Yes, but inflation knocks everything the same—so account for it or not—up to you—but also similarly ding returns of all comparative asset classes.) In general, many folks who don't believe stocks have superior long-term averages tend to believe in secular bear markets.

Fact is, since 1926 through year-end 2010, the S&P 500 has annualized 9.8%.[7] Since 1970 (when we have good data on world stocks), world stocks have annualized 9.6%.[8] And—this is important to remember—those long-term averages include bull *and* bear markets. Even big bear markets! Of *course* they do. Somehow, people miss that. An average is just that—an average . . . of everything. This is basic, and yet, when investors experience down years (which happen—fact of life), it's common for them to feel that one or two bad years ruined it all and they'll never experience anything like long-term equity returns.

And maybe they won't! But probably not because they were hurt by a down year. (More on this later in this chapter—a major reason investors overall don't achieve long-term equity averages is because they in-and-out at the wrong times and don't stick with a strategy.) *Long-term returns have always included down years and will continue to include down years.* Down years are a fact of life. Provided you are well diversified (i.e., not holding huge allocations in just a handful of stocks or not heavy into just one or a few sectors) and stick with an appropriate strategy, history teaches the bad years in stocks get swamped by later, bigger and more frequent positive years. So if you're a long-term growth-oriented investor and are reasonably diversified, you shouldn't be overly focused on the occasional down year. Why? Because bull markets are longer and stronger—*they are by their very nature above average.*

Tables 2.1 and 2.2 show the last 13 bull and bear markets. Note the difference in average duration. Bear markets average 21 months. Remember: An average is just an average, always! Bear markets can be both longer and shorter. And on average, they fall about 40% cumulatively. Now look at bull markets in Table 2.2— they average 57 months (some more, some less) and on average rise a whopping 164%! That's price return—returns are higher still if you include dividends. (I don't here because we don't have good daily data on total returns back to 1926. But price returns tell the story well enough.)

Table 2.1 Last 13 S&P 500 Bear Markets

Start	End	Duration— Months*	Annualized Return	Cumulative Returns
09/07/1929	06/01/1932	33	−51.5%	−86%
03/06/1937	04/28/1942	62	−16.3%	−60%
05/29/1946	06/13/1949	36	−10.9%	−30%
08/02/1956	10/22/1957	15	−18.1%	−22%
12/12/1961	06/26/1962	6	−45.7%	−28%
02/09/1966	10/07/1966	8	−31.7%	−22%
11/29/1968	05/26/1970	18	−26.0%	−36%
01/11/1973	10/03/1974	21	−31.7%	−48%
11/28/1980	08/12/1982	20	−16.9%	−27%
08/25/1987	12/04/1987	3	−77.1%	−34%
07/16/1990	10/11/1990	3	−60.6%	−20%
03/24/2000	10/09/2002	30	−23.3%	−49%
10/09/2007	03/09/2009	17	−44.7%	−57%
Average		**21**	**−35.0%**	**−40%**

For duration, one month equals 30.5 days.

Source: Global Financial Data, Inc., S&P 500 price level returns.

Table 2.2 Last 13 S&P 500 Bull Markets—Longer and Stronger

Start	End	Duration— Months*	Annualized Return	Cumulative Returns
06/01/1932	03/06/1937	57	35.4%	324%
04/28/1942	05/29/1946	49	26.1%	158%
06/13/1949	08/02/1956	85	20.0%	267%
10/22/1957	12/12/1961	50	16.2%	86%
06/26/1962	02/09/1966	43	17.6%	80%
10/07/1966	11/29/1968	26	20.0%	48%
05/26/1970	01/11/1973	32	23.3%	74%
10/03/1974	11/28/1980	74	14.1%	126%
08/12/1982	08/25/1987	60	26.6%	229%
12/04/1987	07/16/1990	31	21.0%	65%
10/11/1990	03/24/2000	113	19.0%	417%
10/09/2002	10/09/2007	60	15.0%	101%
03/09/2009	??	??		??
Average		**57**	**21.2%**	**164%**

For duration, one month equals 30.5 days.

Source: Global Financial Data, Inc., S&P 500 price level returns.

Really, Really *Above Average*

Folks get particularly freaked out by big returns when bull markets start. It seems like too much, too fast—and particularly so since they're still fearful of all the things that freaked them out in the prior bear market. If they can't remember that stocks don't return a safe, predictable 10% each year, then new bull markets (no matter how many they've been through) really send them into a tailspin of myopic fear. People are basically and naturally afraid of heights, and when the market rises more than they expected right after a scary bear market, they fear it will fall back. And since humans hate losses more than they like gains, that fear of heights is doubly scary.

Most folks understand when stocks fall 25%, rising 25% doesn't get them back to breakeven—stocks must then rise 33% for that. To recoup a 40% drop, stocks must rise 67%. So when stocks fall big, as world stocks did from October 2007 to March 2009—down 57.8%[9]—that takes a 137% rise just to get back to previous highs. A common refrain I heard in 2009 and after was, "If stocks rise an average of 10% a year, it could take *eight years* for me just to break even—never mind growing beyond that!" That would be bleak, indeed. Except, as Table 2.2 showed, stocks typically *don't* rise an average of 10% in bull markets, they have risen an average 21.2% annually. And after a bear market, you would expect the future years to be markedly above 10%—whether above or below 21%.

History also suggests the harder and faster the bear market, the swifter the initial return off the bottom usually is. For example, world stocks soared 74.3% and US 72.3% in the first 12 months following the March 9, 2009, bear market bottom.[10] Huge—and vastly more than anyone would have guessed during that very trying bear-market-bottoming period. The fears we fret during the decline cause us to find it unfathomable stocks could rise so much. And our faulty memories blind us to the fact doing so would be normal, not abnormal.

Viva the V

But if you had been through even a few market cycles, that big boom shouldn't have surprised you—nor would you have been fooled into thinking it was just a bear market rally. In fact, you should have expected a big bounce! (Still, most didn't.) In my February 16, 2009, *Forbes* column, "Anticipate the V," I wrote:

> Bear markets have been typically followed by bull markets in a V-shaped pattern. The steeper and bigger the decline, the sharper and bigger the subsequent bull move. The few exceptions to this pattern in the past century have involved the emergence of completely different bad forces than the ones that created and contributed to the bear market.
>
> For example, stocks rallied 324% from July 1932 to March 1937. After a recession-induced big bear market and partial recovery over the next 21 months, stocks encountered an entirely new kind of trouble in 1939. War in Europe sent the market down even lower than the recessionary low of early 1938.
>
> That could happen again, with the economic equivalent of an asteroid coming out of the blue. But, absent such a surprise, we should get the normal V pattern. Its upward swing will swamp any late-stage bear market vicissitudes as they always do.[11]

And a V we got. My timing here, just three weeks from the bottom, was just luck. I expected the V but didn't (and couldn't) know when it would start. How did I know to expect a V? I've been through 40 years of bear markets, and I've studied history. And I've forced myself to remember. I know (and frequently tell readers and clients) you must look beyond averages into what comprise them. Do that, and even if you haven't lived through a few bear markets or have a faulty memory, you learn bull market recoveries happen hard and fast.

Table 2.3 shows the first 3 and 12 months of new bull markets, using US stocks and their longer data history. The first three months of a bull market average 23.1%. Three months! And the first full year averages 46.6%. So basically, the first year of an average bull market about doubles an average bull market year (which is still historically above average overall), and half of that can come in the first three months! Not always, but enough to let you know you don't want to miss a second of it. Plus, that erases a chunk of bear market losses fast.

Many investors today *should* remember the hard fast surge off the October 2002 bottom (which retested lows in March 2003 and then exploded up again). Maybe they got fooled by the 1990 surge—just 6.7%. But the full year would have made up for that,

Table 2.3   First 3 and 12 Months of a New Bull Market—US Stocks

Start	End	First 3 Months Return	First 12 Months Return
06/01/1932	03/06/1937	92.3%	120.9%
04/28/1942	05/29/1946	15.4%	53.7%
06/13/1949	08/02/1956	16.2%	42.0%
10/22/1957	12/12/1961	5.7%	31.0%
06/26/1962	02/09/1966	7.3%	32.7%
10/07/1966	11/29/1968	12.3%	32.9%
05/26/1970	01/11/1973	17.2%	43.7%
10/03/1974	11/28/1980	13.5%	38.0%
08/12/1982	08/25/1987	36.2%	58.3%
12/04/1987	07/16/1990	19.4%	21.4%
10/11/1990	03/24/2000	6.7%	29.1%
10/09/2002	10/09/2007	19.4%	33.7%
03/09/2009	??	39.3%	68.6%
Average		**23.1%**	**46.6%**

Source: Global Financial Data, Inc., S&P 500 price returns.

not to mention the entirety of the 1990s. More grizzled guys (and gals) should remember the super-swift rebounds from the 1987 bear and the one ending in 1982.

Historical precedent is compelling but not enough. Even the most compelling historical pattern is useless unless you find a fundamental reason behind it. And there's a fundamental reason stocks want to V-bounce off a bear bottom. The early parts of bear markets are driven by deteriorating fundamentals. Maybe economic activity is slowing—as are sales and corporate profitability. Stocks see it coming and start pricing in the slowdown, edging lower slowly—fooling people with a grinding top. Headlines often claim, "It's just a correction. Buy the dips."

Later in the bear market, sentiment starts catching up with poor fundamentals. Liquidity usually dries up—this is where you may get a credit crunch or even an outright crisis as we did in 2008 (though not always). You tend to get lots of political jawboning, too, in the end stages of a bear as politicians try to "solve" whatever they think caused the downturn. (Heaven help us.) Unfortunately, ill-considered legislation or regulation or both is frequently a major or even primary cause of a bear market—like accounting rule FAS 157 in October

2007 (which contributed heavily to the subsequent bear market and credit crisis). So the threat of politicians poli-ticking freaks stocks out worse as the market envisions some new debilitating political stupidity. Sentiment turns deeply black, and stocks fall hard and fast—much faster than fundamentals would warrant. It's true through history about two-thirds of bear market losses tend to come in the final third of the bear market duration—the left side of the V. Bear market losses in the final stage are also above average.

Figure 2.1 shows a hypothetical bear market bottom—a classic V. Most bear markets double or even triple bottom—but with a little time, that resolves into a V. What makes the other half of the V? Fundamentals aren't great, but they're nowhere near as bad as most folks believe. And at a perfectly unpredictable point, the hard, fast fall turns into a hard, fast surge. There's usually a sharp reversal in liquidity that greases stocks. And increasing liquidity and reality being not terrific but not-so-catastrophically bad as folks fear create a near-mirror image of the late stage of the bear market. A "V."

Which means the bigger the bear market, the bigger the recovery typically is. So even huge bear market losses can be recouped faster than many commonly think. Figures 2.2, 2.3, 2.4 and 2.5 show real V-bounces—following the bear markets ending in 1942, 1974, 2002 and 2009.

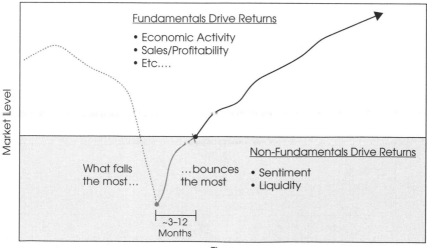

Figure 2.1   Hypothetical V-Bounce

Note: For illustrative purposes only. Not drawn to scale. Not to be interpreted as a forecast.

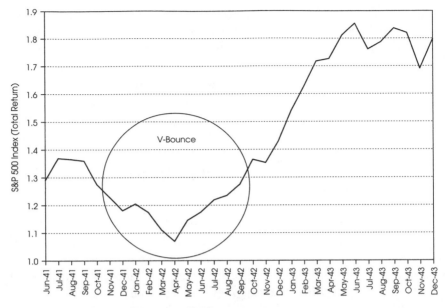

Figure 2.2   A Real V-Bounce—1942

Source: Global Financial Data, Inc., S&P 500 total return (monthly data).

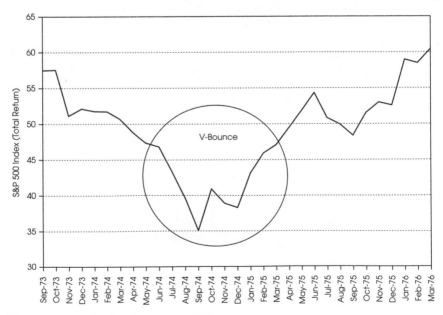

Figure 2.3   A Real V-Bounce—1974

Source: Global Financial Data, Inc., S&P 500 total return (monthly data).

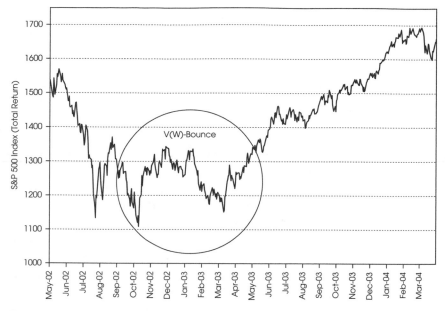

Figure 2.4   A Real V-Bounce—2002

Source: Global Financial Data, Inc., S&P 500 total return (daily data).

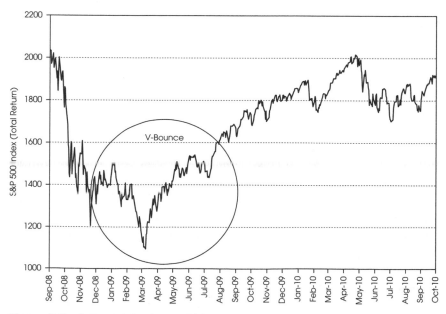

Figure 2.5   A Real V-Bounce—2009

Source: Global Financial Data, Inc., S&P 500 total return (daily data).

This has been going on forever. Figure 2.6 shows a graph from my 1987 book, *The Wall Street Waltz*. It shows industrial and railroad stocks in the Panic of 1907 and after. Stock prices formed an almost perfect V—the speed and shape of the initial recovery about matches the speed and shape of the last stages of the bear market. Many pundits in 2008 and 2009 said the financial crisis was "different this time" and historically more like 1907's financial crisis—concluding that in a financial crisis like that, subsequent returns are more subdued. But had they studied the aftermath of 1907, they would have had to conclude it culminated in a perfect V-recovery.

Some readers may wrongly think this means they should focus on the breakeven point after a bear. Not at all. If you're a long-term investor with growth goals (i.e., most reading this book), you should utterly ignore arbitrary benchmarks like breakeven, high water, round-number index levels, etc. Focus instead on whether your strategy makes sense for your long-term growth goals without thinking about what stocks did last week, last month or last year.

Rather, the V-bounce shows there's nothing average about stock market returns. If you're out of stocks during a bear market and trying to time the precise bottom, don't bother. If you blink, you'll miss it and the huge rewarding surge off the bottom. Also, full bull market returns, being inherently above average, should swamp bear market losses—whether you're in it full time or for just part of it.

Missing the V   History shows bull markets start with a bang. So if you miss that, should you sit out the rest, avoid the next bear and get in for the fireworks next time? No way.

First, not every bull market is like that—like the massive 1990s bull that started with a relative whimper. Plus, if you're sitting out of a bull market because you missed the initial surge, what will tell you to get in for the next big surge? My guess is if you're sitting out, you may not be so keen to get invested again during the deeply dark, terrifying days of a bear market–bottoming period—which are only evident after the surge is well underway and are actually great times to get all in. Whatever scared you last time likely scares you next time.

Bull markets are typically longer and stronger than most realize. So if you miss the initial surge, that's less than ideal. But that's even more reason to not penalize yourself by sitting on the sidelines while a bull market runs on—maybe for many more years.

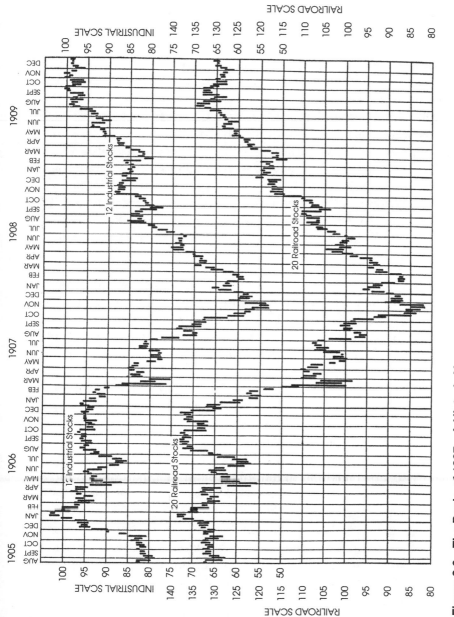

Figure 2.6 The Panic of 1907—A Historic V

Source: Philip L. Carret, "The Art of Speculation," *Barron's*, 1927.

Too Far, Too Fast?

How can remembering big bull market returns are normal and not inherently scary be useful to you? You know to beware the "too far, too fast" concept you hear frequently during bull markets. It particularly pops up in the first year or two, during bull markets' initial massive surges—but any stage of a bull market can be plagued with "too far, too fast" fears. It doesn't mean the bull must stop. Why? Because, say it with me, bull markets are longer and stronger than people remember and above average by nature.

As a rule, stocks can't inherently go too far, too fast. They can boom pretty huge, and there's nothing wrong with that. Some big booms do reverse themselves—like the 1980 Energy bubble or the 2000 Tech bubble—but those crashes were based on fundamentals not supporting sky-high valuations, not specific price levels. That stock prices have gone up a lot doesn't mean they always must fall. In fact, more often than not, they just keep rising in irregular fashion, but people forget—always. For example:

- October 18, 1958: "Among the country's top industrialists, apprehension over the business outlook has been replaced by high optimism and even some fear that the recovery may go **too far, too fast**. . . . The stock market already has gone wild."[12] *Nope! This year-old bull market still had over three more years to run.*
- April 19, 1959: "Securities and Exchange Commission through its chairman, Edward N. Gadsby, warned that it suspected the stock market was going **too far, too fast**."[13] *Again, the 1957 to 1961 bull was still alive and well.*
- July 13, 1962: "Looking at that and other statistics, some analysts were inclined to feel that the market had moved **too far, too fast**."[14] *A new bull market had begun just a month earlier and would run into 1966.*
- January 29, 1975: "The sale of borrowed shares in expectation of price declines—by traders apparently convinced that the market had gone **too far, too fast**."[15] *This bull was a little more than three months old and ran for fully 74 months and 126%.*[16]
- August 14, 1982: "Analysts said many traders concluded that the recent rallies in both the bond and stock markets had gone **too far, too fast**."[17] *Already? This bull market was just two*

days old! It ran until the famously short, sharp bear in 1987, rising 229%.[18]

- August 13, 1984: "Analysts said many traders appeared to believe that the stock market had come **too far, too fast** in its rally of the past two weeks."[19]
- January 2, 1986: "Johnson said both the bond and the stock markets have come **too far, too fast** and some backtracking is overdue."[20] *Nope—this bull still had more than a year and a half to go. Also, US stocks rose 18.6% in 1986, and world stocks a big 41.9%.*[21]
- May 20, 1992: "Investors are troubled. . . . They believe the market is overvalued. They're worried that the stock market has come **too far, too fast**."[22] *The famous 1990s bull ran for over eight more years, rewarding investors with a total 546% in US stocks, 242% in world.*[23]
- March 29, 1995: "It has been clear for a couple days now that investors, particularly institutional investors, were becoming increasingly edgy that the market had gone **too far, too fast**."[24]
- February 27, 1997: "Federal Reserve Board Chairman Alan Greenspan suggested Wednesday that the tremendous increase in the stock market over the last two years may have gone **too far, too fast**."[25] *People credit Alan Greenspan for crying, "Irrational exuberance!" about stocks. Trouble was, he spoke those words December 5, 1996. The bull had over three years and another 75.7% to climb in world stocks, 115.6% in US.*[26]
- July 1, 2003: "The market has gone **too far, too fast**, so investors can expect a 7% to 8% correction."[27] *This was four months into the new bull market, in a year global stocks rose 33.1%. Overall global stocks rose 161.0% from 2002 to the 2007 peak.*[28]
- September 19, 2009: "The stock market has been soaring. It may have gone **too far, too fast**."[29] *Not so—the bull that started in March kept running and runs still as I write.*
- October 15, 2009: "Despite the celebrations on Wall Street on Wednesday, analysts said the rally may have gone **too far, too fast**."[30]

(You see how the same phrases pop up over and over again, yet we always seem to think they're new.)

There's no such thing as "too far, too fast." There's no set amount bull markets are allowed to rise before they must fall again. Nor is there a capped amount they are permitted to appreciate in a given week, month or year. Fact is, in any given year, the bulk of the returns can be the result of just a few weeks—maybe days! You just don't know when those days will be. And when they happen, they will be huge and likely feel like too much, too fast. Markets are wildly unpredictable in the very near term. That's normal. (And by the way, this is all the same in reverse for bear markets.)

People who say a bull market has come too far, too fast fail to remember: If stocks' returns were predictably plodding, they likely wouldn't have as high a return. They couldn't! They'd be perceived as less risky—thereby reducing upside potential. If you want more predictable returns, you must accept lower risk and therefore likely lower overall returns—what you can get from buying laddered Treasurys and holding them to maturity, or similar. (And yes, you must hold them to maturity because Treasurys can and do lose value in the near term.)

Scared of Heights?

Part of the fear of big returns stems from how our brains developed. In behavioral finance, we call this cognitive error *fear of heights*. Our long-ago ancestors learned fast a fall from a high height was instantly deadly or at least crippling (which was effectively deadly). So we naturally fear anything that seems too high. This instinct was (and still is) lifesaving when it comes to actual heights and natural phenomena. But it doesn't work that way with markets.

We express ourselves through metaphors. I do it throughout this book! But returns aren't "high" in the sense that you could fall off them and break a leg—you understand that. Broad market prices can and do reach a certain level, then retreat, then—irregularly and with volatility—reach and surpass past peaks and keep going. Yet when stock prices reach a certain level, many investors frame them in a "high heights" framework. Our brains developed to automatically fear that anything high must eventually fall—and falling from a high height smarts. Bad! But this way of thinking can lead to a variety of investing errors—like bailing out too soon and missing months, if not years, of further stock appreciation, seriously harming long-term results.

What's more, bear markets can be above average, too—like the 2007–2008 bear. What's funny is, in bear markets, there's typically widespread sentiment that stocks can only go down forever—or at least can't go up. You rarely get that kind of widespread optimism to the reverse at any point in a bull market. At sentiment extremes, you do get euphoria—and it's typically a very bad sign. But it's as bad a sign as extreme, uniform bearishness is typically a good sign of better days soon ahead.

Stocks prices can get high and then fall for a time. But they don't fall *just because* they are high. Investors have witnessed that repeatedly and simply forget. When someone says, "Too far, too fast," ignore it. Unless the assessment is rooted in negative fundamentals that are little appreciated and capable of outweighing existing positive fundamentals, someone saying, "Too far! Too fast!" is just showing you how short their memory is.

Normal Returns Are Extreme, Not Average

I'm sure you've heard or read that, after a period of volatility (which is normal, more in Chapter 3), investors should wait to invest until markets behave more "normally." I've been in this business for nearly 40 years. I have much less of my career before me than what's behind me. I've written a regular investing column in *Forbes* for over 27 years and counting. I've written academic papers and books and managed tens of billions of dollars for individuals and institutions. I've done speaking engagements, seminars, TV. I've written, now, eight books on investing and personal finance. I've been exposed to capital markets and investors in every which way you can. And I have never, ever seen the market behave normally.

Actually, that's not true. The market behaves normally all the time—and by that, I mean it's wildly variable, and that's normal. But this isn't what people mean when they say they want the market to behave "normally." They mean they want some sort of signal: "All clear! Everybody in!" Or, "Danger here! Time to exit!" And smooth from there. They want returns to be less variable, more reliable. If you're waiting for that, you will wait a very long time. Because while the market does wildly unpredictable things—which *can include* delivering measured returns for a time—normal returns aren't average, they are extreme.

Table 2.4 is one I frequently show clients and readers. It breaks stock returns into big returns (over 20%), average returns between 0% and 20%, and negative returns. I'm being generous with the average category because my guess is most people (rightly) consider anything above 10% to be above average. But for the sake of creating broad buckets, I delineate this way.

First, and it always surprises me how fast people forget this, you see stocks are positive much more than negative—on the order of over 2.5 times to 1. People who believe secular bear markets are a constant threat (Chapter 4) have either very faulty memories or a very perverted way of measuring returns or some combination. Second, the most common outcome (37.6% of the time) is for stocks to be up over 20%. Average returns are next most common. But that's defining *average* very broadly. Since 1926, US stocks have landed smack dab in the average range (9% to 11%) just three times—in 1968 (stocks up 11%), 1993 (10.1%) and 2004 (10.9%).[31] World stocks have done it just two times since 1970—stocks rose 10.0% in 2005 and 9.6% in 2007.[32]

Table 2.4   Average Returns Aren't Normal: Normal Returns Are Extreme (US)

S&P 500 Annual Return Range			Occurrences Since 1926	Frequency	
>		40%	5	5.9%	Big Returns (37.6% of the time)
30%	to	40%	13	15.3%	
20%	to	30%	14	16.5%	
10%	to	20%	17	20.0%	Average Returns (34.1% of the time)
0%	to	10%	12	14.1%	
−10%	to	0%	12	14.1%	
−20%	to	−10%	6	7.1%	Negative Returns (28.2% of the time)
−30%	to	−20%	3	3.5%	
−40%	to	−30%	2	2.4%	
<		−40%	1	1.2%	
Total Occurrences			85		
Simple Average			11.8%		
Annualized Average			9.8%		

Source: Global Financial Data, S&P 500 Total Return Index from 12/31/1925 to 12/31/2010.

Least common overall are negative returns. And, much as it's easy to forget, history teaches us huge down years happen but are very uncommon. Ironically, when we've had them, people tend to expect them, whereas history suggests when you have had them, you won't have them again for a good long while (usually). Years with annual returns less than –20% have happened just six times— 7.1% of the time. So yes, they happen. They are excruciatingly painful. But with time, even a massive downside gets swamped by the far greater, more plentiful and more extreme upside the market delivers over time.

The Pause That Refreshes (and Confuses)

Now I will totally reverse myself. Bull market returns are indeed, overall, above average. But that doesn't mean all bull market years are above average. Annual market returns are wildly variable, which means it's important to look inside averages to see what comprises them—always. And even within bull markets, there are below-average years.

The Great Humiliator, TGH, that perverted trickster, likes to humiliate as many people as possible for as long as possible for as many dollars as possible. Bear markets are TGH at its finest, but TGH finds ways to humiliate investors all the time, in all ways. Corrections are a great way to terrify people into losing money when they otherwise shouldn't—when markets quickly drop 10% to 20% or a bit more, then quickly reverse, moving to new highs— punishing those who panicked and sold low.

But another easy way for TGH to get you is to throw a pause year at you. If every bull market year were just up huge, that, too, would be too easy. (Again, "too easy" would likely mean lower overall returns over the long haul. So we don't really want investing to be too easy.) In any given year, stocks can do one of four things: They can be up a lot, up a little, down a little or down a lot—all those four things happen. Down a lot is a bear market year. Up a lot is a bull market year—but so, too, is up a little. Heck, even during the course of an ongoing bull market year, you can get a down-a-little year. Sometimes the difference between up a little and down a little is just a little sentiment wiggle at the end of the year before the bull market resurges in earnest. Down a little can still be a bull market year.

Don't Fear Down a Little

If you're a long-term investor with equity-like growth needs, and you expect stocks to be down a little over the next 12 months, should you move heavily away from stocks? Just for a bit? I say don't bother. If you believe you're in an ongoing bull market and not an accelerating bear market—or even if you suspect it's a bear but don't have firm conviction yet—getting out usually isn't worth it.

Why? To start, you could be wrong! What if you get out, and stocks are up a little? *Or a lot?* If you have long-term growth goals, missing out on upside is one of the most harmful things you can do to yourself. Say you miss a 15% up move. That's a lot to make up—you'd have to beat the market, net of fees, by an average annual 1% over the next 15 years *just to get back to where you would have been had you done nothing.* Or resign yourself to poorer overall long-term results.

And you have to nail that forecast dead-on. Forecasting is tough enough without distinguishing with ironclad consistency the difference between up a little and down a little. Then, too, consider transaction costs and maybe tax consequences, which can detract from any benefit. And if you miss a perfect entry point, you can rob yourself of future returns. It's not typically worth it, in my view. Too imperfect.

The Third Year

Pause years—middling or even slightly down years in an overall bull market—are historically peppered in irregularly with up-big years. History shows the third year of bull markets can frequently be pause years (though they don't have to be, and a second, fourth, fifth, etc., year can easily be up or down a little)—like 1960, 1977, 1994 and 2005—pauses that refreshed before the next bull market surge. Table 2.5 shows the third years of ongoing bull markets.

You can see since 1926, third years are usually up a little or down a little. Rarely up big, but never down huge. And then, in these instances, the bull market resurged in year four and after. Pause years (whether third year or otherwise) are normal, happen enough to not be shocking, yet people forget, and their brains go haywire. Pundits who cried, "Too far, too fast!" feel vindicated—momentarily. But bailing on the market fearing a pause year confirms a bear market on the way can rob you—huge! Look at the full market return in Table 2.5's right-most column. Getting spooked

Table 2.5   The Third-Year Pause

	Bull Markets				Total Bull
Start Date	End Date	1st Year	2nd Year	3rd Year	Market Return
06/01/1932	03/06/1937	121%	–4%	1%	324%
04/28/1942	05/29/1946	54%	3%	25%	158%
06/13/1949	08/02/1956	42%	12%	13%	267%
10/22/1957	12/12/1961	31%	10%	–5%	86%
06/26/1962	02/09/1966	33%	17%	2%	80%
10/07/1966	11/29/1968	33%	7%	–10%	48%
05/26/1970	01/11/1973	44%	11%	–2%	74%
10/03/1974	11/28/1980	38%	21%	–7%	126%
08/12/1982	08/25/1987	58%	2%	13%	229%
12/04/1987	07/16/1990	21%	29%	–7%	65%
10/11/1990	03/24/2000	29%	6%	14%	417%
10/09/2002	10/09/2007	34%	8%	7%	101%
03/09/2009	??	69%	15%	??	??
Average		**47%**	**11%**	**4%**	**164%**

Source: Global Financial Data, Inc., S&P 500 price returns.

out of stocks by a third year pause meant, in history, frequently missing a huge chunk of total bull market returns.

Frustrating Bulls and Bears Alike   Pause years are particularly satisfying to TGH. Want to frustrate strong bulls and strong bears simultaneously? Throw a middling year at them. Frustrates everyone.

More frustrating: Fundamentally, these are typically fine years. Nothing usually suggests these years should be middling. Economic growth is usually fine. (Investors easily forget that middling returns can happen against a backdrop of fine or even very strong economic growth.) Rather, pause years generally are the impact of sentiment catching up to reality. The first part of a bull market (look back at Figure 2.1) is driven by liquidity but also the wide gap between sentiment and reality. Bear market losses make sentiment uniformly black. Sentiment catching up is a major force driving those V-bounce returns.

But after a period of big returns, that changes a bit. Not like switching a light, but sentiment improves for some swaths of investors. Their big returns make them feel better, but maybe they can also envision a future that isn't so bleak. Sentiment isn't so broadly bad. Maybe you have a camp of newly bullish folks! People aren't broadly euphoric, but overall and on average, sentiment is better—closer to what reality would warrant. And without that big gap between sentiment and reality, you lose one major driver propelling stocks higher.

That's the pause. It's not bad—it's good. It allows sentiment to reset. Maybe this is a transition year for fundamentals. Coming out the other side of a pause, there's typically a change in leadership categories, e.g., small cap stocks were leading, then big caps take over. Maybe cyclical stocks were leading, then more stodgy blue chips people didn't think were sexy in the front part of the bull take over. But the fundamental feature is not-so-detached sentiment.

The beautiful thing about any pause year is, by the end of it, it shakes out excess optimism. People think the age of big bull market returns is over or maybe fear a new bear market on the horizon because earnings haven't been beating expectations so spectacularly. Here, too, people forget. Part of the pause year's power is people quickly become accustomed to massive returns and huge profit growth. But that's all part of normal volatility.

So as returns turn out to be more middling, you get a resurgence of less optimistic or even outright bearish sentiment. That provides, again, a gap between reality and expectation and more fuel for the next up-leg of the bull market.

Middling bull market years aren't historically rare. They happen, yet people fail to remember or lack the tools to check if their fears about middling returns are correct. But just as big down years don't hurt long-term equity averages and are in fact a part of those averages, neither do middling years. They happen in history: Up a little and down a little are two of four possible outcomes for any given year—expect them all.

As I write this in mid-2011, I've been predicting all year 2011 is likely to be an archetypal third year of a bull market with middling returns—a trend going nowhere fast with a lot of volatility around that nowhere trend. Will that end up being true? Who knows. But what I've been suggesting for 2011 is consistent with the way bull markets usually evolve. I'm trying to use memory and history to my advantage.

Getting Average Returns Is Hard—Really Hard

Knowing returns are variable—knowing it in your bones and not forgetting—can keep you from panicking from fear or heat chasing in greed. But there's a more useful application. If markets return around 10% on average over long periods, and bull markets are *above* average, it must be *easy* to get 10%-ish annualized returns in your portfolio, give or take—right? Actually, that's very tough. Tactically, it's not—it's quite easy. But emotionally and psychologically, there are few things tougher.

Many investors have a stated goal of beating the market. But the truth is, on average, investors not only don't beat the market, they don't even come close to it. If you can truly accept why investors fail to get even average returns, you can likely begin improving your own performance over time.

Naturally, many readers will say, "But I'm above average!" And maybe you are! Like Lake Wobegon's kids, most investors (drivers, too) believe they're above average (which can't possibly be). I hope you're indeed above average. Chances are, however, many readers of this book, whether they admit it to themselves or not (or whether they know how to measure returns properly or not—a common problem), aren't remotely matching equities' long-term average.

Don't believe me? Each year, Dalbar Inc., a research firm based in Boston, releases its study of investor behavior, specifically as it relates to performance. In 2011, its research showed the average equity mutual fund investor got an annualized average return of 3.83% for the 20 years ending in 2010—inclusive of all transaction costs.[33]

To compare, consider the S&P 500 index, which investors in Dalbar's study would have used as their benchmark, annualized 9.1%.[34] Let me put that another way. Had you put $100,000 in the S&P 500 20 years ago and let it ride, you'd have about $571,000. But the average equity investor after 20 years had just $212,000—only 37% as much.

Why did investors on average lag so badly the benchmark they invested against? Inning and outing at the wrong times. Dalbar estimates the average mutual fund investor holds a mutual fund for just 3.27 years. (If you want more on this, I describe this more fully in my 2010 book *Debunkery*.) Most long-term growth-oriented investors buy into the general concept of buy and hold. They bicker about what exactly that means and how it's done. But few would argue holding a mutual fund for 3.27 years *on average* (sometimes less!) is buy and hold.

Many investors I speak with say, "Why do I need to hire a money manager when it's so easy to buy and hold an S&P 500 ETF? Set it and forget it!" And I agree! But in my experience, precious few can actually do that. And that's just what Dalbar observed—overwhelmingly, people can't set it and forget it, especially not when they think they can and that it's easy.

This is an underappreciated value of working with a good professional. Not every money manager can beat or even meet the market. Few have done it long term. But a good professional should be able to guide you to an appropriate long-term strategy and then help you stick with your goals and not in-and-out whenever the going seems tough, or conversely, when you feel like you're missing out on hot performance elsewhere (i.e., heat chasing). Maybe you don't average 10% a year—maybe with some professional help you have the discipline to stick with a strategy that nets you an annualized 7% or 8% long term. That's still much better than what Dalbar observed average investors doing.

Now, to be fair, the mutual fund investors they measured may not have had passive investing as a goal. But if they're actively buying and selling mutual funds, my guess is their goal isn't "to badly lag the market." And you'd think they'd eventually figure out they're doing a terrible job and just pick a decent fund and sit tight. Likely, doing that, they don't beat the market. They probably don't even match it, but they likely don't lag nearly as badly as they do buying and selling every 3.27 years on average.

Not only do investors in-and-out, they do it at the wrong times. Maybe not the perfectly wrong times, but wrong times nonetheless. Big down years frighten investors into thinking long-term equity averages aren't attainable. They panic and radically reduce risk (inconsistent with their longer-term goals). Big up years do damage, too—instilling overconfidence and perhaps greed, so they ratchet up risk (also inconsistent with their longer-term goals), usually in time to get hurt worse than they otherwise would have been in the next downturn. Repeat, repeat, repeat. All of which ultimately dings returns.

What's worse, they forget. They forget chasing heat in the late 1990s hurt bad, then getting excessively risk averse after 2002 also robbed them of returns. And then they chased heat again and reflexively overreacted after 2008, in time to miss a historic bounce off the bottom. They don't learn from past mistakes because they forget: Market returns aren't average. Return variability is huge— and normal. Remember that, and you can do better than the average mutual fund investor—badly lagging what stocks would give them otherwise if they'd stop inning and outing at all the wrong times.

Volatility Is Normal — and Volatile

I s "now" a more volatile time? Read the news, watch TV—odds are someone is saying it is. And that has been true almost every year forever. (It's a twist on "this time it's different" and more evidence investors have faulty memories.) But if you took a time machine back and visited any point 1, 5, 10, 17, 32, 147 years ago, you'd probably still hear folks saying, "Well, now is just more volatile than before!"

This belief—that stocks are increasingly more volatile *now*— doesn't need a bear market bottom to pop up. Undoubtedly, fears stocks have become more inherently volatile do increase in the intensely volatile bear-bottoming periods. But even in relatively less volatile years (and yes, volatility is itself variable) you get folks feeling like stocks are increasingly careening out of control via volatility.

First, stocks are volatile. Can't escape it. Volatility can be terrifying, but the fact the market wiggles wildly shouldn't be surprising. It is now volatile, always has been, always will be, forever and ever, world without end, amen. And you *want* it to be. More on that in a bit.

Readers of this book in 2011 and 2012 likely still intensely remember the terrible market environment of 2008 into early 2009. It seemed the parade of bad news was endless. Banks were going bankrupt, the government response was an unpredictable mess, stock prices were going off a cliff, unemployment was spiking. For a few months, it did indeed feel like the world might end. Of course, 2009 was a terrific recovery year (US stocks up 26.5%, global stocks up 30.0%), as was 2010 (US stocks 15.1%, global stocks 11.8%).[1]

But even 2010 had a big market pullback followed by a full-fledged correction. The world discovered Europe's peripheral economies were weaker than widely thought—threatening the very existence of the euro! Then there was the "flash crash" on May 6 (also known as the "Crash of 2:45") broadly attributed to a string of technical glitches—when within mere minutes, broad markets plummeted. Stocks were down nearly 10% at one point intra-day, only to quickly reverse most of that midday fall (while still ending the day down). Very scary stuff.

But was that proof the stock market is inherently more volatile now? The market more unstable? Of course not. 2008 was indeed a volatile year, but so was 2009! With a few years' distance, people don't remember it that way—they just remember 2008 was horrific and 2009 up big. But up or down, it's all volatility.

Fact is, some years are more volatile than others—always been that way. Some weeks and months are more volatile. But despite ever-present conventional wisdom over the decades that the present is more volatile than the past, there's no discernible trend the market is getting *more* volatile overall—just the same normal variability of volatility there's always been. Plus, whether a year is more or less volatile than average isn't automatically indicative of trouble—stocks can rise or fall on above- and below-average volatility. There's no predictive pattern. It's always been this way, yet people routinely forget. So let's use some history to correct this memory impairment. Doing so, we can see:

- What exactly volatility *is*. (People don't always know!)
- Volatility is itself pretty darn volatile.
- No matter how you slice it, stocks aren't getting more volatile.
- Given some time, stocks can be less volatile than bonds.
- And finally, if you want long-term growth, volatility is *good*, not bad.

What the Heck *Is* Volatility?

Lots of folks complained in 2008, 2009 and 2010 that stocks are more volatile . . . now. And while certainly volatile, that volatility wasn't much outside the historical norm for a bear market and then a big bounce back (read more later this chapter).

- October 1, 2010: "On top of that, **the market is more volatile than usual**. An Associated Press–CNBC poll taken in

August and September found about three in five investors less confident about buying and selling individual stocks because of the volatility."[2] *Remember, stocks were up huge in 2009 and had another fine year in 2010. Further, polls are about feelings and feelings aren't good forward-indicators for stock markets.*

- July 31, 2009: "Though it is undeniable that all of these much-ballyhooed innovations have made markets more efficient, there's good reason to suspect **they also make markets more volatile, less stable and less fair.**"[3] *I'm not sure what "less fair" means. But there's no evidence stocks are inherently more volatile. That's just a variation on "this time it's different."*

Maybe part of the reason people think "now" is a more volatile time is a simple misunderstanding of what volatility is. In general, people think of downside volatility as bad and upside volatility as not volatility at all! It's just "good." But volatility isn't "bad" or "good." It just is.

Typically, industry wonks measure stock market volatility using *standard deviation*. If you remember standard deviation (SD) from your college statistics class, feel free to skip ahead. Standard deviation is just what it sounds like—a measure of how much something deviates from its expected average. And it can be used to measure historical volatility of single stocks, sectors, the market as a whole, anything for which you have enough data points—sunny days in San Francisco, rainy days in Portland. A low SD means results didn't vary much from the average. A higher SD means there was more variability.

As of end-of-year 2010, the S&P 500's annual standard deviation since 1926 was 19.2%.[4] (That's based on monthly returns. You can measure SD based on yearly returns, but you get fewer data points. You can measure based on daily returns as well—but the industry mostly uses monthly.) But that includes the steeply volatile years of the two Great Depression bear markets, which drags the average up. Since 1926, median SD is 12.9%. (See Figure 3.1.)

A few things to remember: Standard deviation is always backward looking. It's a very useful tool, but nothing about SD tells you how volatile or unvolatile anything will be immediately ahead—it just describes how stocks behaved in the past on average. It's a decent guide—but not a useful forecasting tool.

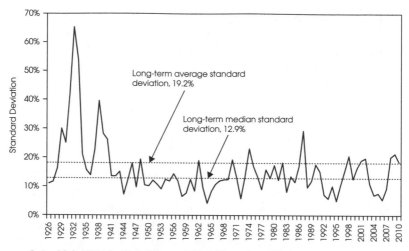

Figure 3.1   Volatility Is Volatile and Not Trending Higher
Source: Global Financial Data, Inc., S&P 500 Total Return Index, 12/31/1925 to 12/31/2010.

Calculating Standard Deviation

For those who didn't take Stats 101 (or can barely remember it) and are burning with curiosity, this is how you calculate a plain-vanilla standard deviation. Understanding the calculation can help you understand what SD is and what it isn't.

Take a series of data points, and calculate the mean (i.e., plain old arithmetic average).

Then, get the difference of each data point from the mean, and square each result.

Add those squareds, divide by the number of data points. Take the square root of that result, and that's your standard deviation.

Better yet, enter your data points into an Excel spreadsheet, and ask Excel to do the work for you. Technology is awesome.

A standard deviation of 0 tells you, historically, returns have never varied. Effectively, that would be like cash stashed in your mattress (ignoring inflation's eroding impact over time). You don't need historical standard deviation to tell you stocks have been pretty darn volatile. I bring it up because, again, stock market volatility is itself volatile. Some years, market volatility is vastly above. Some years, it's vastly below average. And some years, both happen in the same year. An average is an average and bakes in huge variability around it.

Volatility Is Volatile

The most volatile year on record (as measured by SD) was 1932, which included the very bottom of the worst bear market in US history. That probably doesn't surprise you. SD was 65.24%[5]—monthly returns varied hugely. So stocks probably fell huge, right? Wrong— in 1932 stocks fell just –8.41%.[6] Not great, but not disaster. Just the end of a monster roller coaster ride down, ending in a rather blah year overall. The next most volatile year was 1933—SD was 53.8%, and stocks were up a huge 54.4%![7] Big volatility does not mean stocks must fall. Getting past the huge volatility of the 1930s, 2009's SD was 21.3%—well above the median—and stocks were up 26.5%.[8] In 1998, SD was 20.6% and stocks boomed 28.6% despite having a big correction mid-year.[9] In 2010, SD was 18.4% and stocks rose 15.1%.[10] Yes, big volatility has also led to down years. But not always and not enough to make you automatically fear above-average volatility.

The reverse is true as well. Lower volatility doesn't automatically mean big returns. In 1977, SD was well below average at 9.0%, and stocks still fell –7.4%. Amazingly, returns in 1977 were nearly identical to 1932 but with much less volatility.[11] In 1953, stocks fell –1.2% when SD was 9.1%.[12] In 2005, SD was 7.6%, and stocks rose just 4.9%.[13] When SD is around its long-term median (from 12% to 14%), returns also vary hugely! In 1951, SD was 12.1% and US stocks boomed 24.6%.[14] In 1973, SD was 13.7% and US stocks fell –14.8%.[15] Our brains have an impossible time with this, but volatility is not predictive of future returns—or anything else.

Here's a cocktail party fact you can surely stump almost anyone with, including 99% of all investment professionals. Ask them which was more volatile, 2008 or 2009? My guess is most everyone says 2008. But no, in fact 2009 was, though 2008 was a terrible year and 2009 a great one. In 2008, SD was 20.1% to 2009's 21.3%.[16] (When they don't believe you, point them here.) This isn't so strange if you remember that in 2009, US stocks were up 26.5% overall, but that included a huge fall to the March 9 bottom, then a massive 67.8% surge through year-end.[17] Volatile! Also overall positive and up huge.

Lest your cocktail partners feel outraged, you can point out to them we're calculating volatility exactly the way academics, financial professionals and even journalists presume to be the correct way. This isn't some offbeat analysis. But hereto, our feelings exist as they do because our memories are terrible. And our sense of history is zilch.

Not Getting More Volatile

As said before, increased or decreased volatility doesn't automatically translate to worse (or better) returns. But increased volatility is hard to handle—emotionally and psychologically—and *that* can lead to investing errors. Investors regularly flee stocks to avoid volatility—robbing themselves of potential future returns. So if volatility were overall increasing, that could be a cause for concern from a behavioral and emotional standpoint. Except, contrary to conventional wisdom, there's zero statistical evidence volatiliy it is inherently increasing. Look back at Figure 3.1 again—it shows volatility flip-flopping from more to less irregularly with no indication it's long term trending higher. Not at all!

People fear the Internet, greedy bankers and fancy vehicles like collateralized debt obligations add to volatility. The US debt downgrade! Charlie Sheen. Lady Gaga! There's a lot to fret, but there's no sign volatility has trended higher. Yet most folks believe it has—in their bones.

Among other things blamed for increasing volatility is technology like high-frequency trading. A 2010 *Newsweek* article cried, "Trading billions of shares in the blink of an eye has bad stock markets more responsive—and volatile—than ever."[18] Nice sentiment, easy to see why they would believe it, but it's just mindless blather. Where's the evidence volatility in 2010 was markedly higher than ever? There is none.

And those same factors—high-frequency trading, the Internet, etc.—also fully existed in 2003, 2004, 2005, 2006 and 2007—when SD was relatively lower. And none of those things existed way back in 1987 when SD hit a relative peak. (Greedy bankers, sure, but I'm not convinced we want to live in a world without profit-driven bankers.) The Internet was in its infancy in 1998—another relative SD peak—when US stocks were up 20.6%.[19] It wasn't even thought of in 1948 (SD 19.41%, stocks up 5.1%—high SD, middling returns).[20]

See it another way. The Great Depression was wildly volatile—on the downside and upside both—for myriad reasons. One was a relative lack of liquidity and transparency. There just weren't as many stocks then, nor as many transactions, and there were many fewer market participants. Information moved more slowly, so price discovery was tough. Spreads between bid and ask prices for all but the very largest stocks were much greater as a percentage of the total price then, so the bounce between someone hitting the bid or pushing on the ask moved transaction prices a wider percent of the total price. Put all that together and you get much more volatility, regardless of other macro drivers (like a disastrous monetary policy, fiscal missteps, insanely ill-gotten trade policy, a lousy economy, massive uncertainty, Hitler's rise, Huey Long and a whole lot more).

Similarly, thinly traded markets even today are generally more volatile—like penny stocks, micro-cap stocks (frequently the same thing) or very small Emerging Market countries. Because there are vastly more publicly traded stocks now, vastly more participants and easily and instantly available information, markets *should* be inherently *less* volatile overall than the thinly traded Great Depression days. I'm not saying you'll wake up next week and stocks will be less volatile—not at all. (Expect that, and you'll be sorely disappointed.) Just that we're less prone to get the intensely wild swings we saw in the 1930s and still see today in thinly traded markets.

Speculating in Onions—It's a Crying Shame

People also like to blame shadowy speculators for volatility—in stocks, oil prices, you-name-it. But when people blame speculators, they rarely say who speculators are. You, as an investor, speculate prices will go higher. You're a speculator! Eek!

Mostly though, they usually mean folks trading futures—contracts letting people bet on future price direction. There are myriad legitimate reasons to trade futures. Businesses use them all the time to smooth input costs on volatile commodities. Airlines buy oil futures to smooth those costs for travelers. Farmers use futures for feed grain, fertilizer, etc. (And we all know what wildly reckless demons farmers are.)

If you want to know what the world looks like without speculators, look no further than the lowly onion. In 1958, onion farmers convinced Michigan Congressman Gerald Ford (yes, later Republican President Ford) speculators were pushing onion prices down. Hence, futures trading in onions was, and remains, banned—even today! Good old Free-Market Ford. Somehow Ford and farmers didn't understand speculators serve a vital purpose—providing liquidity and transparency. And their market participation can actually *reduce* volatility.

You think oil is volatile? Look at oil prices compared to onion prices in Figure 3.2. Onion prices are much more changeable with more frequent and huger boom/busts. (Peel this onion and you'll be crying, indeed.) Don't just trust your eyes—2000 to 2010, SD for oil was 33.8%, but for onions it was 211.4%![21] And that's something to cry about—10 times as volatile as stocks. How would you like stocks if they were that volatile? (You wouldn't.) All hail speculators for helping mitigate volatility. And to hell with politicians who want to ban speculators in their ignorant and arrogant sense speculators create volatility instead of diminish it. (Hat tip: Dr. Mark J. Perry and John Stossel.)

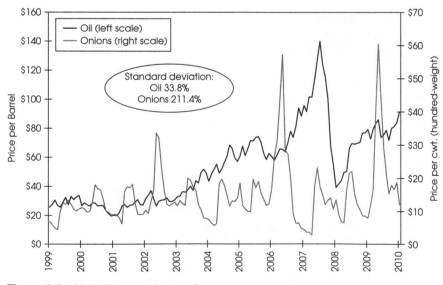

Figure 3.2 Volatility and Onions?

Source: Global Financial Data, Inc., West Texas Intermediate Oil Price (US$/Barrel) and Onions, Average Price to Farmers (US$/CWT) from 12/31/1999 to 04/30/2011.

The Daily Grind

You can see stocks aren't getting more volatile based on standard deviation. But my sense is standard deviation—a wonkish calculation—isn't how people experience volatility. Those most bothered by volatility aren't checking market levels once a year or even once a month. They intensely feel day-to-day moves—which are hugely variable—or even intra-day volatility—which can be more so. As I said in my 2006 book *(The Only Three Questions That Count)*, 2% is what the market calls Tuesday. Five percent? That's Friday.

For example, in 2008 and 2009, single-day moves were massive. On September 29, 2008, the S&P 500 (what most US investors would have been watching) fell 8.8%! It bounced back 5.4% the next day. October 13 stocks were up 11.6%! Two days later, US stocks fell 9.0%. That steep volatility continued through year-end. Even all through 2009, 3% and 4% daily swings—up and down—weren't uncommon.[22] (You would think they were onions.)

Wildly, painfully volatile and very hard to live through for so many. But if the purpose of your money is to take care of you 10 years from now or further out—as hard as it can be—folks shouldn't care about those kinds of daily bounces (so long as they aren't out-of-whack over-concentrated in some narrow category). But people do. It freaks them out. For many people, that kind of super-near-term volatility can be uncomfortable and makes it very hard indeed to remain disciplined to any kind of long-term growth strategy. But as variable as daily returns were in 2008 into 2009, there's no evidence even daily volatility is increasing. Daily volatility is just wildly variable. Always has been.

Setting aside a more technical volatility measure, most would agree a daily 1% fall or more is a big, volatile move. Of course, volatility goes both ways, so a 1% positive move is also big volatility. Historically, we can measure the number of greater-than-1% daily moves, both up and down.

Figure 3.3 shows the average number of 1%-or-more daily moves annually is 61.9. (This graph starts in 1928 because we don't have good daily return data from before then. I again use US stocks because of the longer history.) An average is an average—some years have vastly more big moves, some less. The Great Depression again had a big share of big daily moves, so the median of 51.5 is also a useful gauge. And there's again no evidence more or less 1%-daily swings

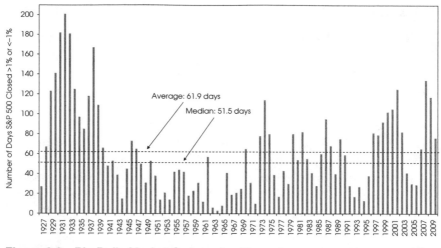

Figure 3.3   Big Daily Market Swings Are Normal

Source: Global Financial Data, Inc., S&P 500 price returns from 01/01/1928 to 12/31/2010.

mean better or worse returns. The 1980s was an overall terrific decade with a brief lousy period thanks to the October 1987 crash, and the 1980s flip-flopped wildly around the median. 1997, 1998 and 1999 all had above-average big daily moves and had terrific returns (33.4%, 28.6% and 21.0%, respectively).[23] 1996 had below-average daily 1%-or-greater moves, and 1996 was still up 23.0%.[24]

This is nothing new—it's just something people forget but markets don't. 1963 had hugely below-average daily 1% moves, and the S&P 500 rose 22.7%.[25] 1936, 1937 and 1938 were all hugely above average, and stocks returned 32.8%, –35.3% and 33.2%, respectively.[26] Nothing predictive there.

You would think a longer-term market participant should, theoretically, get through a few years with big daily swings and notice sometimes they're bad, frequently they're great, and start remembering, "Big daily volatility, on its own, isn't automatically a sign of longer-term trouble." But again, they forget because daily volatility is so painful.

Tune Out for Better Performance

My advice for those significantly bothered by big daily volatility: Turn off the TV and Internet during trading hours or hand the reins to someone else. Utterly ignore daily and even monthly returns or otherwise create some kind of control mechanism preventing you from reacting to big short-term swings. My guess is, if those who watch the market daily (who aren't professionals— professionals must watch daily, of course) can force themselves to look at returns just quarterly, within three years they'd see decided improvement in relative returns. They'd be less prone to make knee-jerk decisions and in-and-out at all the wrong times. That alone can improve performance. (Revisit Chapter 2.) Of course, most people will never do that because most of us are hard-wired to be myopic.

Figure 3.3 also shows daily volatility isn't materially trending higher. Yes, in the late 1990s through the early 2000s, you get a good run of more volatile years—but nothing signifying much of a trend shift. And since there's no clear evidence big daily volatility automatically translates into worse annual returns, it doesn't much matter if you get a few years' run. That's a powerful lesson to remember because focusing on price movement alone can distract you from what is actually fundamentally driving stocks higher or lower. And it can prevent you from making those fear-based (or greed-based) knee-jerk decisions that can, over time, lead to worse results on average.

Stocks Are Less Volatile Than Bonds?

For some, however, daily volatility is just too painful. They acknowledge daily price variability is normal and a fact of life, not unusual or insidiously increasing. But for some investors, they just can't tune out the volatility.

But many investors need some degree of growth to reach their long-term goals. How much that is depends on your personal situation, time horizon, return objectives, cash flow needs and many other factors. But just sitting on a cash-stuffed mattress isn't a solution many investors can live with. And discovering they haven't allowed for enough growth is frequently a mistake investors discover much too late to do much about it.

If you need some degree of growth—and therefore some regular allocation of equities most of the time—and you just can't tune out the market's daily gyrations, try thinking just a bit longer term. In Chapter 4 (just ahead), I show increasing your observation period increases the likelihood stocks will be positive. Still, some folks are willing to trade the probability of superior returns for the nearer-term comfort of a less-volatile asset class like bonds. Fair enough, but despite how volatile stocks can be in the near term, given just a bit of time, stocks historically have not only had superior returns to bonds, but they have had fewer negative periods.

Stocks have had fewer negative periods than bonds? Yes—if you give them a bit of time. How much time?

Figure 3.4 shows three-year rolling periods for 10-year US Treasury real returns. People forget—in the near term, bonds, even US Treasurys, can and do lose value. *Everything traded on a free market carries the risk of loss.* Says so right on every disclosure for every investment product I've ever seen. If you don't see that warning, watch out. (More on that in just a bit.) Not only have Treasurys had negative three-year periods, they've had a number of them in a row. This is not how most people typically think of a less-volatile asset like a Treasury. But all it takes to make bonds have years of negative returns is years of rising long-term interest rates. And from today's historically low levels, it isn't impossible to envision a period ahead in the not-too-distant future when we might run into an environment like that for a few years or more.

Figure 3.5 shows the same thing for US stocks. (Again, I use US stocks here because we have longer and better data, and we want more data for our laboratory.) Yes, the down periods are bigger—

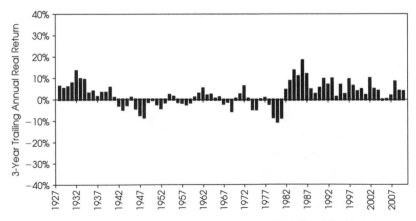

Figure 3.4   US 10-Year Treasurys (Three-Year Rolling Real Returns)

Source: Global Financial Data, Inc., USA 10-year Government Bond Total Return Index from 12/31/1925 to 12/31/2010.

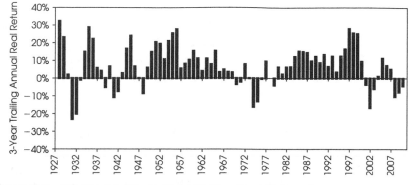

Figure 3.5 US Stocks (Three-Year Rolling Real Returns)

Source: Global Financial Data, Inc., S&P 500 Total Return Index from 12/31/1925 to 12/31/2010.

but there are actually *fewer* down three-year periods for stocks historically. And the up periods simply swamp bond returns. Better returns, fewer negative periods—if you give them just a bit of time. And these figures don't show any meaningful pattern of increasing (or decreasing) stock market volatility—just the normal variability of volatility we've always had.

You may *feel* like stocks are wildly volatile. And you're right. But history—that powerful lab—shows us they become less so if you can think just a bit longer term. Do that, and your relative performance likely improves over time. Don't forget that lesson.

Economic Volatility—Also Normal

Not only are capital markets volatile, but economies speed and slow—even within expansions! And basically, they have in every expansion ever. It's normal, not abnormal. It would be abnormal if quarter-to-quarter GDP growth were not hugely variable. Yet, every time we get a quarter or two of slower growth (as we had early in 2011), folks panic, thinking we're heading for a recession (or that much talked of but rarely seen double dip—see Chapter 1). But there's zero evidence a quarter or two of slow growth (or even isolated quarters of negative growth) means a recession must follow. People just routinely and regularly forget.

Like capital markets, it would be just so much easier and people-friendly if economies expanded at steady, predictable rates.

Would be easier if contractions were steady, too. But economies are much too complex for that. Not only that, let's remember the GDP statistic, as useful as it sometimes is, is a government-produced statistic and therefore naturally wonky. For example, it counts *net* exports—exports minus imports. This means if you're a net importer—as the US is—that counts against you. Which would be fine if there were any evidence being a net importer were inherently economically bad—but there isn't! First, globally, trade balances. Second, nations that are long-time net exporters (like Germany and Japan) don't have long-term records of better-than-average growth. In fact, the reverse! Also, GDP growth rates are regularly and routinely restated long after the fact. And the number is inherently backward looking—it's released at a lag, restated at least twice and gives a snapshot of economic growth of the *past*. It is not now and never has been predictive.

Figure 3.6 shows quarterly GDP rates since 1950—the shaded bars are recessions. Growth rates are, at times, hugely volatile and never predictive. If deceleration were predictive of future recession, Q1 1993 growth of 0.7% would have presaged recession.

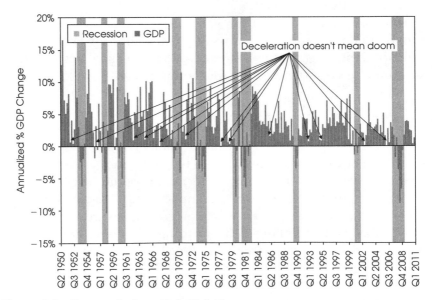

Figure 3.6   Economic Growth Is Volatile

Sources: National Bureau of Economic Research, US Bureau of Economic Analysis, as of 06/30/2011.

It didn't—it was followed by 2.6%, 2.1% and 5.4% growth in Q2, Q3 and Q4.[27] Growth slowed again in Q1 and Q2 1995—to 0.9% and 1.0%—and was followed by another over five years of vibrant (though variable) growth. You can see this pattern over and over again in every expansion of the last 60 years. GDP growth rates often slow down several times within an expansion, as happened in the mid-1990s expansion.

In the big 1960s expansion, growth rates varied hugely—slower growth in Q4 1962, Q4 1964, Q2 1966 and Q2 1967 (1.0%, 1.1%, 1.3% and 0.1%, respectively) didn't spell doom.[28] Even the occasional single quarter of negative growth didn't mean immediate recession—as in 1956 and 1959.[29]

See it another way: *Strong* growth isn't predictive, either. Huge growth of 13.9% and 7.7% in Q4 1952 and Q1 1953 fell off a cliff into recession.[30] You get huge single quarters of growth throughout history—but never do folks say, "Hooray! This is destined to continue!" *No one* (I can find) thought that way after Q2 1978's record-shattering single quarter growth rate of 16.7%—nor after any other single big quarter. If people get big growth isn't predictive, why don't they get slower growth is the other side of the same coin? Partly, as we've discussed, because they fear losses more than they like gains. But also, they simply don't remember—and when you don't remember, you can't connect the dots even if you've seen those dots many, many times before.

Volatility Isn't Inherently Bad

Maybe you'd prefer a world without volatility. But a world without volatility is a world where returns on investments likely can't even beat the eroding power of inflation. To get return, you must take risk—felt frequently as volatility. Maybe your investment goals don't require much growth—fine! But if you want more return, you must steel yourself to tolerate some volatility. If you want less volatility, that's fine—you simply must adjust down your return expectations. And if you want no volatility at all, then you must be satisfied with whatever low interest rate your bank is paying on deposits.

The idea there's some silver bullet—a magical investment—that gets market-like returns with materially less-than-market-like volatility is bewitching. If it existed, everyone would know it, and every money manager in the world would invest in it. Heck, there would *be* no money managers—everyone would do it on their own! But history doesn't support the existence of such a thing. Not legitimately, at least.

Bernie Madoff's victims got fictional returns of roughly 10% a year for years with little annual variation—some of them for nearly two decades or more! And that's why so many people flocked to him and to all perpetrators of Ponzi schemes (as I documented in my 2009 book, *How to Smell a Rat*). People just love the notion of 10% a year with no volatility—too good to be true! But too good to be true is often the ultimate sucker's punch. Now, with Madoff cooling his jets in jail for the next 150 years, it appears many of his victims may get back a bit of their initial investments (minus the pretend 10% annual returns). Which is very good for them—victims of financial Ponzis typically never see a cent. But less good for his other victims who may be forced to forfeit or disgorge billions altogether because they received payouts upon redemption of what they now know were ill-gotten fictional returns. They are victims as much as anyone else—they had no idea their withdrawals weren't rightfully theirs but instead money from new incoming victims' deposits. It's ugly any way you slice it. But without the pledge of smooth, non-volatile returns, Ponzi scheme perpetrators could never get to first base. Making yourself comfortable with volatility actually inoculates you against this type of fraud.

Getting back most of your initial investment in a Ponzi scheme (and nothing else) after a protracted legal battle (if you are fortunate enough to be able to afford a good lawyer or unfortunate enough to have been part of a scam large enough the government assigns one to you) isn't a terrific long-term growth strategy.

But stock-based Ponzis aren't the only scams investors hoping to avoid volatility fall prey to. As I write in 2011, the Iraqi dinar scam is popular. In this scam, con artists approach potential victims (*marks*, to the perpetrator), usually via e-mail or Internet ads, offering to exchange dollars for dinars. They promise some massive return from the strengthening dinar. There are legitimate exchanges for dinars if you have legitimate business in Iraq. However, most of the Internet dinar exchange solicitations are outright scams. And anyone promising you huge returns for arbitraging *any* currency exchange rates is either a con artist, delusional or incompetent. All are bad.

Then there is the ATM leaseback scam. Here, the con artists offer to buy ATM machines on your behalf, then you lease it back to them and they manage the machine for some guaranteed monthly return. You can legitimately buy ATM machines and manage them if you want—machines typically run $2,000 to $5,000, but that's not what this is. You know it's a scam because these con artists tell you the machines run $12,000 or more, *and they guarantee a monthly profit.* No one anywhere can ever guarantee you a return—not even on US Treasurys. I have no doubt some people unknowingly involved in scams like this are collecting monthly checks. What they likely don't know is it's likely all from incoming dupes and the thing will collapse as soon as the stream of new marks dries up—or authorities shut it down. The perpetrators will usually be overseas with most of your money in a place with no extradition.

If someone unknown to you e-mails you and tells you his dad is a jailed prince and he wants your help getting $25 million out of some third world country, and all you need to do is wire $5,000— it's a scam. (It's what the FBI calls an advance fee scheme: You give me some small amount, I'll give you more later—except you never get the more later.) In general, if someone offers you some "too good to be true" proposal and guarantees anything—I can't guarantee you it's a scam, because unlike con artists, I can't guarantee anything. But scams similar to this have been around forever. And you know what? We forget.

Nothing should scare you more than a guarantee of any kind of return. Insurance companies, who can legitimately guarantee things like annuity payments and life insurance payouts, do so because state and federal regulatory bodies require them to have certain levels of cash reserves to cover them, and even their disclosures tell you those payments are only as good as long as that firm is solvent.

You may think these scam examples are obvious—good. But vast numbers of fine, intelligent people have lost significant money to these and other scams. And they do it every cycle. And will this cycle. And the next and the next. After the fact, folks always say, "I should have known." But greed is powerful—as is the idea you can make a quick buck with little risk. Yet our memories failing is even more powerful. (An excellent source if you suspect you're being contacted for a scam is the FBI website—www.fbi.gov/scams-safety/fraud. They list common frauds and how to know if you're a potential target.)

Volatility is good because it's required to get you superior returns over time—history teaches us that. But true volatility is *also* a pretty darned good indication your investment is at least legit—not tied up in a Ponzi fraud. Sometimes, the return *of* your money is more important than the return *on* your money. Unless you think you are particularly skilled at finding Ponzis, profiting, then exiting before the thing collapses or authorities shut it down, and you're confident you won't be deemed complicit or have all your earnings clawed back, and are particularly good at getting your money and yourself out of the country to someplace the US government and courts can't get to—well, then I'm afraid to get market-like growth, you must accept some volatility. If it seems too good to be true, it probably is.

Never a Dull Moment

Part of this fear that "now" is a more volatile time (no matter when "now" is—next week, next year, the year 2047) is tied to the idea the world itself is becoming more unstable. Scarier! Every night, the nightly news says the world is more unsafe—geopolitical tensions are higher. We have more internal political dissent than ever. The world itself is coming apart at the seams, some say—and we have more natural disasters than ever, like the Japan earthquake, hurricanes, tornadoes, etc.

Many have claimed "black swan" events—improbable and wholly unpredictable way-out-the-bell-curve events—are becoming more frequent. Sort of the black swan du jour, which kind of defeats the initial concept of a black swan as a very, very rare event. Then, some say investors must somehow prepare for these most unlikely events on a very likely basis—though the very nature of a black swan is its unpredictability. So how are you supposed to forecast and invest for something that's highly improbable and unpredictable? Investing isn't a certainties game or a possibilities game; it's a probabilities game.

Say that again. Investing isn't a certainties game or a possibilities game; it's a probabilities game. I think if you make yourself say that 200 times in a row, it will make you a better investor because it may get blasted into your brain so you don't forget. It may make you remember to look to history to see what commonly happens and doesn't happen to align yourself with the odds of likely reality.

For example, someone might invest based on the far-out *possibility* an asteroid collides with Earth in 2017, destroying life as we know it. That would be a big black swan! But the far greater *probability* is no such asteroid hits and your strategy of stockpiling canned goods and burying gold bars in a backyard bunker doesn't really help you reach your goals when the 99.99999999974% more probable event becomes reality.

Fact is, the world has always been a dangerous place—and people have always feared it's becoming more so "now." We've always had geopolitical tensions, volatile commodity prices, supply disruptions, hurricanes, tornadoes, earthquakes. Many called Japan's terrible tragedy in 2011—an earthquake and devastating tsunami—a black swan.

It was a historically major earthquake—the loss of life was unaccountably tragic. But Japan sits on a major subduction zone known as the Ring of Fire. They know they get major earthquakes and in fact are perhaps the best-prepared country in the world for even very large ones. That's part of the reason that, as devastating as Japan's April 2011 earthquake was, the infrastructure damage was less than it could have been, thanks to Japan's very strict building codes. Nothing can mitigate the tragic loss of life—but Japan will rebuild stronger, knowing another earthquake will in fact hit them again.

But folks feared it would buckle the market. It didn't. Folks feared Hurricane Katrina would buckle the market when it flooded New Orleans and parts of Mississippi. They forget the market rose that day.

Wars, terror attacks, nuclear emergencies, natural disasters—these aren't black swans. They are and can be devastating—and we hope they're rare in the future—but they've happened throughout history. They are unpredictable, so you can't forecast them or build a portfolio strategy around them—but they aren't wholly improbable.

The good news is, though markets are volatile, history shows they are also resilient. Markets know (though people forget) as terrible as these events are, we always rise above. We dig out and rebuild and go on. Through it all, the profit motive is strong, and human ingenuity never dies. So no matter how trying a setback overall, humanity carries on—and so do our economies and capital markets.

This isn't just my optimistic view of human nature. This is, in fact, demonstrated through history. People think "now" is more trying than ever before—but the fact is, there's never been a dull moment in history. Table 3.1 shows just a smattering of history's major events and the annual market return. You think geopolitics are tense now? How about 1939 when Germany invaded Poland? Or when I was a kid and we US schoolchildren practiced under-the-desk missile drills because Russia's surrogate, Cuba, had missiles pointed at our heads? (I never did quite understand how the desk was supposed to protect us if they really dropped a nuclear bomb on us—but I was a kid and wasn't supposed to ask such questions.)

Table 3.1 Never a Dull Moment

Year	Events	Global Stock Returns
1934	Depression; First margin requirement; Hitler declares himself Führer of Germany	**2.6%**
1935	Spanish Civil War; Italy invades northern Africa; Hitler rejects Treaty of Versailles; Social Security created by law	**22.8%**
1936	Hitler occupies Rhineland	**19.3%**
1937	Monetary policy tightened; Capital spending and industrial production decline severely; Recession	**−16.9%**
1938	World War clouds gather; Wall Street scandals uncovered	**5.6%**
1939	War in Europe dominates headlines; Germany and Italy sign 10-year military pact	**−1.4%**
1940	France falls to Hitler; Battle of Britain; US institutes the draft	**3.5%**
1941	Germany invades USSR; Pearl Harbor; US declares war on Japan, Italy and Germany	**18.7%**
1942	Wartime price controls; Battle of Midway	**1.2%**
1943	Meat and cheese rationed in the US; FDR freezes prices and wages	**19.9%**
1944	Consumer goods shortages; Allies invade Normandy; Bretton Woods system established	**−10.2%**
1945	FDR dies; Postwar recession predicted; Invasion of Iwo Jima; Atom bomb dropped in Japan	**11.0%**
1946	Employment Act of 1946 passed; Steel and shipyard workers strike	**−15.1%**
1947	Cold War begins	**3.2%**
1948	Berlin blockade; US government seizes railroads to avert strike; Israel founded	**−5.7%**
1949	Russia explodes atom bomb; Communists win in China	**5.4%**
1950	Korean War; McCarthy and the Red Scare	**25.5%**

(continued)

Table 3.1 *Continued*

Year	Events	Global Stock Returns
1951	Excess Profits Tax	**22.4%**
1952	US seizes steel mills to avert strike; Top federal income tax bracket is 92%	**15.8%**
1953	Russia explodes H-bomb; Economists predict depression in 1954	**4.8%**
1954	Dow tops 300—common belief that market is too high	**49.8%**
1955	Eisenhower illness	**24.7%**
1956	Egypt seizes Suez Canal	**6.6%**
1957	Russia launches Sputnik; Treasury Secretary Humphrey warns of depression and President Eisenhower agrees	**–6.0%**
1958	Recession	**34.5%**
1959	Castro seizes power in Cuba	**23.3%**
1960	Russia downs U-2 spy plane; Castro seizes US oil refineries	**3.5%**
1961	Bay of Pigs invasion fails; Green Berets sent to Vietnam; Berlin Wall erected	**20.8%**
1962	Cuban Missile Crisis—threat of global destruction; JFK cracks down on steel prices, scaring Wall Street	**–6.2%**
1963	South Vietnam government overthrown; President Kennedy assassinated	**15.4%**
1964	Gulf of Tonkin; Race riots in New York	**11.2%**
1965	Civil rights marches; Rumor of LBJ heart attack; Treasury warns of gold speculation	**9.8%**
1966	Vietnam War escalates—US bombs Hanoi	**–10.1%**
1967	Race riots in Newark and Detroit; LBJ signs huge defense spending bill; Six-Day War	**21.3%**
1968	USS Pueblo seized; Tet Offensive; Martin Luther King and Robert Kennedy assassinated	**13.9%**
1969	Money tightens—markets fall; Prime rate at record high	**–3.9%**
1970	US invades Cambodia—Vietnam war spreads; Money supply declines; Bankruptcy of Penn Central	**–3.1%**
1971	Wage price freeze; US ends Bretton Woods system of exchange rates—ends gold standard	**18.4%**
1972	Largest US trade deficit in history; US mines Vietnamese ports; Nixon visits Red China	**22.5%**
1973	Energy crisis—Arab oil embargo; Watergate scandal; Yom Kippur War; Vice President Agnew resigns	**–15.2%**

(continued)

Table 3.1 *Continued*

Year	Events	Global Stock Returns
1974	Steepest market drop in four decades; Nixon resigns; Yen devalued; Franklin National Bank collapses	−25.5%
1975	New York City bankrupt; Clouded economic picture	32.8%
1976	Economic recovery slows; OPEC raises oil prices	13.4%
1977	Steep market slump; Social Security taxes raised	0.7%
1978	Rising interest rates	16.5%
1979	Oil prices skyrocket; Three Mile Island nuclear disaster; Iran seizes US embassy	11.0%
1980	All-time high interest rates; Health hazards in New York (Love Canal); Carter halts grain exports to Soviet Union	25.7%
1981	Steep recession begins; Reagan shot; energy sector begins collapse; AIDS identified for first time	−4.8%
1982	Worst recession in 40 years—profits plummet, unemployment spikes	9.7%
1983	US invades Grenada; US embassy in Beirut bombed; WPPSS biggest muni bond default in history	21.9%
1984	Record federal deficit; FDIC bailout of Continental Illinois; AT&T declared monopoly—broken up	4.7%
1985	US and Soviet arms race begins; Ohio banks closed to stop run; US becomes largest debtor nation	40.6%
1986	US bombs Libya; Boesky pleads guilty to insider trading; Challenger explodes; Chernobyl; Tax Reform Act Passed	41.9%
1987	Record-setting single-day market decline; Iran-Contra investigation blames Reagan	16.2%
1988	First Republic Bank fails; Noriega indicted by US; Pan Am 103 bombing	23.3%
1989	Savings & Loan bailout begins; Tiananmen Square; SF earthquake; US troops deploy in Panama; Berlin Wall falls; Japanese buy Rockefeller Center	16.6%
1990	Iraq invades Kuwait—sets stage for Gulf War; Consumer confidence plummets; Unemployment rises	−17.0%
1991	Recession; US begins air war in Iraq; Unemployment rises to 7%, Soviet Union collapses	18.3%
1992	Unemployment continues to rise; Economic fears; Monetary supply tightened; Bitter election contest	−5.2%
1993	Tax increase; Economic recovery uncertain—fears of double-dip recession	22.5%

(continued)

Table 3.1 *Continued*

Year	Events	Global Stock Returns
1994	Attempted nationalized health care; Republican revolution in midterm elections	**5.1%**
1995	Weak dollar panic; Oklahoma City bombing	**20.7%**
1996	Fears of inflation; Conflict in former Yugoslav republics; Fed Chair Alan Greenspan gives "irrational exuberance" speech	**13.5%**
1997	Tech mini crash in October and Pacific Rim crisis	**15.8%**
1998	Russian ruble crisis; "Asian Flu"; Long-Term Capital Management debacle	**24.3%**
1999	Y2K paranoia and correction; Graham-Leach-Bliley passed (removes aspects of 1933 Glass-Steagall)	**24.9%**
2000	Dot-com bubble begins to burst; Contested presidential election (Bush v. Gore, hanging chads)	**−13.2%**
2001	Recession; September 11th terrorist attacks; Tax cuts; US conflict in Afghanistan begins	**−16.8%**
2002	Corporate accounting scandals; Terrorism fears; Tensions with Iraq; Sarbanes-Oxley passed; Brazil narrowly averts default	**−19.9%**
2003	Mutual fund scandals; Conflict in Iraq; SARS	**33.1%**
2004	Fears of a weak dollar and US triple deficits; Indian Ocean earthquake and tsunami kills 200,000-plus	**14.7%**
2005	Tension with North Korea and Iran over nuclear weapons; Hurricane Katrina; Oil price spikes to $70	**9.5%**
2006	North Korea testing nuclear weapons; Fear of housing bubble; continued war in Iraq; New Fed chair fear (Bernanke)	**20.1%**
2007	Oil prices at all-time high; Fallout of sub-prime securitizations force US banks to raise capital; Rise of sovereign wealth funds	**9.0%**
2008	Global financial panic; Steepest calendar year stock market declines since 1930s	**−40.7%**
2009	Massive fiscal stimulus plans passed globally; Global central bank interest rates at historic lows; Major debate on US health care	**30.0%**
2010	PIIGS sovereign debt scares; Double-dip recession fears; May "Flash Crash"; Democrats lose House majority; Health care reform passed; Financial reform passed; Basel III banking reform passed	**11.8%**

Notes: Returns from 1970 to 2010 reflect the Morgan Stanley Capital International (MSCI) World Index, which measures the performance of selected stocks in 24 developed countries and is presented inclusive of dividends and withholding taxes. Returns before 1970 are provided by Global Financial Data Inc. and simulate how a world index, inclusive of dividends, would have performed had it been calculated back to 1934.

Sources: Global Financial Data Inc., Thomson Reuters.

People complain inflation is high in 2011 (though it's well below its long-term average). How about 1979 or 1980 when high, double-digit inflation was seen as a fact of life and almost universally expected to rise from there? Stocks were up 11.0% in 1979 and a huge 25.7% in 1980. The world feared the fallout from Japan's Fukushima nuclear reactor, yet the containment structures held and the radiation released was a fraction of the 1986 Chernobyl accident—which was 400 times more potent than the nuclear bomb dropped on Hiroshima. (Stocks soared 41.9% in 1986. So much for a nuclear disaster's ability to melt the markets.) Throughout history, stocks have fallen here and there. But overall, capital markets have continued charging irregularly higher eventually, vastly increasing overall global wealth along the way. This goes back to Sir John.

It's human nature to misremember history and say, "I wasn't so scared then. That wasn't nearly so painful." Our brains evolved this way to help us survive our hunter-gatherer days. It's the same with volatility. History shows us "now" isn't an inherently more volatile time—just that volatility ebbs and flows. So we forget long-past volatility. Even if you've lived through massive volatility a number of times, it's so easy to forget within just 5 or 10 years. But you forget at your peril. You might end up knee-jerking at what's otherwise some normal volatility in an overall fine year and robbing yourself of who-knows-how-much future return. Or, worst case, you could find yourself wiring your life savings to a con artist. Neither outcome is great.

I'm not trying to advocate everyone always be 100% in equities all the time—not at all. An appropriate asset allocation decision requires myriad inputs. However, I see far too many people frightened out of appropriate investments because of what is, in reality, very normal volatility. Never forget: Volatility is normal—and volatile. History teaches us. Memory fails us.

CHAPTER 4

Secular Bear? (Secular) Bull!

Have you heard the phrase, "This is just a cyclical bull in a secular bear market?" If not, good for you. Skip this chapter. If yes, read on.

A *secular bear market* is theoretically just a very, very long bear market that goes on for maybe a decade with bumps and wiggles along the way. For example, those who believe in secular bear markets don't see 2007–2008 as an above-average bear market, but a part of a many-years-long bear—maybe a decade or more. Yikes!

I don't think secular bear markets much exist—at least not enough historically to deserve much fuss. Big bear markets strung together with shorter- or smaller-than-average bull markets? Sure! A long period with a lot of volatility within, that point to point is overall flat or down? Absolutely—the 2000s were like that. But a bear market lasting 10 years? *Seventeen years* in one popularly (and very incorrectly) cited case? Nah. And if they did, you can't forecast anything lasting that long anyway. Folks forget quickly: Even in seemingly overall flattish longer periods, there have always been shorter intervals (maybe a few years' worth) of upside volatility—sufficient to spin people's heads and convince most everyone nirvana is ahead. But in general, I just can't find secular bear markets in history.

Oddly, those who believe in secular bear markets tend to see bull markets (that's right, entire bull markets) as countertrends in an overall downward trend—frequently calling them "cyclical bull markets in a secular bear" or even "bear market rallies." Hence, any period of upside is inadequate to justify investment.

It's true in bear markets you get countertrend rallies—just as in bull markets you get corrections. But an entire bull market a countertrend? This *Financial Times* quote captures it well: "I recall all too well that the 2003–07 bear market rally—yes, that is what it was . . ."[1] A five-year, 161% up-move in global stocks a bear market *rally*?[2] (In US stocks, 121%![3]) If it had been another two years and another 30%, would the same folks have *still* seen it as a cyclical bull within a secular bear?

Let's clear this up now. As shown in Figure 2.1 in Chapter 2, bear markets last, on average, 21 months. That's skewed higher by the massive late Great Depression bear market, which was nearly twice as long as the next-longest bear market. But even the very longest bear market on record lasted just over 5 years—and that was 75 years ago.

On average, bear markets typically don't last two years. Bull markets last much longer—averaging 57 months. See it another way: The *average* bull market is nearly as long as the *longest-ever* bear market from the Great Depression! If you're expecting bear markets to be so long, you're expecting something historically very unusual (and easy to remember if you've lived through even a bit of investing history yourself).

Typically, identifying "secular bear markets" requires a bit of "data mining" (otherwise known as fudging). Believing in them requires 1) a very short memory and 2) a complete disregard of history. Folks who believe in secular bear markets want you to think long term, but from having done so, it's quite clear to me secular bear markets don't much exist, but secular *bull* markets actually may. However, forecasting either is a fool's errand. (More on why in Chapter 6.) In this chapter, we examine:

- What makes secular bears see the world the way they do.
- The two culprits—the two periods secular bears point to most.
- Do secular bull markets exist?

Seeing the World Through Bear-Colored Glasses

Research shows the human brain is hard-wired from many thousands of years to focus more on danger than the absence of danger (from Daniel Kahneman's Noble Prize–winning prospect theory). This is why folks tend to fear airline travel much more than car travel—though vastly more people die in cars than in airplanes each year in every country.

And it's the same in investing. Though secular bear markets are hard to find, secular bears, as individual people, aren't—you can find them easily on TV and in print. This is the opposite of how it works for people biased to bullishness. Secular bears are wrong much more than they are right—except during bear markets, *which occupy much less time historically than bull markets.* Then, they are vindicated—but for some reason, folks quickly forget that more than two-thirds of the time, they were bearish and wrong.

My guess is long-term perma-bear types get a lot of media play because human nature tends to bestow automatic credibility on the skeptic. The pessimist. They don't call the movie critics *critics* for nothing. They sure don't call them movie *analysts*. It's critics. Criticism is seen by most as sophisticated and smart. Scientific even! On the flip side, humans tend to see optimists as dupes—Pollyannas seemingly unaware of all the trouble all around us, whistling their way through rose-colored lives. (Almost all of Sir John's life, he was seen as a Pollyanna.)

Mind you, in capital markets, history is solidly on the side of the more-optimistic-than-not set. (Not the perma-bullish—but the bullish-much-more-than-bearish.) But there's still something power-fully persuasive about a snarky pessimist.

Plus, it's just *easier* to be a dug-in bear. If stocks are up big, you can say, "It's just a correction in a secular bear." The higher they go, the more they might fall—and the prospect of falling frightens people more than opportunity makes them feel good. And for some reason, people are more forgiving if you're wrong and miss upside than if you're wrong and expose them to the downside—though history shows over time, being bearish and wrong can be much more damaging to long-term results than being bullish and wrong. I think it's because of what behavioralists have proven—that people hate losses fully twice as much as they enjoy gains emotionally.

It may be easier to be a bear market *pundit*, but as an investing *professional*—whose livelihood depends on managing other people's money—it's more profitable (for both the firm and its clients) to be more bullish than not over time. Why? History shows stocks are positive much more than negative (which you already know from Chapter 3 and I show in more ways later this chapter). It's pretty simple. If stocks do better more often than not in the long term and you've been a dug-in bear, you miss that upside—and in the long term, you lose most of your clients. That's why few dug-in bears run firms that manage very much money. There is a time for bearishness, yes, but dug-in bears eventually get left behind and wiped out of the money management business. Because while there are times to be bearish, there are more times to be bullish.

Two Secular Bear Markets?

Two past periods widely pointed to as secular bear markets include the famous (but quite incorrect) "17 years of zero returns" from 1965 through 1981. Second, and more recently, the decade of the "aughts," from 2000 to 2009.

Whether either was a secular bear market depends on how you measure and what you define as a bear market. For example, it's true, from 1965 to 1981, stocks annualized a scant 0.01%—if you measure using the bizarrely constructed, price-weighted Dow Jones Industrial Average (aka, the Dow) and *exclude* dividends.[4]

But why would you? No serious academic or trained professional would. There's a reason the industry calls indexes that include dividend reinvestment *total return*—these are the ones they typically use for market measurement. Dividends are part of your *total return* and should be counted. Sure, for long-ago periods, daily total return data can be hard to get. In this very book, I occasionally use price data (i.e., without dividends) to measure very general historic trends—but only because I sometimes can't get reliable total return data for that phenomenon or period. It's a limitation of the historic data—total return data better reflect reality.

When you do include dividends, the Dow annualized 4.5%—or 111% cumulatively over that supposedly flat period.[5] Below average, but not a bear market and still 111%! Put another way, over those 17 years, your money doubled, plus some!

There's still yet another problem: The Dow is inherently wonky and broken as a measuring stick for long-term economic results. Why? It's price weighted as opposed to market-capitalization weighted. Again, no serious academic or formally trained professional today would use price-weighted indexes if they could possibly avoid it because they don't reflect economic reality. What's more, for these periods commonly deemed "secular bear markets," there are abundant correctly calculated indexes. (In fact, you can well argue that when someone points to the Dow for an intermediate- or long-term return analysis, they are telling you, without meaning to, that they were never formally trained. Had they been, they wouldn't use the Dow without explaining thoroughly that it isn't at all accurate or reflective of anything economic.)

I wrote at some length about the fallacy of price-weighted indexes in my 2006 book, *The Only Three Questions That Count*, and wrote further on it in my 2010 book, *Debunkery*. Briefly, in a price-weighted index like the Dow, a stock's influence on index returns is dictated by the pure cosmetics of the share price relative to the average share price of other stocks in the index. A stock with a $100 share price has double the impact of a $50 stock, though the $50 stock might come from a firm 10 times bigger by actual size, i.e., market capitalization.

People are reluctant to believe this because the Dow is cited so often in the media—but it is simply true. If you had a two-stock price-weighted index in which one stock price is $100 and the other is $50, and the $100 stock drops 5% and the $50 stock rises 10%, the index level won't change at all. But if you owned equal amounts of both stocks, you would have made 2.5% from those two price movements.

On top of the lack of dividends mentioned earlier, that's what happened between 1965 and 1981—the higher-priced stocks in the Dow didn't do as well as the lower-priced stocks. So the Dow as an index underperformed the economic returns of owning the 30 Dow stocks—and that dog won't hunt. Absurd.

Further, and this is really pretty insane, stock splits (and reverse splits, which happen less often for stocks big enough to be in the Dow, but still happen) have a very real impact on index returns— because they impact the price per share of the stock. And how high the price per share is relative to the index's other stocks really matters in these bizarrely constructed indexes. In a given year, returns can be purely random tied to which stocks split and which don't.

Said simply, if the stocks that split do better than the stocks that don't split, the index will do worse than the economics from owning equal amounts of the stocks. And vice versa! You should utterly ignore any price-weighted index for any form of intermediate- to long-term return analysis—always—and instead prefer market-capitalization indexes, which better reflect reality. (It's telling that Dow Jones hasn't created a new price-weighted index in years—recognizing the pitfalls.)

Simple fact and case in point: The S&P 500, a market-cap-weighted index, annualized 6.3% from 1965 to 1981 (total return), 180% cumulatively.[6] And yes, those famous 17 years are below the long-term average, but not disaster and not remotely a secular bear market. That doesn't make the period bad. Remember, too, from Chapter 2—to have an average, you must have things above it and below it. So there will always be above- and below-average periods—true for any and all time series. For an awful lot of people in 2011, with 10-year Treasurys yielding well under 3% and a past 10-year period that was overall flat, a 17-year return of 6.3% annualized may not seem so bad.

But suppose for some reason you wanted to measure using an inherently broken index and not reinvest dividends. Those 17 years still aren't a secular bear market. Why? Because a bear market is a period marked by overall *falling* securities prices—not one of below-average, but rising ones. And it's hard and maybe impossible to find falling stock prices over long periods.

A bear market is formally and technically defined as a drop of more than 20% over some prolonged period. This is to distinguish it from a market correction, which is a drop of 10% to 20% over a shorter period—a few weeks or even months. Corrections happen almost every year at some time. We had one in 2010—then global stocks finished the year up 11.8%.[7] As I write, we appear to be having another one in mid-2011. Stocks can fall far and fast—but they can recover quickly, too. Corrections—even huge ones—are normal during the course of bull markets and don't hurt overall returns—as long as you don't panic and sell at relative lows.

But bear markets are by definition bigger and longer. Where are the 10-year negative returns in stocks? Historically, there are just a very, very few—and if you wait just a bit after that, they disappeared as stocks bounced back. The only one that really endured for any long period is the one that began in 1929.

But if you want to create a phony image of low long-term returns, that's easy—use a price-weighted index that excludes dividends. And even then, from 1965 to 1981, the Dow was exactly flat. Not down. And that's ignoring the huge volatility in the period in between. There were three distinct US bull markets within that period—ones big enough to spin your head and make you dizzy. It wasn't a long period of sustained negative returns. It was just a long, gyrating, wild ride with overall positive returns.

The Aughts

Then there were the "aughts." Aught not have been, but they were. During the 10 years from 2000 through year-end 2009, the S&P 500 annualized –0.95% and the MSCI World annualized –0.24%.[8] Including emerging markets, the MSCI ACWI annualized 0.89%.[9]

Flat—slightly up or slightly down, depending on where you invested. Hardly something to cheer. But *flat*, again, isn't down big and doesn't capture what the 2000s really were. There was a very large bear market starting in 2000 (the third largest since World War II), a normal-sized bull from 2002 to 2007, another monster bear market (the biggest since World War II), and then 2009 boomed huge, kicking off another bull market that continues as I write. (And still, two out of the three biggest bear markets in over 50 years—back to back—and the 10-year period was only flat. That is evidence of a stunningly resilient market—a point few seem to recognize today because our memories are so short.)

Plus that middle-of-the-aughts bull market wasn't trivial—five years! Bull markets last, on average, about 60 months. I always say don't be fooled by averages, but unusually, this one was smack-nose average. Is *five years* a countertrend? That's all of college and a year of graduate school. Think about how much time that is! That's long enough for your grandchild to be born, learn to ski, ride a horse, read basics and figure out Santa is really your son or daughter. Pretty long.

What's more, if you were out of the market from 2002 to 2007, you weren't saying, "Phew, I'm ok with missing this because I know it's a secular bear market." You were saying, "Holy cow, I'm missing a huge, years-long, 161% (world) or 121% (US) boom in stocks."[10] Only in retrospect can you know a 10-year period was flat, overall. And flat overall doesn't make a bear market.

Make That Secular Bear a Secular Bull   Another way to see this— flip the whole argument on its head and it becomes totally silly immediately, and the perma-bears' logic dissolves. If perma-bears can discount four or five years of overall upside as a countertrend rally within a secular bear market, then why aren't the much shorter periods true, formalized bear markets occupy countertrend corrections within long-term secular *bull* markets?

No one ever suggests such a thing. No one has ever called a bear market a mere correction in a secular bull market. No one even talks about secular bull markets. In the vernacular of our culture, the phraseology of "secular bear market" exists; "secular bull market" doesn't. That shows you what our biases are. Despite stocks rising vastly more than falling over our long history, we've never commonly coined the phrase *secular bull market*. Not even Sir John used those words. That ought to tell you something about our societal cognitive dissonance whether discussing the oughts or the aughts. We look for downs and fear them and put them front of conscience, but our memories fail to recall the longer sweep of ups and progress.

Anyone can cherry-pick specific periods when, from point to point, you get a flat or negative return—while ignoring all the upside volatility within that would have been agonizing to miss. But let's play the same game a different way. Shift the time just a few years forward or back.

If re-focusing on those 17 years from 1965 through 1981, tack on just a few more years—make it a nice round 20! From 1965 through 1984, stocks rose 342.3% (annualized 7.7%).[11] Not too shabby. Heck, tack on five more—from 1965 through 1989, stocks rose 1,015.2% and annualized 10.1%—just above average.[12] That secular bear just became a secular bull (remembering it was never a bear in the first place because using a correctly calculated index, the returns were below average but positive—not negative).

Twenty-five years is a pretty reasonable time horizon to consider for most folks who are long-term, growth-oriented investors (see why in a bit). You can play the same game with the aughts—tack a few of the mid- to late-1990s to the start, and overall you get positive returns. I don't know what the next few years hold, but my guess is, in the future, you can tack on some 20-teen years and get the same effect.

Taking a longer-term view, history (not using the Dow, price-weighted, funky, non-reflective-of-reality index that it is—*particularly* if you don't reinvest dividends) quickly dissolves even the most dreadful periods into overall positive trends.

Past Performance Isn't Indicative

In a book heavy about using history as a tool, you may be surprised that I say (repeatedly) past performance is no indicator of future results. It's not! History is a useful tool for shaping forward-looking expectations. But it's never a guarantee. You know that, and most investors understand that. Yet amazingly, in 2009 and 2010, many were citing *past* overall flattishness as a reason the period *ahead* would be lousy and flat—and claiming it was a reason to move heavily away from stocks. There were endless media cries about a new US "lost decade" similar to Japan's in the 1990s. Which runs counter to history (as I'll show in a bit). The longer stock returns are poor, the more likely you are to soon run into a period when forward stock returns are good. But that's not the way our myopic memories want to work. For example, in 2009 and 2010 it was easy to find media quotes like these:

- September 27, 2009—"However, when, at the conclusion of the 20-year period that ended in February 2009, bonds had outperformed stocks by a margin of 0.40%, the news was impossible to miss. I know this because, for those few weeks, the phone lines in my office lit up with calls from clients who wanted to exit equities and put their entire nest eggs into bonds because they'd heard talk of a **'lost decade'** for stocks."[13] *Anecdotal evidence about investor behavior, but likely pretty reflective of how many felt. We'd just gone through a flat period, which made people feel bad about the period ahead.*
- September 31, 2010—"It won't take much in this climate to turn fears of a US *'lost decade'* into a reality."[14]
- October 11, 2010—"Advanced economies risk a **'lost decade'** unless policy makers recognize the severity of the wounds left by the financial crisis."[15]

To nail a "lost decade" call, you had to make that call *in late 1999*. But very, very few (none I can find) were saying, "The next 10 years will be lousy," in 1999 while Tech fever was epidemic. Instead, you heard things like valuations didn't matter, it was a new economy, etc. *BusinessWeek* had that famous cover touting "The New Economy"—on January 31, 2000, a little over a month from the Tech peak and the start of a big bear market.[16] The cover story didn't ponder if the go-go times were about to end. It said they'd soon be replicated outside of Tech—and globally!

My March 2000 *Forbes* column Tech bear market call (see Chapter 1) by pure luck was mere days before the actual global Tech peak. But I wasn't saying the next 10 years would be flat—I always look out the next 12 to 18 months—24 months at the outside. Even so, at the time, I was very much alone in my forecast—regardless of the duration of my bearishness. (Professionals, too, can become too euphoric—although it happens less often than when they become too dour.)

That no one was predicting a flat decade in 1999 or 2000 should underscore the fallacy of trying to make long-term forecasts. (More on that in Chapter 6.) Though many try, I've never seen anyone do it, outside of people who, overall, think stocks should rise over time. But even they don't know the nitpicky details behind why stocks should rise in any particular year in the far future—outside the fundamental principles of capitalism, which make stocks rising more than falling over long periods a greater likelihood.

Also, it should remind you what just got done happening has little or no bearing on what happens next. For example, in retrospect, no one would say now the 1990s being overall hot was a great reason to be bullish for all of the aughts. In the same way, that the aughts were overall flat is no reason to be bearish for the next 10 years! The immediate past is never predictive about the immediate future. It's easy (but frequently costly) to think that way because the immediate past is so familiar to us. But if the period behind were in any way predictive of the period ahead, stock markets would be uni-directional, and they're not.

Stocks—Up Vastly More Than Down

Consider this: If we're in a string of secular bear markets, how did the US get to $16 trillion in market cap? And the world to $54 trillion?[17] And just how long must a positive countertrend be before it's no longer a secular bear market? Because if five years is a countertrend, I'm not sure how long a non-countertrend must be. Six years? Seven? Twelve? Twenty-seven? Eternity? If you make the time period long enough, by definition it becomes effectively impossible to ever prove the perma-bear wrong.

This isn't an argument for always being a screaming bull. There are years when stocks have more muted returns (as discussed in Chapter 2). And near-term returns can be agonizingly negative (as in 2007 to early 2009). There is a right time to be bearish. But the fact is, in history, stocks overall rise much more than fall.

Day-to-day, that may not seem so—which may be why people forget this so fast. See Table 4.1 which shows daily, monthly, yearly, rolling 1-year, rolling 5-year and so on trading periods, as well as the number of times they've been positive or negative. Stocks (again, using the long history of US stocks) are positive daily about 53% of the time—little better than a coin flip. The positives and negatives tend to come in clumps, too, so when in the throes of an overall more negative period, it's easier to forget stocks like to be positive more than negative.

Stretch your observation a bit longer, and 62.3% of calendar months historically have been positive. Again, positive and negative months tend to clump, so you typically get a string of negative months during bear markets. But you must have a very short memory indeed to not remember calendar years are positive 71.8% of history. Well over two-thirds! Rolling 1-years have been positive

Table 4.1 Stocks' Historical Frequency of Positive Returns

	Number of Periods			Percent of Periods	
	Positive	Negative	Total	Positive	Negative
Daily Returns*	11,375	10,098	21,473	53.0%	47.0%
Calendar Month Returns	635	385	1,020	62.3%	37.7%
Calendar Quarter Returns	230	110	340	67.6%	32.4%
Calendar Year Returns	61	24	85	71.8%	28.2%
Rolling 1-Year Returns, Monthly	736	273	1,009	72.9%	27.1%
Rolling 5-Year Returns, Monthly	835	126	961	86.9%	13.1%
Rolling 10-Year Returns, Monthly	847	54	901	94.0%	6.0%
Rolling 20-Year Returns, Monthly	781	0	781	100.0%	0.0%
Rolling 25-Year Returns, Monthly	721	0	721	100.0%	0.0%

*Daily return data from 1/31/1928 to 12/31/2010, based on price-level returns.

Source: Global Financial Data, S&P 500 Index from 12/31/1925 to 12/31/2010.

72.9%, rolling 5-years 86.9%, 10-years 94% and every single rolling 20-year period historically has been positive. That is a heck of a lot of upside volatility, and some pretty bad memories most investors have—even professionals. Especially professionals! And don't forget, even within those few longer periods that were overall negative, they included shorter interludes of hugely positive returns—they weren't 10-year periods of nonstop consistent downside.

If someone argues the period ahead will be long-term negative, they're arguing something that, historically, has happened rarely, if at all. (You can't find a rolling 20-year big negative bear market return!) So if they can't find that, they must explain why the period ahead will so strongly buck the odds and be an almost-never or first-ever event. They must also explain why they have suddenly discovered a way to make long-term forecasts when in the history of professional money management, no one has done it successfully except perhaps coincidentally by accident. That's all a very tall order.

Flat Decades Don't Lead to Flat Decades   Overall negative 10-year periods are pretty rare—they occur just 6% of the time. If you want to base your future on something that happens 6% of the time, plan to be wrong about 94% of the time. What's more, those few periods weren't that negative on average. Most were pretty flat. On average, they fell just –14.2% cumulatively—just –1.6% annualized.[18] Flat. Not great, but not disaster. And around that average, the returns of all the negative periods are grouped pretty tight.

The worst 10-year period, ending August 1939, was down –40.2% cumulatively or –5.0% annualized.[19] Again, not great by any means. But that wasn't a reason, on its own (as many believe), to think negatively about the future from there. (And no reason to presume the negativity of 2007 to 2009 means more future negativity.) Note the following 10-year period from 1939 to 1949 was overall fine—up 138.4% cumulatively—making up for the previous decade and then some.[20]

Not surprisingly, more than half of history's negative 10-year periods culminated in the big bear market that ended the Great Depression. And the 10-year periods in the Great Depression were worse—they averaged –16.4%. The rest were sprinkled in the bear-market–bottoming period of 2008 and 2009, and a couple ended during 2010's big mid-year correction—together, they averaged just –11.4% and annualized –1.24%. Pretty flat. There are none elsewhere—that's how rare they are. (Again, they're just 6% of total 10-year periods.)

The big question is: What will the *next* 10 years be like? I have no idea. I never forecast that far out. However, history being some guide, we can contemplate what has happened before to shape probabilities. Consider negative 10-years from before—Table 4.2. Following negative 10-years, *every subsequent 10-year period was positive.* There's no evidence a down or flat 10-year period is predictive of a subsequent down 10-year period. Could happen in the future, but hasn't so far, so it isn't terribly likely. In fact, the opposite is normal. The following periods averaged 156.2% cumulatively, 9.7% annualized—just about average.[21]

The worst 10-year period following a negative 10-year was January 1939 to January 1949, and stocks still rose 98.6%, or 7.1% annualized[22]—below average, but generally fine. And that negative 10-year wasn't that negative. It was down just –8.6% overall—an annualized –0.9%.[23] Negative or flat 10-year periods aren't predictive of a flat forward period—that's never happened. Could it? Sure, but the odds aren't great.

And remember, none of these 10-years were straight shots down. Figures 4.1, 4.2, 4.3 and 4.4 show some famously flat-to-negative 10-year periods. In all—even 1929 to 1939—there were intervening, legitimate bull market periods. Then, too, in each, the next 10 years were fine. Lots of volatility, but overall fine.

Past performance is never indicative of future results. If you expect the immediate past period to repeat—particularly over a 10-year period, which is essentially impossible to forecast—you're most likely making a costly mistake.

Stocks Are Historically Positive *and* Beat Bonds   The unvarnished truth is over longer, "secular" periods, stocks are overwhelmingly more positive than not. There simply aren't enough past, long periods of sustained negativity to give credence to the nonstop hunt for and fixation on many-years-long secular bear markets. Could one happen? Sure! But, as always, investing is a probabilities game. You have to at least consider if what you expect is an outside probability or not before committing your dough.

Table 4.2   Negative 10-Years Have Historically Been Followed
by Positive 10-Years

Period Ending	10-Year Trailing Return		10-Year Forward Return	
	Cumulative	Annualized	Cumulative	Annualized
12/31/1937	−1.3%	−0.1%	151.7%	9.7%
03/31/1938	−26.0%	−3.0%	205.9%	11.8%
04/30/1938	−18.0%	−2.0%	174.9%	10.6%
05/31/1938	−22.4%	−2.5%	209.3%	12.0%
08/31/1938	−2.9%	−0.3%	127.4%	8.6%
09/30/1938	−3.6%	−0.4%	117.2%	8.1%
11/30/1938	−11.7%	−1.2%	99.5%	7.2%
12/31/1938	−8.6%	−0.9%	98.6%	7.1%
01/31/1939	−19.4%	−2.1%	113.9%	7.9%
02/28/1939	−16.3%	−1.8%	99.4%	7.1%
03/31/1939	−27.4%	−3.2%	138.0%	9.1%
04/30/1939	−28.9%	−3.4%	134.8%	8.9%
05/31/1939	−21.1%	−2.3%	113.2%	7.9%
06/30/1939	−33.5%	−4.0%	127.6%	8.6%
07/31/1939	−29.4%	−3.4%	118.6%	8.1%
08/31/1939	−40.2%	−5.0%	138.4%	9.1%
09/30/1939	−26.7%	−3.1%	109.9%	7.7%
10/31/1939	−9.7%	−1.0%	119.7%	8.2%
11/30/1939	−0.9%	−0.1%	131.7%	8.8%
12/31/1939	−1.0%	−0.1%	136.6%	9.0%
01/31/1940	−10.1%	−1.1%	149.8%	9.6%
02/29/1940	−11.3%	−1.2%	151.1%	9.6%
03/31/1940	−16.9%	−1.8%	149.8%	9.6%
04/30/1940	−16.5%	−1.8%	162.7%	10.1%
05/31/1940	−35.3%	−4.3%	258.9%	13.6%
06/30/1940	−16.4%	−1.8%	213.9%	12.1%
07/31/1940	−16.8%	−1.8%	207.5%	11.9%
08/31/1940	−15.2%	−1.6%	209.7%	12.0%
09/30/1940	−1.3%	−0.1%	223.7%	12.5%
02/28/1941	−4.5%	−0.5%	291.3%	14.6%
Average	**−16.4%**	**−1.9%**	**156.2%**	**9.7%**

Source: Global Financial Data, Inc., S&P 500 total return from 12/31/1925 to 12/31/2010.

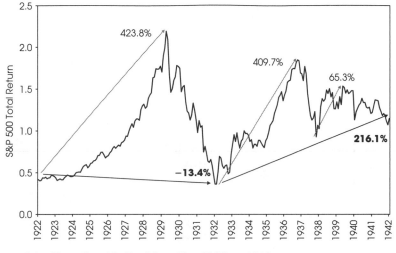
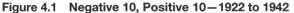

Figure 4.1   Negative 10, Positive 10 — 1922 to 1942

Source: Global Financial Data, Inc., S&P 500 total return from 05/31/1922 to 05/31/1942.

Figure 4.2   Negative 10, Positive 10 — 1928 to 1948

Source: Global Financial Data, Inc., S&P 500 total return from 03/31/1928 to 03/31/1948.

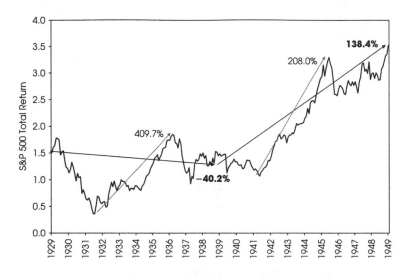

Figure 4.3   Negative 10, Positive 10—1929 to 1949

Source: Global Financial Data, Inc., S&P 500 total return from 08/31/1929 to 08/31/1949.

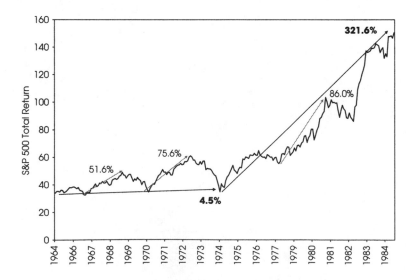

Figure 4.4   Flat 10, Positive 10—1964 to 1984

Source: Global Financial Data, Inc., S&P 500 total return from 09/30/1964 to 09/30/1984.

The likelihood of stocks having positive returns over long periods—based not only on historical precedent but also fundamental theory—isn't all you should care about. Over long periods, they also overwhelmingly beat other similarly liquid asset classes—like bonds. Table 4.3 shows average performance of stocks versus bonds over 20-year rolling periods.

Most of history—97% of 20-year rolling periods—stocks beat bonds, and by a wide margin. Cumulative stock returns over 20-year periods historically average 889% to bonds' 246%—stocks beat bonds by a 3.6-to-1 margin, on average. The two periods when bonds did beat stocks, it wasn't by much—bonds beat stocks by a 1.1-to-1 average margin, *and stocks were still positive.* You didn't get much by making a bet that works out just 3% of the time. And you're unlikely to get much in the future, despite many people currently leaning hard that way with US long-term bonds yielding under 3% (particularly if long-term interest rates rise much at any point).

Over even longer periods, there's simply been no contest. Table 4.4 shows 30-year rolling periods. On average, stocks have returned 2,473% and bonds 532%—stocks beat bonds by a 4.6-to-1 margin on average. And bonds have never beat stocks over 30 years.

Table 4.3   Stocks Versus Bonds—20-Year Periods

	Average Total Return Over 20-Year Rolling Periods
US Stocks	889%
US Bonds	246%
	Average Total Return Over 20-Year Periods When Bonds Outperformed Stocks
US Stocks	243%
US Bonds	262%

Sources: Global Financial Data Inc., S&P 500 total return for US stocks; USA 10-year Government Bond Total Return Index from 12/31/1925 to 12/31/2010.

Table 4.4   Stocks Versus Bonds—30-Year Periods

	Average Total Return Over 30-Year Rolling Periods
US Stocks	2,473%
US Bonds	532%

Sources: Global Financial Data Inc., S&P 500 total return for US stocks; USA 10-year Government Bond Total Return Index from 12/31/1925 to 12/31/2010.

Take Time to Consider Time Horizon You may think 30 years is a long time. But in my view, many people think about investing time horizons wrong. They may think, "I'm 60. I plan to retire at 65. I've got only five years to invest, so my time horizon is five years. At that point, I must utterly change how I invest by moving heavily away from stocks. Or, with only five years, I should start moving heavily away from stocks now!" In my view, this cookie-cutter approach in which age is the only or primary input for an investment strategy is all wrong. It utterly ignores critical personal factors, like what your ultimate goal for the money is, what your income needs are, what your return expectations are, what your tolerance for risk is, on and on and on.

Plus, for many investors, it potentially robs you of superior returns—meaning maybe you must seriously dial back your lifestyle later on. Your time horizon shouldn't be how long it is until you retire. In my view, a more appropriate way to think about time horizon is how long you need your assets to last—which, for most, is their entire life *and* that of their spouse. (For gents reading this, remember, odds are your wife lives longer. Plan for that, too, and you'll increase the odds she remembers you fondly rather than spends her widowhood cursing your name.)

You can read more on time horizon in my 2010 book *Debunkery*, but for your average 60-year-old male, planning to live another 25 to 30 years isn't unreasonable. Average life expectancies are getting longer, not shorter, and probably keep extending thanks to ongoing medical innovation, improving health, etc. Plus, my guess is most readers in their 50s and 60s today are probably more active (and healthy) than their parents were at the same age. Then, if a 60-year-old man is married to a 50-year-old, healthy woman, suddenly time horizons get a lot longer. And if you have a longer time horizon and need growth, odds are in your favor stocks outperform bonds. I'm not saying you must always be 100% in stocks—there are other considerations besides time horizon. And there is definitely a time to be flat-out bearish. But the longer your time horizon, the more it makes sense to consider a larger dose of stocks most of the time.

In myriad ways, it's easier—emotionally—to be bearish always than bullish most of the time. If you're bearish and wrong, you can say "Oh well, at least I didn't lose money." Which is true, sort of—as we saw earlier in this chapter. If you have a short time horizon, or your long-term objective is to "never lose money on an absolute basis, inflation be damned," then being always bearish might be appropriate. But if you're long-term-growth oriented—to any degree—being bearish and holding minimal or no stocks and not experiencing equity-like upside for very long periods can be quite damaging to long-term results. History teaches us stocks are positive much more than negative. It's just our faulty memories that regularly forget this.

Debt and Deficient Thinking

This chapter will undoubtedly anger many readers because it's going to tell you your memory is wrong—almost backward—about something people feel quite strongly about and almost certainly won't change their mind about: government debt. And if your memory can be seriously wrong about something you feel strongly about—that's scary. And the aftermath of fear is usually anger.

Then, too, I'm fully aware some people will read this book, siphon off one or two sentences and discount the rest. That's superficial. Then again, those aren't the people I wrote this book for since they likely never improve their memories or want to. They will always, as Bernesian psychologists would say, see what they want to see.

Debt is such an emotional issue for many folks it's virtually impossible to have a rational discussion about it. Just a discussion! Every time I talk about it, no matter what I say, most people still walk away believing what they want to believe anyway, which is what they believed before—and then hammer me on TV, in print, in blogs as unrealistic, demonic or worse.

What they don't get is 1) I don't care what people say about me, 2) this message is so important and so little understood I'm willing to be publicly and widely mocked by those who don't understand and 3) by slamming me, they may actually direct a few people to what I originally said, and some few of those may read, understand and actually change their minds. I consider that a public service. So, for that, I thank them.

It shouldn't be such an emotional issue, but it is. (And media takes advantage of that—hyperbolic headlines about debt are sure-fire sellers.) The fear the world is overindebted is one of the more common, most repeating fears in investing history. *It is nothing new.* Always through time, debt fears cycle in and out—people just forget today's fears aren't so unique:

- September 15, 1868: "The colony is already greatly **overindebted;** most of the wealth of the country is absorbed in the payment of interest of public and private debts to English capitalists."[1] *From a New Zealand newspaper. They (and we) seem to have done ok since.*
- March 12, 1972: A *Time* magazine cover asked, "Is the US **Going Broke?**"[2] *Well, we didn't then.*
- 1983: Another *Time* magazine cover warned, "The **Debt Bomb**: The Worldwide Peril of Go-Go Lending."[3]
- February 18, 1988: "The **overindebted** consumer is likely to be cutting back his spending this year. This sets the stage for a recession."[4] *What happened was another two years of expansion, a shallow recession and a huge market and economic boom for the entirety of the 1990s.*
- November 22, 1991: "Yet, corporations generally also are seen as **overindebted.**"[5] *Again, the 1990s were an overall pretty darn good decade—globally—for corporate profitability, economic growth and stocks.*
- April 2, 2001: "There are risks in the boom—**overindebted** homeowners could be taking on too much debt."[6] *Mind you, the 2001 recession ended a few months later, and the bear market about a year after that. The start of the 2007–2008 bear market was more than six years away.*
- March 15 2011: "This is the conundrum, the potential economic catastrophe, confronting the **overindebted** developed world right now."[7] *We shall see. . . .*

We could fill the whole book with similar headlines. And despite all the fears about debt that continuously crop up, the world carries on, gets richer overall and stocks tend to rise (irregularly). Yes, there have been times and places when debt has bitten back but, overall, the world progresses despite these fears. Doesn't take much more than thinking back a few years to see that's true.

Even after the severe credit crisis in 2008, as I write, corporate profits are at all-time highs and so is global GDP. (As pointed out in Chapter 1, global GDP actually doubled from 2000 to 2010.) Readers in 2011 and 2012 may think this is nuts—aren't Greece and the PIIGS proof too much debt kills you? Not really—they're proof too much socialism is fiscally deadly. If Greece (and other eurozone nations) were now and had been more capitalistic, they'd have more growth and more confidence from the world their economy isn't so long-term troubled. They could grow out of debt problems and have lower interest rates—making their debt more affordable! More on that in a bit.

I frequently write about how investors' brains go haywire on debt and how they'd be less apoplectic if they studied just a bit of history. Critics of mine like to say I love debt and am dangerously blasé about it. Not at all. I don't actually want the government to endlessly increase debt—but more because I'd prefer a much smaller government. I believe in my bones you, reader, are much smarter about spending your money than any politician could ever be. I want you to spend more of your money, them less. When you spend your money, you make choices that make sense to you. You start a business or buy stuff from other businesses. You buy stocks. You buy bonds. You save some other way. You send your kids to school and buy them orthodontia. You do whatever it is that makes sense to you. Maybe you recklessly blow some of it. Up to you! Mind you, recklessness is in the eye of the beholder. But still, even when blowing your money frivolously, that's your choice, you enjoy it (presumably) and benefit from your enjoyment. And the recipient of your frivolity (a trip to Vegas, a $400 bottle of wine, an antique car) gets the benefit of the money you spent. And while your memory is likely vastly worse relative to money than you think it is (the point of this book), it is far better than that of any government—local, state or federal, domestic or foreign.

When governments spend your money, they don't think about how it benefits you. They think about how it benefits the people who can provide them with money that helps get them re-elected.

People also see my views on debt as ideological. Oddly, I regularly have Republicans accuse me of being a strong Democrat and vice versa. I'm actually neither and loathe politicians of both parties equally. I think people who identify Republican or Democrat are fine—I just can't abide either party's politicians. I am an equal-opportunity politician hater.

The Fundamental Things Apply

My guess is most readers understand the fundamental economic benefits of a certain amount of leverage—at the corporate level. You understand that many firms use leverage responsibly all the time. Maybe they borrow to build a new plant. They presume a higher long-term after-tax return from the plant than their borrowing cost. It's rational. Maybe they're right, maybe wrong. But my guess is most readers think it is socially ok to take this rational risk in a world in which some win and some lose and society is overall better off in the long term by rational firms taking those risks.

Yes, sometimes they use it irresponsibly—no one refutes that. When they do, their earnings get whacked, and maybe they go broke. Stocks tank. Shareholders get angry. Maybe the CEO gets fired, vilified, dragged in front of a congressional hearing. There are real-world consequences for irresponsible use of corporate debt. Legitimate business owners know this and want to minimize the risk the business they've worked years to build goes poof because of a few bad decisions. Yet it is all part of a process you accept.

The benefits of this type of leverage are clear. Without it, many firms couldn't grow, do research, add product lines, hire or innovate. CEOs will rationally weigh the cost of leverage against the future benefit of increased spending and decide what debt level makes sense.

And despite what some say, there is no magical debt level that is right for all firms or even all industries. Some industries are just more debt-heavy than others. Have to be! If you're a mining company, it's very difficult to bootstrap the exploration and then the opening of a new mine. That can take years and massive amounts of huge, heavy equipment, lots of labor—all capital intensive. But the payoff can be worth it. A mining firm is just going to require more debt than, say, a services firm. There, the costs are more limited to hiring smart people and putting a roof over their heads.

Since most folks fathom all this, corporate debt doesn't normally bug them so much. What bugs them is personal debt and, more than that, government debt. This book isn't about preaching how much debt you or anyone else personally should have. That is up to you, your spouse, your creditors and whatever spiritual adviser you cotton to. But it's the same concept as corporate debt—used responsibly, the benefits are real. You (probably) used leverage to buy a house, a car, a college education maybe. Debt for a college education can be very economic. Yet we all know there are real-world consequences to having too much debt—but despite widespread assumption, there's no fact-based evidence society overall is recklessly over-indebted.

For example: Overall debt service in America as a percent of income has fallen steadily in recent years and hasn't been this low since 1995.[8] Few fathom that, and it's almost never mentioned in media.

No doubt, some reading this will say, "Well, yes, but *this time it's different.*" But people *always* think this time is different (see Chapter 1). This is the part where people can't remember that just last month, last year, last decade, they had identical sets of concerns that failed to materialize or failed to be as big as feared. The fear the world is dangerously indebted is nothing new. Through history, individually, people run into trouble. Even disastrously! But societally, we carry on.

This chapter focuses largely on government debt because it's government debt people most fear will tank the economy, bring down stocks and leave the country a smoldering ruin. In this chapter, we address:

- How people fear budget deficits, but history shows it's the surpluses they should fear.
- Looking at the long history of government debt helps put it in perspective.
- Developed world defaults are incredibly rare; emerging world ones are not.

Deficits Aren't Bad, but Surpluses Will Kill You

Fill in the blanks. Historically, US federal budget deficits have been _____ for stocks and surpluses _____.

If you answered *good* and then *bad,* congratulations. You can skip the rest of this section. If you got that backward, read on.

Politically, both parties attack deficits. They blame them on their opponents, on the previous administration, on anything but themselves. But if they understood some basic economic fundamentals, maybe they wouldn't be so keen to deflect blame.

Figure 5.1 shows the US federal budget balance as a percent of GDP. I've noted relative highs (budget surpluses) and lows (deficits). Then, Table 5.1 shows subsequent 12-, 24- and 36-month returns after relative peaks and troughs.

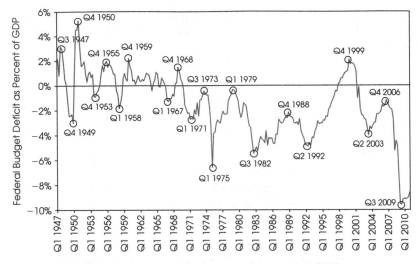

Figure 5.1   US Federal Budget Balance as a Percent of GDP

Sources: Global Financial Data, Inc., US Bureau of Economic Analysis as of 03/31/2011.

Reflexively, most expect stock returns to do much worse after very big deficits and much better after surpluses. An important lesson: Never reflexively believe anything! History, that useful lab, shows it's actually the reverse. Twelve months after surplus peaks, stocks returned 1.3% on average. They returned just 0.1% cumulatively after 24 months and just 7.1% cumulatively after 36. And that's not just a few big negatives dragging the averages down—there's big return variability after big surpluses.

Much more so than after big deficits. Returns 12, 24 and 36 months after deficit troughs are nearly uniformly positive. And the returns are much better—20.1% after 12 months, 29.7% after 24 and 35.1% after 36. If your instinct is to sell when deficits are exploding higher—*just because you fear the deficit*—you're likely making the wrong move. The reverse is true: A huge surplus isn't necessarily a sign all is clear ahead. (Another key lesson: Don't make market moves based on one factor—capital markets are much too complex.)

This is true through history. And it's also true globally. (In my 2006 book, *The Only Three Questions That Count,* I showed the same relationship between deficits, surpluses and the stock market is true in Germany, Japan, and the UK.) And every time we start getting big deficits, you hear the same drumbeat about big deficits meaning doom. And yet, on average, the doom fails to materialize.

Repeatedly. Yet no one learns from their past misperception on this because they forget too fast.

And routinely, surpluses are treated as some sainted, holy state of fiscal existence, but they don't uniformly lead to better stock returns. What's going on here? Why is this so dead backward from how people perceive it?

Backward—But Fundamental

When a government runs a deficit, they're forced to borrow money—then they spend it. They won't borrow it if they won't spend it. Then, as said earlier, when the government spends money, they spend it very stupidly. But when the government, you, or any one or thing borrows and spends money, it changes hands six times on average in the first year (in America—it varies by country).

So the government borrows money and spends stupidly—on bullet trains to nowhere and limousine fleets for politicians. But no matter how dumb you think those things are, the money goes to one of three places—a person, an institution or other governments. No other possibilities. Those recipients take that money and spend it again—that money going mostly to people or institutions. And again and again. This concept—how fast money changes hands—is called *velocity*. And every time money changes hands, someone benefits. And the more money changes hands, the more money moves through the economy, benefiting more people.

While I wish the government wouldn't spend money stupidly and would leave most everything to the private sector, it can at times be economically better for the government to borrow and spend money than for that money to not be borrowed and spent at all. The proof is in the stock market—which does pretty well following big deficits and is consistently lackluster following surpluses.

Leave Ideology Out of It This might make many readers think of the fiscal stimulus following the 2008 credit crisis—which may make you insanely angry or very happy, depending probably on your ideology. But investing is a game best played in an ideology-free zone. (More in Chapter 7.)

Was Obama's 2009 stimulus plan the right thing to do?

Doesn't matter! Could they have done a better job? Well, no. You and I could have, but they're politicians and by definition will do a dastardly job. Could they have done worse? Sure, I guess—I can

Table 5.1   S&P 500 Returns Following Deficit and Surplus Peaks

Surplus Peaks		Subsequent S&P 500 Price Return		
Date		12 Month	24 Month	36 Month
Q3 1947	Annualized	2.6%	1.6%	8.8%
	Cumulative	2.6%	3.2%	28.8%
Q4 1950	Annualized	16.5%	14.1%	6.7%
	Cumulative	16.5%	30.2%	21.6%
Q4 1955	Annualized	2.6%	−6.2%	6.7%
	Cumulative	2.6%	−12.1%	21.4%
Q4 1959	Annualized	−3.0%	9.3%	1.8%
	Cumulative	−3.0%	19.5%	5.4%
Q4 1968	Annualized	−11.4%	−5.8%	−0.6%
	Cumulative	−11.4%	−11.3%	−1.7%
Q3 1973	Annualized	−41.4%	−12.1%	−1.0%
	Cumulative	−41.4%	−22.7%	−2.9%
Q1 1979	Annualized	0.5%	15.7%	3.3%
	Cumulative	0.5%	33.9%	10.2%
Q4 1988	Annualized	27.3%	9.0%	14.5%
	Cumulative	27.3%	18.9%	50.2%
Q4 1999	Annualized	−10.1%	−11.6%	−15.7%
	Cumulative	−10.1%	−21.9%	−40.1%
Q3 2006	Annualized	3.5%	−20.2%	−7.7%
	Cumulative	3.5%	−36.3%	−21.4%
Average	**Annualized**	**−1.3%**	**−0.6%**	**1.7%**
Average	**Cumulative**	**−1.3%**	**0.1%**	**7.1%**

Sources: Global Financial Data, Inc., US Bureau of Economic Analysis, S&P 500 price returns, as of 03/31/2011.

imagine much worse scenarios. But they do stuff pretty stupidly no matter what. But whether you agreed or disagreed at the time, it doesn't matter—not for your portfolio. You can't change it. Maybe you're a top economic adviser and Obama (or any president) listens to you and does everything you say (fat chance)—then this doesn't apply to you. However, for everyone else, it does no good from a stock market forecasting perspective to get exercised over whether you think policy is right or wrong. Argue about it at a cocktail party, fine. But leave it out of your portfolio decisions.

Deficit Peaks		Subsequent S&P 500 Price Return		
Date		12 Month	24 Month	36 Month
Q4 1949	Annualized	21.8%	19.1%	16.6%
	Cumulative	21.8%	41.8%	58.6%
Q4 1953	Annualized	45.0%	35.4%	23.4%
	Cumulative	45.0%	83.3%	88.1%
Q1 1958	Annualized	31.7%	14.7%	15.6%
	Cumulative	31.7%	31.4%	54.5%
Q1 1967	Annualized	0.0%	6.1%	−0.2%
	Cumulative	0.0%	12.5%	−0.6%
Q1 1971	Annualized	6.9%	5.4%	−2.1%
	Cumulative	6.9%	11.2%	−6.3%
Q1 1975	Annualized	23.3%	8.7%	2.3%
	Cumulative	23.3%	18.1%	7.0%
Q3 1982	Annualized	37.9%	17.4%	14.8%
	Cumulative	37.9%	37.9%	51.2%
Q2 1992	Annualized	10.4%	4.3%	10.1%
	Cumulative	10.4%	8.9%	33.5%
Q2 2003	Annualized	17.1%	10.6%	09.2%
	Cumulative	17.1%	22.3%	30.3%
Q1 2009	Annualized	8.0%	??	??
	Cumulative	8.0%	??	??
Average	**Annualized**	**20.2%**	**13.5%**	**10.0%**
Average	**Cumulative**	**20.2%**	**29.7%**	**35.1%**

Your job as an investor isn't to endlessly bemoan what you see as policy mistakes or congratulate yourself for agreeing with your favorite politician. Your job is to consider what's likeliest to happen and consider what the likely fallout is. It's also to consider what most people think is likeliest to happen and whether you think that's reflective of reality. And consider what happens if reality and expectations are pretty well matched or not—because what moves stocks over the next 12 to 24 months is that gap between expectations and reality.

What matters is trying to figure out if expectations are too dour or too gleeful, and then trying to find opportunities in the expectation gap. And because many investors are frequently blinded by ideology and their reflexive debt-fear, they miss this point: Big budget deficits aren't automatically disastrous. In fact, they could be signaling good stock returns to come. And the reverse!

Don't take this to mean you should try market timing deficit troughs. I don't know how you would. However, you should take it to mean that you shouldn't automatically bail on stocks just because you fear a big deficit. History shows that wouldn't work so well. In fact, it would have worked badly. Remember this, because the next time we see big ballooning deficits, pundits will caution about coming doom. They won't say, "Oh yeah! The last time this happened, we suddenly remember it all turned out fine."

The History of Big Government Debt

One major reason folks hate deficits and love surpluses is deficits add to overall government debt, whereas surpluses can be used to reduce it. And it's the total debt people really hate. Hate, hate, hate, hate, hate!

You hear politicians, both sides, claiming our grandchildren will be saddled with debt, and aren't we all horrible people for being so profligate? Or, isn't the opposition party a bunch of grandchildren-hating jerks? Don't vote for them, vote for me! I *love* grandchildren.

Fear of debt is partially ingrained in us from a time when being indebted was seen (in many cultures and in some cultures is still seen) as immoral. But also, it's simply a short-term memory error. Use history to see this right. But quick: When in the last century was our low point in debt? When was our high point? Figure 5.2 shows US net federal debt as a percent of GDP as far back as we have decent data—were your guesses right? (Most people I show this to usually get it wrong.)

Figure 5.2 shows *net* debt, which means the debt held by the public—you, corporations, state and local government, foreign investors, foreign governments, etc. It doesn't include intra-government debt—debt one federal government agency owes another—because that debt effectively cancels itself out. (It's rather like not including the fiver you borrowed from your spouse on your household balance sheet, because you know you'll get straight with each other eventually. [Well, maybe.])

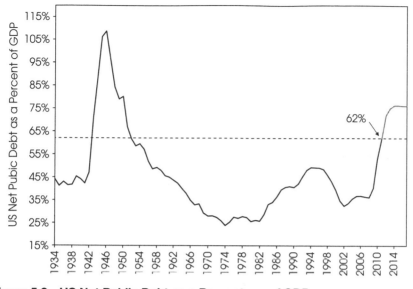

Figure 5.2   US Net Public Debt as a Percentage of GDP

Source: Treasury Direct, Congressional Budget Office, May 2011 release.

Recently, debt levels have increased—news that's not shocking any readers. But we're still well below peak levels seen during World War II. Some may say, "Yes, but that was going to finance a war, so that's different." Actually, it's not. Debt is debt is debt. Debt doesn't care if it's seen as morally right (fighting Nazis) or morally ambiguous ("shovel-ready" fiscal stimulus). What matters is it exists, and it has some interest rate that must be paid. Lenders demand to be repaid. That's it.

Remember the late 1940s and 1950s? This is a period of great nostalgia for many Americans—whether they lived through it or not. It saw a boom of suburbs, cars, home ownership, technological innovations, medical advances. It saw the explosion of TV, Howdy Doody, Elvis, I Like Ike and Marilyn. It was not (and isn't remembered this way) a period of severe economic austerity to pay for the sins of the high debt of the 1940s. The 1980s through 1990s was another period of relatively elevated debt after the debt lows of the 1970s. But the 1980s and 1990s were pretty darn economically vibrant, featuring two back-to-back, near-decade-long booms in stocks. Interestingly, the 1970s—when net debt was lower—are recalled as being more economically lackluster.

I'm not saying—at all—that the lower debt caused the lackluster, or the higher debt caused the boom. I'm saying, for all the fear about debt, you'd think there was some learning experience—some point in the past when high debt levels in the US incontrovertibly led to widespread economic fallout. I don't see it. There is no evidence America's periods of higher debt levels led to lower future economic progress or vice versa. None. Nor in other developed Western nations.

Debt Payback Disaster

US history students will remember there *was* a time the US had no debt. Andrew Jackson paid down all of America's debt in 1835 with proceeds from Western land sales. And the period immediately following was filled with overwhelming economic vibrancy, stability and world peace. Just kidding! It effectively led to the Panic of 1837 and the Depression of 1837 to 1843—which made any modern recession look like a walk in the park. It was one of the three worst recessions in US history (the other two being those starting in 1873 and 1929).

Maybe 80 years of history isn't enough for you. Or maybe you think the US is unique, and some other developed nation's history can prove an absolute debt level that's problematic. Fine! Figure 5.3 is one of my all-time favorite visuals—it shows UK debt as

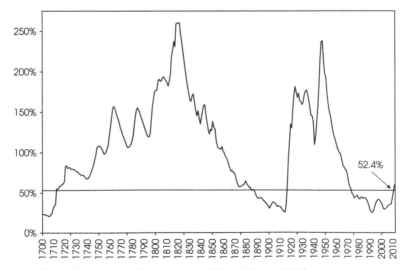

Figure 5.3   UK Debt as a Percent of GDP (1700 to 2011)

Source: HM Treasury, UKpublicspending.co.uk, as of June 2011. Includes budget projections through 2011.

a percent of GDP *since 1700.* Very careful stewards of economic data, those Brits.

First, note their recent debt levels as a percent of GDP aren't very different from ours. Then, too, the UK had much higher levels of debt in the 1940s and even through the 1950s—it had a lot of war-related rebuilding to do—much more than we did, for obvious reasons. There were long periods when the UK lagged the US in economic growth in the postwar era, but the UK isn't a smoldering ruin thanks to its high debt levels. In fact, over the last three decades, its GDP grew at almost exactly the same rate as ours did—some years a bit more and others a bit less—but that must be true with any two countries growing at similar rates. What's more, the UK lagging in the 1950s, 1960s and 1970s was likely tied more to its intensely socialist bent up until the Thatcher era and had much less to do with its debt load. (I can't say this enough: Socialists don't do economic growth well.)

But here is the cooker: For most of the eighteenth and nineteenth centuries, the UK had debt levels vastly higher than today. Debt was above 100% of GDP almost uniformly from 1750 to 1850, above 150% for about half that period, and peaked above 250%! And the UK was far from economically troubled then. This was when the UK was indisputably the world's dominant economy—and an innovation leader. The global Industrial Revolution kicked off in England—much earlier than in the US—and England was the center for revolutionary manufacturing practices worldwide. This was when news traveled by foot, horse, carrier pigeon and, only much later, train. If the Brits could have debt levels above 100% of GDP for a full century and remain the global economic and military powerhouse while they were sending memos on horseback, I think the US may squeak by ok with its current debt levels—or even higher—because what truly matters is the affordability of that debt.

Can We Afford It or Not?

Pundits like to state some unequivocal level when debt becomes unsustainable. Pegging it at 90% or 100% or 160% or, or, or, or. It tends to move around. (Mind you, somehow Britain survived with levels higher than that.)

As said earlier, corporations have wildly different levels of debt—varying from firm to firm and industry to industry. There's

no one right level of debt at the corporate level—why is there one
for nations? Inherently, countries with all the right stuff leading
to higher levels of future growth can afford to carry more debt.
Why? They can typically better afford the repayment. But projecting future growth rates, for reasons we've already seen, is
always tricky.

And yes, at some point, debt levels can be unsustainable. I don't
know what that is for the US because we haven't seen it yet. But the
level is when the debt becomes unaffordable. And for the US, even
at its current relatively elevated level, our debt is still very affordable. Historically so! Easy to see! Amazing to me so few folks ever
contemplate the evidence. What you are about to see no newspaper
or magazine will carry. No politician cites. No fear-monger toler-
ates. But it is based on hard facts—pure and simple.

Figure 5.4 shows US federal debt interest payments as a percent
of GDP. Currently, they're just above 2%. This is lower than the
entirety of 1979 to 2002. That period included the two mega bulls
of the 1980s and 1990s and overall vibrant economic growth. From
about 1984 to 1996, federal debt interest payment levels were
nearly *double* what they are now (as I write in 2011)—with no ill
effect. Let me say that again: Interest payments on our federal debt

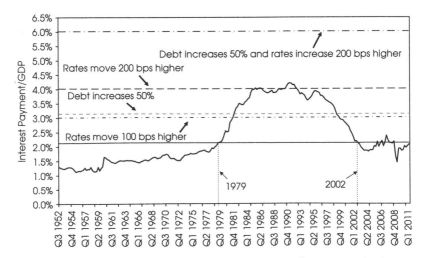

Figure 5.4   US Federal Debt Interest Payments as a Percent of GDP

Sources: Thomson Reuters, Federal Reserve Flow of Funds, US Bureau of Economic
Analysis, US Treasury (Q3 1952 to Q1 2011).

as a percent of the size of our economy are half what they were 20 years ago!

How can it be we have more debt but lower debt costs? Well, part of it is the economy is bigger, too. Part of it is interest rates are low. And part of it is the government owns more of its own debt than it used to and merely pays itself. But our debt is much more affordable today than it was 20 years ago. Simple fact.

Could our debt become more expensive? Sure. See Figure 5.4 again. If rates jumped a full percent or debt were to increase fully 50% relative to GDP from today's elevated level, debt interest costs would be about 3% of GDP—where they were for most of the 1980s and 1990s. If rates moved fully 2%, they would hit a level that still didn't prove problematic in the past. If you think about debt this way—the ability to pay—suddenly, the situation seems not so dire.

Look at this a different way—federal debt interest payments as a percent of federal tax revenue (Figure 5.5). Again, at 9.1%, it's half of what it was 20 years ago and shows almost the exact same phenomenon as in Figure 5.4. Our debt is more affordable today than it was 20 years ago, which means we're not in a debt crisis just when people think we are. That has to be bullish.

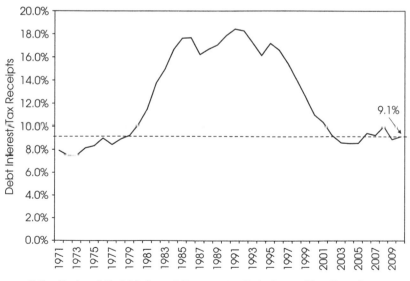

Figure 5.5   Federal Debt Interest Payments Relative to Tax Receipts

Source: US Congressional Budget Office, as of 12/31/2010.

Should we endlessly add debt? No. And, eventually, if we do keep adding debt and that makes investors nervous about America's economic sustainability, that likely makes interest rates rise, making our debt less affordable. But we aren't at the crisis stage so many froth at their mouths over.

An interesting point: As I write this in 2011, S&P just downgraded the US credit rating from AAA to AA+. (Moody's and Fitch just reaffirmed the AAA rating, but the pack thinking is strong among the three-stooge raters—Moody's and Fitch may eventually follow suit.) What happened to US Treasury rates? They *fell*—to near all-time historic lows. Treasury bond prices rose. That's so beautiful. In fact, Treasury rates fell as bond prices rose basically all 2011 (with minor volatility), even while Congress was debating a new debt ceiling (an arbitrary marker that's been raised now 103 times since 1917 and will be raised again many more times).

Think about that. If the world really felt US default risk were higher now, it would demand higher rates to lend us money. Yet, rates are lower—making debt interest costs still cheaper. We have a long way to go just to get past a debt-interest-cost point that wasn't even remotely troublesome in the past.

That's just in 2011. But all through recent years, while the US has been increasing debt relative to GDP, interest rates have stayed pretty darn low or fallen. That's the market telling us that, though politicians love to bemoan our debt and our memories fail us, markets know we're nowhere close to disaster.

Just Who Is at Default Here?

Another reason debt was a particularly sensitive topic in 2010 and 2011—PIIGS. Before 2010, pigs were something you barbecued. But in 2010, Greece surprised the world by admitting they'd done a bit of book-cookery and had much more debt than previously realized. That led investors to take a harder look at other peripheral eurozone economies. Portugal, Ireland, Italy and Spain were also found fiscally wanting, though Spain less so and Italy much less so. They were dubbed, cutely, the PIIGS—though their situations weren't cute. And everyone feared the little PIIGSies would blow the eurozone down.

Rightly, too, because the eurozone didn't have a way to deal with very fiscally weak members. They had no way to expel members who failed to meet the eurozone's required fiscal benchmarks (debt as a percent of GDP, deficit size, etc.)—and the Maastricht Treaty (and subsequent treaties establishing the eurozone) didn't have a bailout framework.

And Greece couldn't, for example, just print money to inflate its way out of its elevated debt. (Not the best solution either, but at least an option desperate countries have used many times before.) Why? Because Greece shares a currency with Germany and France and 14 other eurozone members.

There was endless talk of contagion and a potential renewed credit crisis. Worse, there were fears if Greece defaulted, it could have meant the end of the euro in a very fiery, disorderly fashion—a very material global negative. But I rather doubted it would happen that way—not in 2010 or 2011 at least. Why would the other eurozone members let it?

However Germany and France feel about the euro, no one ever wants anything monetarily major to happen in a sudden, disorderly way. Hence, the European Central Bank, IMF and EU pulled together $1 trillion to backstop the PIIGS—which covered all their debt financing needs (minus Italy, which was overall in much better shape) through 2013. This bought the eurozone time to sort through its (many) issues and plan a way forward—and it meant no true disorderly defaults and the euro would survive, at least until 2013.

Except suddenly, folks saw defaults everywhere. Headlines screamed, "Is the US the next Greece?" Well, no. As per Figure 5.4. Unlike Greece, the US has never defaulted. No offense to Greece, but they've spent more time in default than out. Last time was effectively in the mid-1990s, but we forget.

What's more, if being perfectly frank, Greece could have afforded their debt but just didn't want to make the tough choices necessary to avoid default. Figure 5.6 shows Greece's debt interest costs as a percent of GDP. In 1993, Greece paid 12% of its GDP in interest payments annually. In 2010, as Greek debt woes came to light, it was less than *half* that. What's more, from 1989 through much of 1992, Greece issued no long-term debt (see Figure 5.7). Zero! None! Zip! No one would lend them any—didn't trust them with their money for 10 years because of default risk. Instead, Greece had to pay 18% and 19% on three-month debt!

If Greece afforded their much higher short-term debt interest costs then, they could afford them now if the world forced them to.

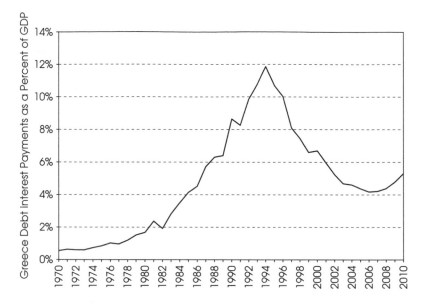

Figure 5.6   Greece's Debt Interest Costs as a Percent of GDP

Source: Thomson Reuters.

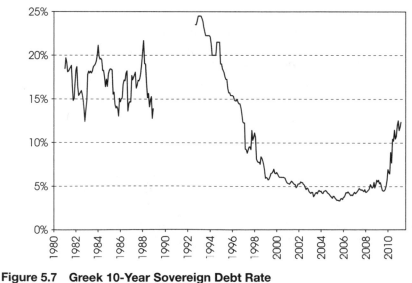

Figure 5.7   Greek 10-Year Sovereign Debt Rate

Source: Global Financial Data, Inc., as of 07/31/2011.

They had options. They could have sold state assets. They could have ratcheted back pensions for public workers. Amazingly, 40% of Greece's GDP is the public sector, and 25% of Greek workers work for the government! A little less socialism and a little more free market capitalism would probably go a long way to fixing what ails Greece.

Note in Figure 5.7 when Greece couldn't get long-term financing in the early 1990s, it forced them to scale back for years, improving the debt rates. Thus, Greek overall borrowing costs fell as per Figure 5.6. Free-market discipline is tough. But they did it in the 1990s, so they could do it now if the world put their feet to the fire. Yes, free-market discipline would be tough today—higher interest rates and angry, rioting teenagers and public employees—all politically tough to handle. You've got to fear those teenagers.

That said, the fear of Greece defaulting might have roiled the eurozone—possibly the world. So eurozone nations were cowed by Greece fears, and Greece opted for the easier way—a bailout. Everyone wants a bailout these days.

In sympathy with Greece (not that I have much), they were in a weird situation because its eurozone membership means it can't make unilateral monetary policy decisions in its own best interest. But defaults in less-developed nations are hardly groundbreaking, totally unforeseen events. We've seen them forever. Greek defaults and debt restructurings are commonplace. South American countries make a perfect habit out of it. And, again, all their defaults were tied not to absolute or relative levels of debt, but rather the relative affordability of their debt.

A US Default? But the US default? Not when our debt is as affordable as it is. But never say never. Still, for all the fear surrounding a Greek-like debt meltdown in the US, you'd think there were some pattern of major, developed nations defaulting on certain levels of debt, debt costs, etc. But I can't find one. Not one! And maybe that's what scares folks—fear of the unknown.

During the summer of 2011, pundits babbled about a US debt default because politicians were bickering over a new debt ceiling (a wholly arbitrary marker—among developed nations, only Denmark has one). Nonsense. The US was never—not ever—in any danger of defaulting. Our tax receipts monthly are super-more-than-sufficient to cover interest payments. All the default talk was just typical nonsense political scare talk.

The US as a nation has never defaulted—not once. Some municipalities, yes. Defaults in big municipalities are rare, but they have happened—New York City in 1975, Cleveland in 1978, Orange County in 1994. And maybe California as a whole soon—and maybe that's good because all these kinds of places seem to wise up and behave better after they default. But the US as a whole never has and can't for a very long time from now because our debt is relatively affordable—historically so.

What's more, when people think "default," they think "lose all money." But that's rarely the case. Defaults can be just *delayed* interest payments. Or the government misses a couple, but makes up the rest. Many municipalities make contractual deposits to a sinking fund tied to muni debt—they default if they miss a sinking fund payment *even if investors get paid on time*. I'm not trying to gloss over the seriousness of default, but default doesn't automatically mean investors are always totally wiped out the way you would envision from reading media.

The worst period of US muni defaults ever was, unsurprisingly, the Great Depression. Between 1929 and 1937, about 4,800 municipalities defaulted on 7% of outstanding debt.[9] A big chunk, but not widespread disaster. But here's the kicker—during that very wretched time, the recovery rate was 99.5%.[10] I seriously doubt you've read that anywhere in media. That's the good news they don't like to print. Put that another way—muni investors during the worst global economy of the modern era lost just 0.5% of their muni investments.

Muni default fears were particularly potent as 2010 ended (and will be again after the next recession). Why? State budget gaps broadened, leading to fears states couldn't make good on their obligations. But state budget gaps always broaden in the aftermath of recession because income, corporate and sales tax revenues fall. Then, too, state (and local) governments commit to some higher level of spending based on assumptions of increasing tax revenues just when revenues fall—leading to a deficit. Then, when the economy recovers, incomes recover at a lag, and then state tax revenues do, too. By then, states usually realize they must ratchet down spending or they're toast—so the combination of unexpectedly higher tax revenue and slowing spending helps close the gap. Repeat. Repeat. Repeat.

So by mid-year 2011, default fears that were so prevalent in 2009 and 2010 had largely evaporated because, as typically happens, investors realized states' income tax revenues were above expectations, helping close funding gaps. This, too, happens after every recession (people just forget)—people panic and fear mass defaults that never materialize. Some municipalities do default, no question. But never at the magnitude headlines predict.

Outside the US, Canada and Australia have also never defaulted. Since World War II, developed Europe is default free. Russia defaulted in 1998—a big country but not classified as developed. Moldova in 2002—but no one argues Moldova is developed. Ukraine in 1998 with Russia and again in 2000. That's about it.

Can a major, developed nation default? Sure. But before panicking, at the very least, check how affordable that nation's debt is. Because even if a country has debt 400% of GDP, but total interest costs of 1% of GDP, their debt load could double, and if interest rates didn't move much, they likely aren't defaulting. Debt affordability matters.

A Debt-Free World Isn't a Better World

Even if current debt jitters fade, the fears will be back at some future point—count on it. And if nothing disastrous happens because of current elevated debt levels, overall, investors won't remember and will have the same set of fears they have now.

A good exercise if fear of "too much debt" has you pondering making a major portfolio strategy change: Ask, "Is a world without debt better?"

If we had no debt, some might think that would be ideal. People would pay cash for everything. Companies and governments, too! There would be no reckless spending of money we don't have. Seems ok, on the surface.

But a world with no debt is a world without US Treasurys or other government debt. Without Treasurys, we'd effectively have no monetary policy. Global central banks couldn't function—not as they do. I'm having a hard time wrapping my brain around how you have monetary policy without Treasurys (and other government debt like gilts, bunds, etc.). How do we have a modern banking system that lends readily without Treasurys, which make up the bulk of bank reserves? I suppose we could revert to the gold standard, which I don't advocate for myriad reasons. (Why do you want to tie global money supply to a finite metal with limited industrial use? And for those who think a gold standard gets the government out of monetary policy—think about what's involved in maintaining a currency peg to gold.) But even if we did, we had Treasurys when we were on the gold standard before.

A world without government debt is likely to be far worse than what we have now—just like it was after Andrew Jackson eliminated all government debt. We don't want to ever do that again. Your real issue should be how affordable our overall debt is and, in that regard, right here and now in 2011 and 2012, it's pretty darned affordable.

CHAPTER 6

Long-Term Love and Other Investing Errors

There's a school of investors who believe, with their very souls, small cap stocks are inherently best for all time. There's another subset that feels the same about small-cap value. Who's right?

There are those who believe large cap is best; no, large-cap growth is best—steady and safe; no, Tech; no, high-dividend stocks; no, German mid-cap Industrials. Name a category, no matter how big or narrow, there are adherents—rigid in their orthodoxy, absolute in their canonical beliefs.

But it's not blind faith (so they'll have you believe)! They can show you data *proving* their category is best! And sometimes they can—if they use shorter time periods. Or oddly define the category. Or use faulty indexes. Or do some other bogus calculation. There are myriad ways data can be altered (or tortured) to get there—false nonetheless.

Now, in some instances, some categories have had an edge historically. For example, small cap, as far back as we have decent data, has outperformed the market overall! Small caps have annualized 12.0% to the overall market's 9.9% (since February 1926).[1] Before tattooing "Small Cap 4-Ever!" on your forehead, know a lot of that outperformance ignores huge bid/ask spreads that were common in small caps in the 1930s and 1940s—sometimes up to 30% of the purchase price. Simply buying and selling these stocks took a major chunk out of returns—not accounted for in long-term index returns. Then, too, small caps tend to bounce huge off bear market bottoms. Ignore the four biggest small cap booms off bear market bottoms (1932–1935, 1942–1945, 1974–1976, 2002–2004), and large caps overall beat small caps—and typically for agonizingly long periods.

Even if you can figure when those bounces off the bottom are (hard to do), there are lots of other ways to make huge returns that actually beat small cap then. But some of those times when big stocks beat small are long enough to drive you absolutely crazy—bonkers. Just look at most of the longest bull markets in history and you will see that they've been dominated by big stocks. Plus, the descent of most big bear markets has seen small caps do worse than big caps. Again, if you can time markets, the small cap versus big cap argument becomes superfluous.

Believing one category is inherently long-term better is, again, the fault of faulty short-term memory—perusing history can help dispel this misbelief. What's more, believing in one category's superiority requires a lack of fundamental understanding of how capital markets work.

Like many of this book's memory mishaps, this isn't merely about misremembering history. Believing in category superiority and rigidly adhering to one size/style/sector/however-you-define-it category can lead to some serious errors—like over-concentrating in one area and giving up chances to enhance performance and manage risk. It can also lead investors to lag broader markets for long periods. And lagging for a long time can cause your brain to want to make even more serious errors, like chasing heat, switching out of an appropriate long-term strategy, panicking and selling low, etc.

In this chapter, we examine:

- Why no one category is inherently better.
- How long-term love (in markets) is like long-term forecasting—both are wrong.
- How rational investors become heat chasers.
- And ways to use history, rationally, to know when some categories are likelier to outperform.

No One Category Is Best for All Time

I myself am a bit sentimental about small-cap value. That's where I got my professional start. Way, way back when, I was instrumental in formalizing small-cap value as an institutional investing style and the now commonly used six-pack definition—large-cap growth, large-cap value, mid value and growth, and small value and growth.

It may be hard to believe, but until the late 1980s, small-cap value wasn't really a defined investing category. Hardly anyone managed it professionally. My first book, *Super Stocks*, published in 1984, introduced a valuation I created and then championed—the price-to-sales ratio (PSR). (Before that book and my articles on PSR, there's simply no literature on it. It didn't exist.)

The PSR was really aimed at identifying smaller, super-undervalued stocks, i.e., small-cap value stocks. The idea being if you could identify decent firms that hit a rough patch and had no earnings (and therefore no P/E ratio frequently), when earnings sprung back, their stock prices would, too. Like super stocks!

PSR worked great for a long time, then became less useful as a forecasting tool on its own. (If you want fuller detail, I wrote about this in my 2006 book, *The Only Three Questions That Count*.) But today this ratio is widely used, available widely online and, hence, is less useful. Part of that was my fault—I wrote a book about it and promoted it in my *Forbes* columns (which I began writing in 1984) and elsewhere. Anything that becomes widely known loses power—this includes information but also investing tools, methods and valuations. Why promote it? I didn't think I was so smart that I'd figured out something no one else could, so I expected PSR to lose power. It still remains useful in evaluating stocks against their peers—like the P/E, price to book and any number of valuations. And at certain times, it has more power as a forecasting tool than at others (usually when people think it has none). But on its own, not the PSR nor any other valuation can tell you when a stock is more or less likely to outperform.

As sentimental as I am for the small-cap value category, I don't now and never did think it inherently superior. It has periods it leads and others it lags—like all equity categories. History bears that out. For good reason—fundamentally, all properly constructed equity categories should net similar returns long term. Why?

Can't Predict Long-Term Supply? Can't Predict Long-Term Returns

Stock prices, like everything else bought and sold in a free market, are driven by supply and demand. Supply and demand shifts are taught to you in school as functions of eagerness. How eager are people to have something at any given price? How eager are providers of that something to provide it to you at any given price? Eagerness has a very emotional quality to it on top of rational qualities.

In the very near term—like over the next 12 months or so—supply is relatively fixed. Supply is increased by firms doing initial public offerings or new issuances and decreased by bankruptcies, stock buybacks and cash-based mergers and acquisitions. When valuations are high, firms rationally become more eager to issue new stock—to them it's cheap money. And they get more emotionally eager to do it when they see all their peers doing it. Issuances take a long, long time to do—tied to regulatory functions and other investment banking requirements—and firms must disclose their intentions. Buybacks and mergers don't happen out of the sky, either. So for the next 12 months (24 at the outside), you can estimate pretty well what stock supply will be—and it's hard to budge those numbers very much. Therefore, near term, shifts in demand for equities mostly drive stock prices—up and down. And demand is fickle and can move fast—up or down.

But longer term, stock supply can expand or contract nearly endlessly—swamping all other drivers. What stock prices will be 3, 5, 7, 10 and 37 years from now has much more to do with far future supply pressures than anything else. And supply is wholly unpredictable in the long term.

The Supply Shuffle

Why? Investment bankers, for one. Still in 2011, investment bankers are almost universally reviled. Whatever you think of them, they provide a very basic societal service in helping firms access capital markets—through equity or debt issuance. Or by helping firms complete mergers and acquisitions. And without capital markets and the ability to issue stock or buy back stock, firms can't raise money and can't grow or optimize their capital structure and shareholder value. And you want firms to grow—it's what allows them to hire, innovate, do research, create cool new gadgets and life-saving drugs. If you like firms that hire and develop vaccines that wipe out childhood illnesses, you can still dislike investment bankers (and don't have to be one yourself), but you should at least begrudgingly let them exist.

When a certain category heats up (I describe this more fully in my 2010 book, *Debunkery*, if you're interested), there's more demand for those kinds of shares (think Tech in the late 1990s, Energy in the late 1970s). Investment bankers see this demand and aim to satisfy it by helping firms—new and old—issue shares. Done right, this is very profitable for them. Newer firms realize the demand for this category makes it easy for them to raise capital—so they want to go public. More established, already public firms realize they, too, can raise capital easily to launch a new product line and maybe compete in the now-hot category. Or maybe they raise capital to buy a smaller, newer firm—same result.

The investment bankers keep printing new stock in that hot category until supply surpasses demand—demand falls and so do prices, causing the firms they represent to want to back off. Sometimes, prices fall suddenly (like in the Energy bubble in 1980 or the Tech bubble in 2000). Sometimes, they fall more slowly. But then, demand increases for a different category and investment bankers create supply to meet it. Meanwhile, excess supply in the now-cold category gets mopped up as firms buy back shares or go bankrupt or get swallowed by other firms in cash takeovers. Repeat. Repeat. Repeat.

So supply can expand and contract near infinitely as demand floats from category to category—irregularly and forever. And there's nothing inherent about one category over another that makes investment bankers more apt to increase (or decrease) supply for it over another—other than what they can move at the moment. Each category—if well constructed—will travel its own erratic path but ultimately net pretty similar returns in the very long term. Any fluctuations are tied to supply shifts that are impossible to predict. Or you get oddities like the bid/ask spread in small-cap stocks early on.

This is why perma-love with any one category is fruitless. Yes, certain categories can lead overall for a long time—just long enough for too many folks to think it will go on forever—which is usually just before it reverses course and starts lagging. But your preference for a certain category (in an overall well-diversified portfolio) should be driven by your forward-looking assessment of why fundamentals favor that category for the next 12 to 18 months—24 months on the outside. It should not be driven by your belief that category X is better "just because."

Figure 6.1 — No One Style Is Best for All Time

1991	1992	1993	1994	1995	1996	1997	1998	1999	2000	2001	2002	2003	2004	2005	2006	2007	2008	2009	2010
Russell 2000 Growth 51.2%	Russell 2000 Value 29.1%	MSCI EAFE 32.6%	MSCI EAFE 7.8%	S&P/Citi Growth 39.4%	S&P/Citi Growth 25.7%	S&P/Citi Growth 33.5%	S&P/Citi Growth 41.0%	Russell 2000 Growth 43.1%	Russell 2000 Value 22.8%	Russell 2000 Value 14.0%	Barclays Agg 10.3%	Russell 2000 Growth 48.5%	Russell 2000 Value 22.2%	MSCI EAFE 13.5%	MSCI EAFE 26.3%	MSCI EAFE 11.2%	Barclays Agg 5.2%	S&P/Citi Growth 34.6%	Russell 2000 Growth 29.1%
Russell 2000 46.0%	Russell 2000 18.4%	Russell 2000 Value 23.8%	S&P/Citi Growth 3.9%	S&P 500 Index 37.6%	S&P/Citi Value 23.9%	S&P 500 Index 33.4%	S&P 500 Index 28.6%	S&P/Citi Growth 35.9%	Barclays Agg 11.6%	Barclays Agg 8.4%	Russell 2000 Value -11.4%	Russell 2000 47.3%	MSCI EAFE 20.2%	S&P/Citi Growth 9.3%	Russell 2000 Value 23.5%	S&P/Citi Growth 10.3%	Russell 2000 Value -28.9%	Russell 2000 Growth 34.5%	Russell 2000 24.9%
S&P/Citi Growth 44.1%	S&P/Citi Value 9.5%	Russell 2000 18.9%	Russell 2000 1.3%	S&P/Citi Value 37.2%	S&P 500 Index 23.0%	Russell 2000 Value 31.8%	MSCI EAFE 20.0%	MSCI EAFE 27.0%	S&P/Citi Value 6.5%	Russell 2000 2.5%	MSCI EAFE -15.9%	Russell 2000 Value 46.0%	Russell 2000 18.3%	S&P/500 Index 4.9%	S&P/Citi Value 19.7%	Russell 2000 Growth 7.1%	Russell 2000 -33.8%	MSCI EAFE 31.8%	Russell 2000 Value 24.5%
Russell 2000 Value 41.7%	Russell 2000 Growth 7.8%	S&P/Citi Value 16.6%	S&P/Citi Value -0.6%	Russell 2000 31.0%	Russell 2000 Value 21.4%	S&P/Citi Value 31.5%	S&P/Citi Value 16.3%	Russell 2000 21.3%	Russell 2000 -3.0%	Russell 2000 Growth -9.2%	S&P/Citi Value -16.2%	MSCI EAFE 38.6%	S&P/Citi Value 15.3%	S&P/500 Index 4.7%	Russell 2000 18.4%	Barclays Agg 7.0%	S&P/Citi Growth -35.5%	Russell 2000 27.2%	S&P/Citi Value 17.1%
S&P 500 Index 30.5%	S&P 500 Index 7.6%	Russell 2000 Growth 13.4%	S&P 500 Index -1.8%	Russell 2000 Value 28.5%	Russell 2000 16.5%	Russell 2000 22.4%	Barclays Agg 8.7%	S&P/500 Index 21.0%	S&P/500 Index -9.1%	S&P/Citi Value -9.6%	Russell 2000 -20.5%	S&P/500 Index 31.6%	Russell 2000 Growth 14.3%	Russell 2000 4.6%	S&P/500 Index 15.8%	S&P/500 Index 5.5%	S&P/500 Index -37.0%	S&P/500 Index 26.5%	S&P 500 Index 15.1%
S&P/Citi Value 22.2%	Barclays Agg 7.4%	S&P 500 Index 10.1%	Russell 2000 Value -1.5%	Russell 2000 Growth 25.7%	Russell 2000 Growth 11.3%	Russell 2000 Growth 12.9%	Russell 2000 Growth 1.2%	S&P/Citi Value 4.7%	MSCI EAFE -14.2%	S&P/500 Index -11.9%	S&P/500 Index -22.1%	S&P/Citi Value 28.7%	S&P/500 Index 10.9%	Russell 2000 Growth 4.2%	Russell 2000 Growth 13.4%	S&P/Citi Value 1.9%	Russell 2000 Growth -38.5%	S&P/Citi Value 21.6%	S&P/Citi Growth 14.1%
Barclays Agg 16.0%	S&P/Citi Growth 4.5%	Barclays Agg 9.8%	Russell 2000 Growth -2.4%	Barclays Agg 18.5%	MSCI EAFE 6.0%	Barclays Agg 9.7%	Russell 2000 -2.5%	Barclays Agg -0.8%	S&P/Citi Growth -22.2%	S&P/Citi Growth -19.5%	S&P/Citi Growth -30.2%	S&P/Citi Growth 26.8%	S&P/Citi Growth 6.3%	Barclays Agg 2.4%	S&P/Citi Growth 11.4%	Russell 2000 -1.6%	S&P/Citi Value -38.9%	Russell 2000 Value 20.6%	MSCI EAFE 7.8%
MSCI EAFE 12.1%	MSCI EAFE -12.2%	S&P/Citi Growth 0.2%	Barclays Agg -2.9%	MSCI EAFE 11.2%	Barclays Agg 3.6%	MSCI EAFE 1.8%	Russell 2000 Value -6.5%	Russell 2000 Value -1.5%	Russell 2000 Growth -22.4%	MSCI EAFE -21.4%	Russell 2000 Growth -30.3%	Barclays Agg 4.1%	Barclays Agg 4.3%	S&P/Citi Value 2.3%	Barclays Agg 4.3%	Russell 2000 Value -9.8%	MSCI EAFE -43.4%	Barclays Agg 5.9%	Barclays Agg 6.6%

Figure 6.1 No One Style Is Best for All Time

Source: Thomson Reuters.[2]

128

Figure 6.1 shows this a different way. It shows annual performance for some broad categories—large-cap US stocks, small-cap US, growth, value, foreign, bonds (Barclays Aggregate Bond Index). It should look like a mishmash quilt to you because it *is* a mishmash quilt. Leadership rotates—frequently and at times violently. Something can be hot for a long time, like large-cap growth from 1995 through 1998, when it becomes a worst performer. What was best doesn't always become worst—sometimes categories just bounce around irregularly. But there's no discernible pattern and, even over this 20-year period, no evidence one category served you best year after year.

More amazing: It doesn't take much to see no one category is superior. Just checking a few years' history should dispel that misbelief. Believing one category is best means you truly must ignore even very recent history—which we know many investors do.

Another key takeaway from Figure 6.1: If you don't have a fundamental reason for favoring something other than *it's been hot*, you are, effectively, heat chasing. Sometimes that works out for a while! But usually not. (More on that later this chapter.)

Long-Term Love Is Like Long-Term Forecasting—Both Wrong

Another problem with perma-love with a category—it's akin to long-term forecasting. Long-term forecasting rarely works (more on this in a bit) but people still attempt it, and their attempts frequently get big media play. Why? My guess is folks who like to say, "Stocks will do X, Y and Z over the next 10 years," know investors widely suffer from myopia, and by the time we get even a few years out, they will have forgotten about their forecast. So there's little harm to the prognosticator in making bold, long-term proclamations that don't come true. Very few folks check back later! (And journalists almost never do.)

I say with confidence you can safely ignore any attempt at a forecast longer than 24 months, because to know what category will be best 3, 5, 7, 10 or 37 years from now, you must know what category toward the end of that time—long from now—investment bankers will be increasing supply for or what category will experience shrinking supply. How can anyone know that? Investment bankers (CEOs and CFOs, investors and anyone else involved in the business of shifting stock supply) in 3, 5, 10 and 37 years will be responding to far distant drivers no one has any way of predicting.

Of course, going forward, any one asset class, size, style, sector, industry, etc., can lead for a long, long time. But there's no way now to forecast that. I always caution investors just because something has led for a long time, doesn't mean it must stop leading now. This is the same idea people wrongly apply to stocks more broadly. Many believe if a bull market runs too long—i.e., longer than average—the bull market must end. No! (See Chapter 2.) Averages have huge variances underneath, and any single category can have fundamentals—even shifting ones—that support outperformance for far longer than average. But there's simply no way to know what category will lead over the next full 10 years unless you know something about that category's share supply relative to the supply of other categories' shares over the next full 10 years (i.e., you can't).

History Is Full of Long-Term Market and Economic Forecasts—Most Are Wrong

In 1894, someone predicted in *The Times* the streets of London would, by 1944, be buried under nine feet of manure! The growth in popularity of horse-drawn carriages made it a certainty.[3] (Utter manure, obviously.)

In case you haven't been to London in the last 70 years, rest assured, it's not covered in nine feet of dung. A little something called the combustion engine staved off the inevitable. People tend to fantasize about the world pre-automobile, as if society were somehow living in a clean, idyllic, carbon-free utopia. (People who think this way likely have never spent time on farms.) Horse manure isn't very green. It's quite bad for our water supply. What's more, in late-nineteenth-century metropolitan areas, people suffered terribly from respiratory diseases because, among other reasons, they *inhaled* manure. There was so much of it getting kicked around, it *floated in the air.* And you think cars spew a lot of greenhouse gases? They can't hold a candle (whoa—don't do that) to the rear end of horses, cattle and other livestock. The world's biggest carbon output, even today, comes not from cars but from livestock. Believing our world is getting *less* clean, not *more* clean, takes a lot of myopia.

Maybe some people have a dimmer view of humanity than I have. But I happen to believe profit-motive is a powerful engine for societal good—including improving our environment. History shows consistently capitalistic countries have had cleaner environments than communist, socialist or any form of despotic totalitarian governments. As capitalistic societies get richer, they get more innovative—*and more clean*. No one really *likes* a mode of transportation that requires a massive pooper scooper.

True environment lovers wouldn't fear for the future. They would be inspired by whatever as-of-yet unimagined innovation would make our world cleaner, faster, more powerful. They wouldn't fear industry—they'd embrace it because industry is what makes a society richer. And history shows a richer society is a better steward of the environment.

What does any of this have to do with investing? It's the same myopic error investors make when attempting long-term forecasts. They make long-term bets based on current assumptions, which can change—radically. London isn't covered in manure—someone invented the car! No one would have thought of that then, just as no one knows what will influence stock supply among various categories 5, 10 or 20 years from now.

An ERP Is Just a Fancy Long-Term Forecast

Academia has its own form of misplaced long-term forecasting, usually called an *equity risk premium* (ERP). There's nothing wrong with this concept—the idea that for the additional volatility risk you take in equities, you should get some sort of premium over a risk-free rate like a Treasury over long periods. I don't know any sane person who disagrees with that as a rough theory. It's when you try to forecast from it that things get wacky.

It's easy to calculate a backward-looking ERP—take the annualized return of equities over some period, take the same for Treasurys, and subtract. (Some people say you should use a 1-year rate; others, a 10-year rate—and that is all too fine a point). Since equities are a long-term investment, I tend to think it best to use the 10-year, but feel free to quibble. It won't really change the outcome in a meaningful way. Since 1926 through year-end 2010, US stocks have annualized 9.8% and 10-Year US Treasurys 5.3%—so the equity risk premium since 1926 for US stocks is 4.5%.[4] Fair enough—you got a nice premium on average for the extra volatility. Just as you'd expect.

The problem with many academic ERPs is they attempt to calculate a *forward* ERP. So, if the 10-year Treasury rate is currently 3%, and someone predicts a 10-year ERP of 2.5%, then they think stocks will average 5.5% annually over the next 10 years, which isn't disastrous but is well below average. Mind you, in my experience, most ERPs I've seen usually predict very low forward stock returns, though not always. These are simply extensions of the practitioner's own biases, or the mind-set of the time when they are making them or both. A bearishly biased academic will tend to bearish projections, and a bullish one will make bullish projections. ERPs tend to be lower when society is more bearish than when it is, overall, more optimistic.

What's more, at the end of the 1990s, it was fashionable (for some) to predict *big* stock returns for the next 10 years because the previous 10 had seen big returns (as covered in Chapter 4). Of course, that didn't happen. And today (as I write in 2011), most ERP models are pretty dour. They are just projecting forward what we just lived through—not a great way to make forecasts.

Believers in forward ERPs (and other long-term forecasting models) usually suffer from myopia. I've never seen any model that stood up well to back-testing consistently. If it did, it got a few periods right, not the majority, and only by happenstance.

The Fatal Flaws

There are a few common fatal flaws among all ERP models, no matter how different they are. First, like the manure prediction, most academic ERP models I've seen take current or even past conditions and project them forward. They do something like take the *current* dividend yield, the *current* inflation rate, the average earnings per share over the *past* 10 years, subtract the *current* bond yield and mix that together somehow for a forward projection. Naturally, what earnings-per-share averaged over the past 10 years says nothing about anything going forward, nor do current inflation rates, dividend yield, bond yields or any other current or past components that may go into an ERP mix. If the past predicted the future, stocks would be uni-directional. They're not.

Second, they seem to ignore other forms of history—even very recent history. Most ERP models usually spit out modest projections—2.0%, 2.5%, 3.0%. But long term, actual equity risk

Table 6.1   Historic ERPs by Decade

Decade	10-Year Treasurys Annualized Returns	S&P 500 Annualized Returns	ERP
1930s	4.0%	–0.1%	–4.1%
1940s	2.7%	9.0%	6.3%
1950s	0.4%	19.3%	18.9%
1960s	2.8%	7.8%	5.0%
1970s	6.1%	5.8%	–0.3%
1980s	12.8%	17.5%	4.7%
1990s	8.0%	18.2%	10.2%
2000s	6.6%	–0.9%	–7.6%

Sources: Global Financial Data, Inc., USA 10-Year Government Bond Total Return Index, S&P 500 total return from 12/31/1929 to 12/31/2009.

premiums by decade have been hugely variable. Table 6.1 shows historic equity risk premiums by decade. First, you notice actual 10-year annualized stock averages are themselves variable (Chapter 3). Stocks annualized 19.3% in the 1950s, 18.2% in the 1990s. Negative full decades are rare—stocks annualized –0.1% in the 1930s and –0.9% in the 2000s—flattish. But the ERPs themselves had huge variations. The 1960s and 1980s ERPs were close to the long-term ERP average of 4.5%—though stock returns themselves weren't "average."

Another takeaway—many investors fear the flat decade of the 2000s portends long-term trouble for stocks. But see how long ERPs were hugely positive following past negative periods. (Recall Chapter 4.)

This is also why some very famous P/E predictability models fail—they aim to forecast long-term returns—5 and 10 years out. Folks who think today's P/Es (or past averages) say anything about long-term equity returns don't realize that, first, on their own, the P/E isn't predictive. Can't be! Why?

One huge reason (people tend to forget fast): There are two moving variables to the P/E. A high P/E could be the result of temporarily depressed earnings. And when a stock (industry, sector or entire market) has very depressed earnings, that can be a great time to buy (e.g., P/Es were historically high in early 2009—a superb time to buy). Just one reason a high P/E says nothing about forward-looking risk or return on its own.

But as important—nothing about the P/E is predictive of long-future stock supply shifts. And no ERP model or any other long-term forecasting model I've ever seen even attempts to address long-term shifts in supply. Anyone trying to make long-term forecasts without addressing supply is telling you more of what they don't know about capital markets than what they do know. For the most part, they implicitly assume in the long term, supply shifts overall will be what they have been in the long-term past, which may or may not be true or even close to true.

It's Still Heat Chasing Even When It Seems Safe

Another problem with long-term love a little study of history can solve—people have a strong tendency to believe something that's had a good run recently is inherently safer. (Also known as *heat chasing*.)

In the cold, rational light of day, most people would say they know just because something has done well doesn't make it safer. But heat chasing happens all the time—usually after something has a particularly good run. Think Energy in the late 1970s before that bubble popped in 1980, Tech in the very late 1990s, residential real estate in 2005 and 2006. Maybe gold now.

This isn't a new problem—people forget bubbles aren't unique to modern markets. Recall the famous "tulip bubble," when in the space of just a few short months during 1636, values of tulips skyrocketed—costing many multiples more than what an average worker earned annually. In 1637, values plummeted. Similarly, in 1720, we had the South Seas bubble, shown in Figure 6.2.

South Seas trading mania had picked up in 1711, when Lord Treasurer Robert Harley chartered the South Seas Company (SSC), made himself its governor and granted it sole rights to South Seas trade (basically the Pacific Ocean). Assessing the commercial potential was impossible. Who could value an entirely unknowable thing? But manias are built on phenomena that can't be detailed precisely.

Lord Harley and his promoters were likely much more interested in doing deals than doing trade. As stocks soared in 1719, they concocted a scheme to swap the entire English debt for SSC stock—plus a take of future (pipe-dream) profits. Politicians loved it—who doesn't want something for nothing?

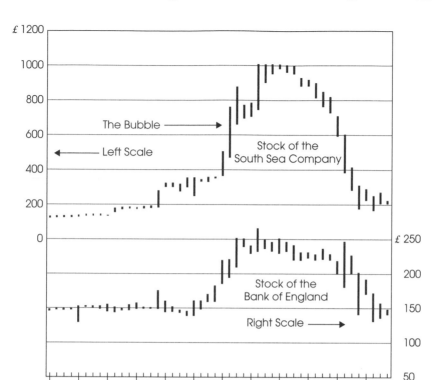

Figure 6.2   The South Seas Bubble, December 1719 to October 1720

Source: James E. Rogers, *A History of Agriculture and Prices in England, 1703–1793* (New York: Clarendon Press, 1902).

More and more people bought in—the government's involvement gave it an air of credibility. Stocks overall rose, too—buoyed by speculative fever. Figure 6.2 also shows Bank of England stock, normally quite stodgy, getting caught in the fever. Though, Bank of England stock rose just 33% in the period shown, while SSC boomed 225%.

As these things go, more investors flocked to SSC stock. SSC issued ever more shares because, to them, they were just printing money. Other similar ventures were started during this time, taking advantage of the mania.

But SSC didn't want upstarts siphoning off potential investors. Since all of Parliament was invested in SSC, they persuaded Parliament to outlaw all companies not royally chartered. Problem was, no one knew who was chartered and who wasn't. All but the biggest stocks plunged. SSC was chartered and didn't fall at first. But loss-ridden investors, particularly those who bought on margin, soon needed to liquidate even from those firms whose stock prices hadn't fallen—like SSC and the Bank of England. They got hit with what I call "sympathy selling" (and happens still today in all bear markets). Problem was, SSC had no legitimate business to keep it afloat amid the selling. They, and many other firms, went kaput. Oh well! On to the next cycle.

If you want an excellent history on bubbles, and why we will always be prone to them periodically, read Charles MacKay's excellent book, *Extraordinary Popular Delusions and the Madness of Crowds*. My guess is speculative bubbles existed back to the earliest marketplaces in Mesopotamia. As long as humans exist, we'll have bubble manias from time to time. And we'll have heat chasers.

If You Knew You Were Chasing Heat, You Wouldn't Do It

Fact is, if you knew you were chasing heat, you wouldn't do it, right? No one would. Everyone knows heat chasing is bad. But heat-chasers don't chase heat because they know it's risky—they chase heat because they think the hot asset class is inherently safer and permanently better.

It's very difficult behavior to overcome—it's evolutionary. Long ago, humans learned to follow patterns to stay alive; e.g., I saw my buddy eat these berries, and he didn't die. I ate them, too, and I didn't die. I should probably keep eating these berries and not those other ones that made my other buddy very sick. There was safety in patterns.

In the same way, if something has a consistent run of good returns, our brains want to tell us, "Look at that pattern. That means that's safer." (This, of course, is tied to the fact we have short-term memories—and bad ones at that. If we remembered what happened the last time we wanted to follow a hot investment, we wouldn't do it again.) Or, if we don't think it's inherently safer, we think, "I better get in now while the getting is good. I'll know when to get out."

It doesn't always happen that way and not universally. Humans are a mess of behavioral responses, which is partly why capital markets are so darned tricky. Frequently, if something has a good run, that starts another evolutionary reaction—fear of heights. But the desire to see safety in a pattern is equally as potent an ingrained response. Both of these responses lead to big costly errors.

Not So Safe as Houses

Asset classes seen widely as "safe" (when they're not) come and go. Residential real estate was one recent example. Readers in 2011 and 2012 may say, "Yes, well, everyone knows now homes can be a lousy investment." Except in 2005 and 2006, you probably read about investors liquidating 401(k)s to buy condos in Miami and Las Vegas—even raw land!

People like to point fingers for the real estate run-up. Former Fed head Alan Greenspan is a favorite scapegoat—for keeping rates so low for so long. I don't know that we can blame him so directly. Interest rates had been trending lower since the early 1980s—globally. Lower interest rates means borrowing is cheaper, which means people could afford more house. That's pretty clear to see, but it wasn't the only factor.

In my view, one major contributor was a 1997 tax-law change. Before 1997, homeowners got a once-per-lifetime capital gains exemption on the sale of residential real estate—$250,000 for singles and $500,000 for couples. That changed to an exemption every two years. Before that tax law, folks tended to stay in their homes longer. Or, if they moved, they'd roll gains into the next property. With the tax-law change, people suddenly had an incentive to sell homes—they wouldn't get dinged by the tax man. People forget a reduction in capital gains tax is an increased incentive to sell and often motivates increased selling. Stocks, contrary to what many think, have typically done badly in the short-term right after capital gains taxes are reduced because sellers hold back waiting for that lower tax to sell and then all dump at once.

Then, too, in America, GDP kept rising. So more folks every decade could afford to buy homes. And because homes prices rose in such a steady fashion for a long time and credit was so easy, there was a pretty widespread attitude that real estate was safe. It was tangible—unlike those persnickety stocks that are now nothing more than digital ones and zeroes.

The problem with housing, even during the best of times, is it's a large single transaction with huge transaction costs and ongoing deferred maintenance costs and taxes. Then, too, if a significant portion of your net worth is tied up in a single type of asset—a home—with no geographical diversity, that can be risky. You wouldn't put all your money in one stock, would you? Many folks see that now with the benefit of hindsight, but many folks didn't see it that way then. They just saw real estate as the latest in a long line of can't-lose investments. Can't-lose investments eventually do.

Will Rogers Versus Bernard Baruch

Another problem: Many think (still) the housing weakness that started in 2005 and 2006 (push that forward or back depending on where you live) was unusual—unprecedented! Takes a very short-term memory to forget that, yes, real estate can and does lose value. In 1980, I remember folks having the same feeling they had in the mid-2000s—that real estate was an ironclad investment. I remember a 19-year-old kid who did some maintenance work around my office giving me tips on where to get some cheap land. He quoted Will Rogers to me (19 years old!) saying, "Buy land; they ain't making any more of it." Which brought to mind another famous quote from investor Bernard Baruch, "When beggars and shoeshine boys, barbers and beauticians can tell you how to get rich, it is time to remind yourself that there is no more dangerous illusion than the belief that one can get something for nothing."

Before 1980, rural real estate had risen by 15% a year for years—thanks in part to spiraling inflation in the Nixon-Ford-Carter years driving up farm-product prices. But then, blessedly, Fed head Paul Volcker (appointed by Carter then reappointed by Reagan) successfully ended the inflationary death spiral. When he took office, inflation was in the high teens. When he left, inflation was low single digits and trending lower—a trend that was mirrored globally and continued for decades.

That and the government curtailing some silly price supports and farm loan programs helped end inflation for farm products—but made farmland look less attractive. Figure 6.3 is another old graph I like—showing change in farm real estate per acre from 1981 to 1985.

There were some regions that did ok. Texas prices rose during that period, but it worked out to less than 10% annually—less than the prior dizzying pace of appreciation. Overall nationally,

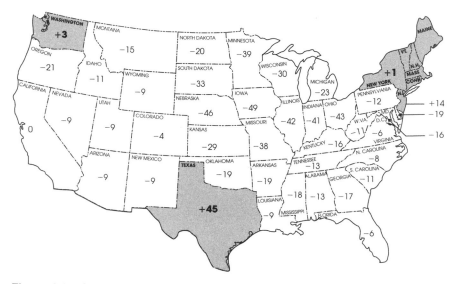

Figure 6.3   Change in Average Value of Farm Real Estate per Acre 1981 to 1985

Source: US Department of Agriculture, Economic Research Services, Agricultural Land Values, June 7, 1985.

prices crashed. Iowa down 49%. Illinois down 42%. Bottom line: If everybody believes something will make big bucks, it probably won't. Why? If everyone believes it, they've probably already spent their money on it, which means there's no more buying power to push prices higher.

There are more examples. Commercial real estate crashed in the 1990s. Real estate in Japan did lousy in the 1990s and beyond. New York City had a real estate downturn in the 1970s. Denver in the 1980s. San Francisco real estate languished before the Tech boom in the early-to-mid-1990s. You can find examples of smaller, more regionalized booms then busts—because real estate is normally localized, though the 1980s farmland bust and the more recent one were decidedly national.

Those are shorter-term boom-bust cycles. But the truth is, real estate has always been a pretty lackluster long-term investment. Since we have decent data (1978), a dollar invested in real estate would have grown to $16.65.[5] However, that same dollar in world stocks would have grown to $23.22 and in US stocks to $32.99— almost double![6]

But that real estate return is from an index measuring institutional investors investing in mostly commercial properties. *Residential* real estate property prices over the same period annualized just 4.5%—in other words, $1 invested became *just $4.30.*[7] Now, that's just an average, and individual markets have seen bigger (and smaller) increases. But that's just one of the problems with thinking about your primary residence as an investment like stocks. You probably don't own a geographically diverse portfolio to mitigate location risk. And even if you do, the average returns don't look so hot.

So why is it common for people to think real estate—their home—is a good long-term investment? Well, possibly because it's a *big* investment. But also the power of leverage. Most folks don't buy a property using cash. They borrow—heavily—putting down 20% or less!

If you buy a $250,000 house and put down 20% ($50,000) and sell five years later, maybe the house has appreciated to $275,000. That's a 10% total increase—just about 2% annualized—and less than what you'd likely get from a Treasury bill. Lower than inflation. But, that's not really your return. Because you only put down $50,000! That $25,000 gain is a 50% increase on investment and about 8.5% annualized and pretty darn good!

Now, this ignores things like transaction costs to buy and sell, which can be over 4% coming and going. Then, too, you didn't live there for free—you paid interest costs. Plus, you paid property taxes and association fees, you had to fix the roof, paint the inside, keep up the lawn, etc. These are all costs many homeowners forget to account for when calculating their gain. Yes, you'd have to pay rent if you didn't own the house—maybe that was more or less than your interest and upkeep costs—but that cost should be factored in when thinking about a house as an *investment* instead of a pleasant roof over your head. Still, it's the leverage that can make real estate gains seem outsized, and readers know all too well leverage can go against you.

Figure 6.4 is another older chart I like, showing farm prices from 1912 to 1976 in constant dollars (chained to 1967) and also current dollars at the time the chart was created (in 1978). From 1912 to 1975, in current dollars, your average annual return was just 3.3%—*before property taxes.* That's about equal to inflation or what you get from US Treasurys. In constant dollars, there's almost no real, after-inflation appreciation for an entire lifetime. (Again, before property taxes, which means you likely had a loss.)

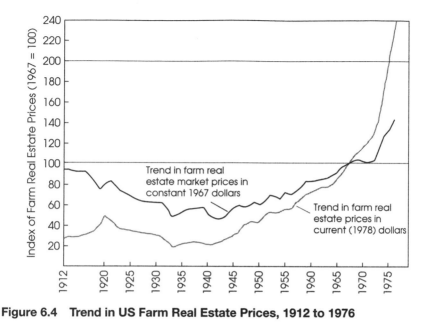

Figure 6.4   Trend in US Farm Real Estate Prices, 1912 to 1976

Source: Raleigh Barlowe, *Land Resource Economics: The Economics of Real Estate* (Englewood Cliffs, NJ: Prentice Hall, Inc., 1978).

This chart also disproves the idea real estate can be an inflation hedge. If you bought in 1912 and needed to sell in 1942, you were down 40%. That's not an inflation hedge. That's *actually* a secular bear market (see Chapter 5). To break even, you had to wait until 1968. Including transaction costs, property taxes and upkeep, you probably never broke even.

Yes, there's value to owning real estate. For most of us, it may be the value of a roof over our heads. There are other intangibles to real estate, of course. And yes, there are many successful real estate investors—but the best I've seen have very diverse portfolios, both in product (commercial versus residential versus mixed use versus industrial) and geography.

As fresh as the housing downturn is today still in people's minds, memories are short. The next time real estate cycles in as a hot, can't-lose investment, don't forget. I don't care if it's Tech stocks, real estate, gold, pork bellies, the Malaysian ringgit, whatever—if everyone you know thinks something is "can't lose," it can and will. Maybe soon.

All That Glitters

As difficult as it is to make long-term forecasts, it's also difficult to predict when a currently hot asset class will turn cold. Why? Because even if something leads for a long time, it can keep running. That something *has been* hot doesn't mean it *must* go cold. It's just never a reason to buy something on its own, without other fundamental reasons supporting that decision.

As I write this in 2011, gold has been super duper hot. People like to think gold has some inherent value, but it's a commodity,

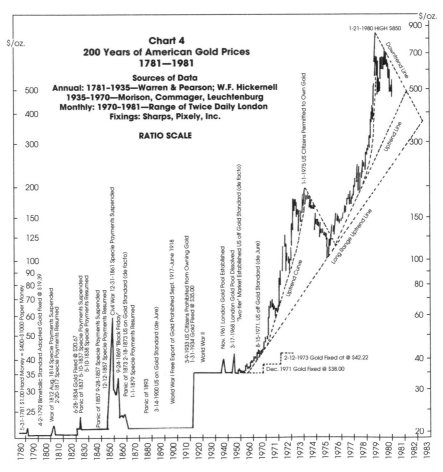

Figure 6.5   200 Years of American Gold Prices 1781 to 1981

Source: Copyright ©1981 by the foundation for the Study of Cycles.

like any other—forcing your memory out just a bit shows that. It's worth what people are willing to pay for it—and commodities are notoriously volatile, prone to boom and bust. Gold is no different. And that's been true basically forever.

I like Figure 6.5 because it highlights a few points. First, it shows some big gold booms and busts back to 1780. The booms were few and far between and ended fast. Also, for much of that period, gold prices were fixed! Gold didn't start trading truly freely until late in 1973. The world effectively went off the gold standard in 1971, but gold price controls remained in place until late 1973 in part to ease the transition.

I also like this chart because it's a bit deceptive—and even deception can be instructive. The left side of the chart takes up about 170 years, and the right side about 30. When gold began trading freely, it took off like a shot—a boom, a mini crash, then another boom.

Folks who like gold and claim it's a terrific store of value, a good inflation hedge and/or a good this-that-or-the-other, are basing that claim on the 40 years of decent, freely traded data. Which is fine! You must work with the data you have, and you can learn even from smaller pools of data. So let's see what the data say.

Figure 6.6 shows gold just during the period it traded freely (starting when post-Bretton Woods controls were dropped in 1973). Here, you see the same two brief booms in Figure 6.5 in the 1970s. Then a bust, followed by a smaller boom in 1982. Then . . . nothing. Anyone investing through the 1980s and 1990s should remember—gold moved sideways with some volatility for over 22 years with some smaller positive runs but never surpassing the 1980 peak, never mind the smaller 1983 peak. This is a slightly longer sideways and flattish trend than stocks have ever had (per Chapter 4). If you bought anywhere in the period from 1978-ish to 1982, you basically went sideways or sideways and down for over two decades. (See my 2010 book *Debunkery* for more details on why gold is the ultimate timing issue.)

Then, starting in 2005, there were three quick booms in succession. So, the history of freely traded gold tells us: boom, sideways, boom, bust, boom, agonizingly long sideways and downtrend, then boom again.

Another way to think of that is Figure 6.7, which shows growth of a dollar in global stocks, US stocks, Treasurys and gold.

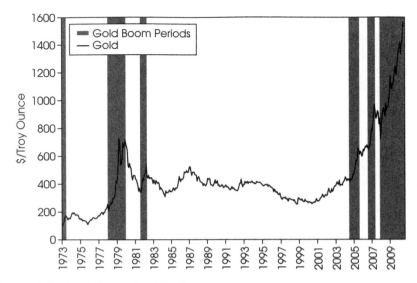

Figure 6.6   Gold Boom Bust Cycles

Source: Global Financial Data, Inc., Gold Bullion Price–New York (US$/Ounce) from 11/30/1973 to 06/30/2011.

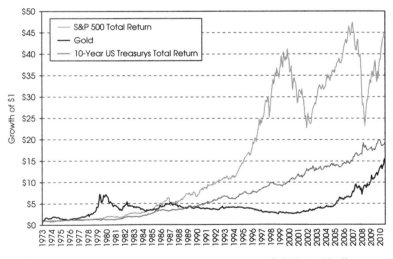

Figure 6.7   Growth of $1: Stocks, Bonds and Gold (1973 to 2010)

Sources: Global Financial Data, Inc., Gold Bullion Price–New York (US$/Ounce), S&P 500 total return, US 10-Year Government Bond Total Return Index from 11/30/1973 to 06/30/2010.

Yes, stocks are volatile, but more often than not they're positively volatile (see Chapter 3). And with all that volatility, and including the overall lackluster returns in the 2000s, stock returns were vastly superior.

A more shocking discovery—Treasurys had a better return than gold over the entirety of the period gold traded truly freely. Yet gold was much more volatile! (See Figure 6.6.) For all that bouncing around, you'd want better long-term returns. But you didn't get them.

No—to invest in gold well (as well as most industrial metals and indeed most commodities), you usually must time the boom/busts well. And if you want to give it a try, ask yourself, "What was the last, good, short-term timing call I made?" Then ask yourself—and be honest, "What was the last, good, short-term timing call I got wrong? Have I been wrong more often than right? Or right more than wrong?"

For example, did you buy US Tech stocks in the mid-1990s? Did you then short Tech in March 2000? Did you short global stocks in 2001, then buy them back in March 2003 and hold through 2007? Did you buy oil in January 2007, right before its last steep surge, and sell in July 2008? Did you buy Emerging Markets in Fall 2008? Or global stocks in early 2009, when sentiment was black? Did you sell euros and buy dollars in April 2008? Then reverse that in March 2009? Were you overweight Materials, Energy and Consumer Discretionary for the year or so following the bear market bottom, because they fell most in the bear and then bounced the most in the new bull?

If you didn't get those right—some pretty big swings in some fairly broad categories—then what makes you think you can time the next gold boom? Or the next gold bust? If you aren't a proven, more-right-than-wrong hot hand at market timing, don't bother with timing gold.

Better Ways to Do Long-Term Passive   Maybe that's fine by you. You won't time it. Instead, you're ok being passive to gold and simply waiting out what could be long sideways periods in the future. But if that's the case, then why not be passive to an asset class that has superior long-term returns and a greater likelihood of better returns over long periods going forward? In the period shown in Figure 6.7, stocks far and away outperform gold. (And in almost all intermediate periods.) One dollar invested in US stocks became $43.84, in world stocks $27.40, while in gold became just $14.82.[8] Even Treasurys beat gold—$1 invested became $19.25[9]— better returns with less volatility! If you have the discipline to hang on to something that does dreadfully for two decades, you have the discipline to hang on to something that traditionally is more positive than not—and in shorter periods—and is likelier to yield better returns.

Is gold the next category to go bust? No idea. I don't get in the business of trying to time gold because it is devilishly tough without much evidence of a long-term payoff. I know I don't know how to time gold. And if you really think you're a good enough timer to time gold well—well, you don't need any advice from me. (And whether you're right or not about your timing skills, you certainly won't accept any advice from me.)

Whether it's gold, silver, pork bellies, real estate again or some equity category like Energy, Tech, Consumer Staples or Discretionary— don't be fooled into thinking long-term outperformance means long-term diminished risk. The future is always the future, and risk is ever present. That something has been hot means just that—it was hot. That says nothing about risk or return going forward.

Use History to Your Advantage

Are stocks likelier to outperform bonds, cash, real estate and gold long term? Most likely—strong historical precedent and finance theory and basic business fundamentals all suggest that should be so. But within the broader asset class of stocks, long-term bets on narrower categories likely lead you to some periods of outperformance, but also periods (sometimes long) of relative underperformance.

That's long term. Short term, of course, performance dispersion can be massive—and timing it well (not even perfectly, but well) can be very profitable if you can do it. Note you don't have to time leadership swings if you don't have the time, inclination or expertise. Just being fairly passive to stocks—if you have the discipline—is likely to net you better returns than what most investors get over time. (See Chapter 2.)

But if you want some extra portfolio juice, history is one useful tool in deciding if something is likely to lead for the next 12 to 24 months.

(Again, it's a good tool, but just one tool in forming forward expectations. To determine likely outperformance of narrower categories, you also want to consider a myriad of economic, sentiment and political drivers.)

But history can tell you coming off the bottom of a bear market, owning small caps is typically a good bet. Of course, that would require you to time bear market bottoms well—and if you could do that, you wouldn't really need to time narrower categories. But still, small caps near the end of a bear and in the earlier stages of a new bull typically outperform.

The flip side of that is during the mature stages of a bull market, you want to own larger cap stocks. The more mature the bull market, the bigger you should likely go. Of course, history alone can't tell you whether a bull market is in its early or more mature stages because bull markets don't run a predictable length of time. (See Chapter 2.) But there's a strong historical precedent for owning small caps early on and then large caps in the later course of a bull market.

Also, history teaches, at the end of a bear market, you want to own those narrower categories that fell most in the late stages of a bear. They tend to bounce huge in the early stages of a bull. Figures 6.8 and 6.9 show sector performance into and out of the last two bear market bottoms. Almost uniformly, those sectors that had the worst performance in the six months to the bear market bottom had the best performance in the six months after.

So if you truly believe you're at the tail end of a bear market, you pretty well know what sectors to load up on.

History (and fundamentals) also says, generally, if you expect the spread between long-term interest rates and short-term rates to narrow (a so-called flattening yield curve) growth stocks tend to do better than value stocks. And if you expect the reverse to occur—so that the spread between long-term interest rates and short-term rates gets wider (a so-called steepening yield curve)—value stocks typically do better than growth stocks.

Since a steeper yield curve means a bigger spread between short-term rates and long-term rates, that spread is, in essence, profit banks can make from lending. The greater the spread, the greater the potential profit, the more banks want to lend. An environment when banks are eager to lend tends to favor value firms—they typically raise capital by borrowing rather than issuing stock.

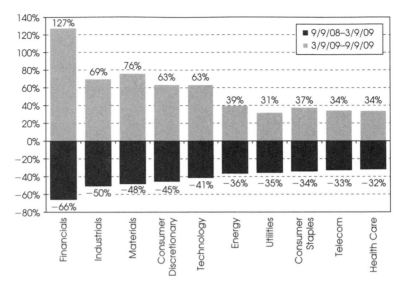

Figure 6.8   What Falls the Most Bounces the Most—2009

Source: Thomson Reuters, MSCI Financials Index, MSCI Industrials Index, MSCI Materials Index, MSCI Consumer Discretionary Index, MSCI Technology Index, MSCI Energy Index, MSCI Utilities Index, MSCI Consumer Staples Index, MSCI Telecommunications Index, MSCI Health Care Index, all price returns from 09/09/2008 to 09/09/2009.

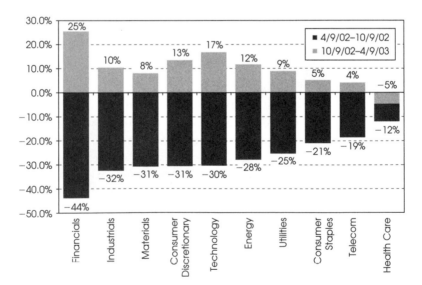

Figure 6.9   What Falls the Most Bounces the Most—2003

Source: Thomson Reuters, MSCI Financials Index, MSCI Industrials Index, MSCI Materials Index, MSCI Consumer Discretionary Index, MSCI Technology Index, MSCI Energy Index, MSCI Utilities Index, MSCI Consumer Staples Index, MSCI Telecommunications Index, MSCI Health Care Index, all price returns from 04/09/2002 to 04/09/2003.

And when firms are raising more capital, they're presumably doing it to grow and increase future profits. Value stocks like that.

When the yield curve flattens out relatively, banks are less eager to lend. Value stocks don't like that. But investment bankers (of course) are happy to help firms raise capital by issuing stock. Here, the growth stocks have the advantage because while they can and do borrow, it's frequently easier for them to raise capital through stock issuances, so an environment when banks are less eager to lend tends to favor growth stocks.

These are a very few examples (you can find more in my 2006 book, *The Only Three Questions That Count*, and my 2010 book, *Debunkery*). You can use history in myriad other ways to help shape forward-looking expectations. Once you get in the habit, it's not hard. Use historical data and consider what conditions existed then, and if they're at all similar to what you see today. See how they played out, and how narrower categories were impacted. This doesn't tell you what *will* happen now. Nothing can! But it can help you form reasonable expectations and shape probabilities for the next 12 months or so.

But if you want to know where stocks or any category will be in 5 or 10 years, you'll have as much luck with a magic 8 ball. Unless you can figure out how to forecast far future stock supply swings. (And if that's the case, give me a call to clue me in.)

CHAPTER

7

Poli-Ticking

Want to see investors' memories utterly fail? Ask them about their politics. Folks have myriad reasons (misguided or not) for liking one political party over another. And something you commonly hear is Party X is better for stocks and/or the economy while Party Y is disastrous.

Simply ain't so. And investors blinded by partisan preference may miss very real patterns driven *not* by ideology but by very fundamental factors.

Amazingly, just a cursory review of even recent history could keep folks from misremembering. But then, folks who are particularly ideological can find "yes, but" ways around that, i.e., "Yes, I like Party X better, and stocks fell hard when my Party X guy was elected. But you must look at longer-term averages." The problem is, when you look at longer-term averages (which most don't do), that's still wrong.

The way the human brain works, you tend to remember things and years and elections that conform to your pre-set prior bias but ignore or forget years and elections that contradict your biases. If someone points out you're wrong—even if they can prove it cold—you tend to want to dodge that by reframing to another time frame, the reason it's an exception, or some other fluky thing.

This tactic, called *reframing,* is a common, natural defense mechanism folks often use to explain away instances when stocks don't behave the way their biases tell them they should. It's just another way investors' memories are faulty and an example of what behavoralists call *confirmation bias*—a common cognitive error.

But by stretching your memory a bit longer and studying a bit of market history, you can overcome this problem. Do that and you discover:

- No one party is materially better or worse than the other for stocks long term.
- Folks blinded by ideology miss a useful forecasting tool that can help shape better forward-looking expectations.
- No one party is better, but sometimes party does matter—it just flip-flops.
- This isn't a quirk; other nations can be similarly impacted by politics.

Enter the Ideology-Free Zone

As mentioned in Chapter 5, I'm occasionally accused of being both a strong Democrat and a strong Republican by people who don't like something I say. I'm neither—nor do I identify as Independent—and haven't claimed allegiance to a political party for a long time. I prefer neither party and find plenty to criticize (and, very rarely, applaud) in both.

My personal ideology aside, it still wouldn't matter if I were a Democrat, Republican or some other perversion. (And official political parties are, almost by definition, perverse. I mean the parties themselves, not those normal citizens who normally identify with them, who are, by and large, normal, lovely people.) As a money manager, my aim is to be ideologically agnostic. Why? A political preference is just another bias. Biases are deadly in investing. They color your analysis, making you blind to certain things while giving others undue weight.

Biases aren't a failing—they're normal—just the way our brains evolved. Biases are cognitive shortcuts, if you will—an offshoot of our need to follow patterns. But just like falling in long-term love with a category can cause major investing errors (Chapter 6), falling in love with one set of folks because you believe you're generally like-minded is similarly dangerous.

You may love your political party, and they, in fact, may love you back (in their perverse way)—particularly if you frequently donate. But neither party loves your portfolio.

I doubt that you believe that now but hope you do soon. You may believe something else—like, "My party doesn't love my portfolio but that other party really hates my portfolio." I hope to get you to change your mind on that, too. Neither party commandeers a majority of sense about how capital markets work. Quite the opposite, really.

Your Party Isn't Better

Folks who identify strongly Republican tend to think Republicans are more business friendly and therefore better for the economy and stock markets. Strong Democrats will say their party is best economy- and market-wise. They're both wrong. History shows neither is materially better for stocks long term. However, that doesn't stop folks from misremembering this:

- September 10, 1992: "Some analysts suggest getting out now because a win by Democrat Bill Clinton in November will send the market plunging for six months. (Wall Street prefers Republican administrations, which are perceived to be better for business.)"[1] *Except stocks boomed for nearly the totality of Clinton's administration.*
- August 16, 2009: "Measured by simple price appreciation on the Dow Jones industrial average, Democratic presidents have been better for the stock market than Republican ones." *Oops—just the opposite of the previous quote. Also, as discussed in Chapter 4, if you must use a faulty index (like the Dow) and ignore dividends, your hypothesis probably doesn't hold much water.*[2]
- December 12, 1971: "If the Dow-Jones industrial average is higher on the Monday before election day than at the start of 1972, President Nixon will undoubtedly be reelected. But if the average is lower than on the first of the year, then the Democratic party will most likely take over the Presidency."[3] *This . . . makes no sense.*
- October 31, 1996: "A USA TODAY/CNN/Gallup Poll finds Democrats were rated better able to handle most key issues, such as the economy, education and Medicare."[4] *Fine, but a poll just measures people's feelings and faulty near-term memories. And feelings change fast.*
- September 21, 2010: "Additionally, public opinion about which political party is better for the US economy has swung in favor of the Republicans, according to the Pew poll."[5] *See? Feelings change—fast. Don't trust them—not yours or anyone else's.*

Many folks have a very hard time with me saying neither party is better—because they're just sure theirs is. Taking it personally, even! Again, I say that identifying with either party is normal and fine and a majority of Americans do it. And voting for either party does not inherently make you a better or worse person or investor.

In history, there have been excellent, long-term successful investors who voted either way (although the investor class has typically leaned more Republican than not—for reasons I explain a bit further on—but again, that hardly matters). The danger is in framing forward-looking expectations through an ideological prism.

I can't tell you how many Republicans told me as Barack Obama took office that the market had to do terribly under him because of what he and the Democratic party would do. Note, the market bottomed within a few weeks of his taking office and has done markedly better than average under his tenure—so far. How can that be? (We'll see in a bit.)

Whether you love or hate the person in the White House, or think the majority party is a bunch of criminals—doesn't matter—not for your portfolio. Hereto, readers in 2011 and 2012 will remember the heated debate over ObamaCare. Like it, loathe it—your feelings matter not one whit for stocks. What you think *should* have happened or *ought* to happen doesn't matter, either. ObamaCare (or any other piece of legislation) may make you giddy or may make you want to shake your fist at the sky. But leave all that out of your investing decisions because it doesn't much matter. I know that is hard for you to believe. Maybe impossible. That's your problem.

Sure, it matters to you personally when you decide whom to vote for. But instead of grinding your teeth over what you see as bad decisions or policy directions you wish we'd go, *when it comes to investing*, instead of fretting, ask:

- Utterly free from my political biases and what I wish would happen, what seems like a range of likely outcomes over the next 12 months or so?
- Using all the tools at my disposal, what do I think is most likely? Least likely? In between?
- What do most people think is likely to happen?

- Is there a huge gap between what I rationally view as likely outcomes, and what people expect?
- And if that likely reality happens, how would that upside or downside surprise impact stocks over the next 12 months or so?

That's what matters more to stocks. Not whether some group of people is happy while another is miserable based on who's in the Oval Office. Again, using ObamaCare as an example—it creates winners and losers, like all pieces of legislation. Your feelings about it won't change that. Focus instead on discovering what industries and firms likely win, and which lose—and then see if you can't game those opportunities. Parts of ObamaCare may get overturned, and many parts change. Which? And how does that likely impact stocks? That's what you should care about when you wear your money manager hat.

Again, forecasting markets over the next 12 to 24 months is, in large part, about shaping a set of likely outcomes, understanding what most people expect, and then understanding how divorced expectations are from that likely future reality, for good or bad.

This is why markets can soar on lackluster economic growth or lower corporate profits. This is why markets can have a lousy year even if economic growth is strong. It's not about what happened or what you hope happens. It's about what most people were expecting and how they react when a better- or worse-than-expected reality plays out. If most people expect a lousy economy, even flattish or tepid growth is better than expectations—and stocks can boom. If people's expectations are too rosy, even if things are fine, stocks can be lackluster.

So stop thinking in terms of, "I like this guy. I think he's tops for the economy. That other guy is an idiot and possibly hates puppies!" You can say those things at home, at cocktail parties, at political rallies, on Twitter, wherever. But when it comes to making investing decisions, drop the ideology. It's deadly.

Presidents and Risk Aversion

Table 7.1 shows US presidents since 1926 (when S&P 500 data starts), each year of their term and annual stock returns. Overall, stocks average 9.3% annually under Republican presidents and 14.5% under Democrats.[6]

But wait . . . didn't I just say neither is better nor worse? It's true, stocks overall under Republican presidents have worse average returns. But much of that is tied to the massive volatility of the first big bear market of the Great Depression, then the massive bounce back in FDR's first term. And all that was a long time ago. Strip out that one see-saw and the averages are much closer—11.1% to 13.6%—not enough to make a material market bet.[7] (Another trick to remember when looking at stock market averages: If you remove outliers and the numbers change a lot, reconsider whether the straight average is a compelling reason to make a market bet.)

But then, perhaps you think it's still true the Democrats are better. Yes, but if you throw out Hoover and FDR, there are just a lot more Republican years than Democrat years to begin with. They're not level playing fields. If you stop looking for ideological superiorities and focus on the amazing patterns within these numbers, you can see some real consistencies.

Table 7.1 divides returns into first, second, third and fourth years of each president's term. For now, ignore individual years; just look at averages. First and second years average 8.1% and 9.0%, while third and fourth average 19.4% and 10.9%.[8]

Interesting enough pattern. Now look at individual years. The back half of presidential terms—years three and four—are nearly uniformly positive. Year three doesn't have a single negative since 1939, which was barely negative. Year four has just four down years. And returns are not always but frequently are double-digit positives.

Now look at the front half. Returns are more variable, with year one a touch more variable than year two—but not too different. Historically, your odds of a down year were much higher in years one and two and much less in years three and four (with notable exceptions, of course—no one thing is a silver bullet).

But so what? Weird patterns happen all the time when dealing with something as chaotic as capital markets. Folks love finding patterns in charts and price graphs. A pattern is nothing more than a quirk and you shouldn't make market bets based on it—unless there's a good explanation for it, rooted in sound fundamentals.

And here, there's an excellent fundamental explanation—tied to when *legislative risk aversion* is increasing or decreasing. Legislation—no matter how it's couched or how many thousands of pages it's on—typically results in a redistribution of money, property

Table 7.1   Presidential Term Anomaly

President	Party	First Year		Second Year		Third Year		Fourth Year	
Coolidge	R	1925	N/A	1926	11.1%	1927	37.1%	1928	43.3%
Hoover	R	1929	*–8.9%*	1930	*–25.3%*	1931	*–43.9%*	1932	*–8.9%*
FDR – 1st	D	1933	52.9%	1934	*–2.3%*	1935	47.2%	1936	32.8%
FDR – 2nd	D	1937	*–35.3%*	1938	33.2%	1939	*–0.9%*	1940	*–10.1%*
FDR – 3rd	D	1941	*–11.8%*	1942	21.1%	1943	25.8%	1944	19.7%
FDR/Truman	D	1945	36.5%	1946	*–8.2%*	1947	5.2%	1948	5.1%
Truman	D	1949	18.1%	1950	30.6%	1951	24.6%	1952	18.5%
Ike – 1st	R	1953	*–1.1%*	1954	52.4%	1955	31.4%	1956	6.6%
Ike – 2nd	R	1957	*–10.9%*	1958	43.3%	1959	11.9%	1960	0.5%
Kennedy/ Johnson	D	1961	26.8%	1962	*–8.8%*	1963	22.7%	1964	16.4%
Johnson	D	1965	12.4%	1966	*–10.1%*	1967	23.9%	1968	11.0%
Nixon	R	1969	*–8.5%*	1970	3.9%	1971	14.3%	1972	19.0%
Nixon/Ford	R	1973	*–14.7%*	1974	*–26.5%*	1975	37.2%	1976	23.9%
Carter	D	1977	*–7.2%*	1978	6.6%	1979	18.6%	1980	32.5%
Reagan – 1st	R	1981	*–4.9%*	1982	21.5%	1983	22.6%	1984	6.3%
Reagan – 2nd	R	1985	31.7%	1986	18.7%	1987	5.3%	1988	16.6%
Bush, GHW	R	1989	31.7%	1990	*–3.1%*	1991	30.5%	1992	7.6%
Clinton – 1st	D	1993	10.1%	1994	1.3%	1995	37.6%	1996	23.0%
Clinton – 2nd	D	1997	33.4%	1998	28.6%	1999	21.0%	2000	–9.1%
Bush, GW – 1st	R	2001	*–11.9%*	2002	*–22.1%*	2003	28.7%	2004	10.9%
Bush, GW – 2nd	R	2005	4.9%	2006	15.8%	2007	5.5%	2008	*–37.0%*
Obama – 1st	D	2009	26.5%	2010	15.1%	2011	—	2012	—
Average			**8.1%**		**9.0%**		**19.4%**		**10.9%**

Source: Global Financial Data, S&P 500 Total Return Index from 12/31/1925 to 12/31/2010.

rights or regulatory changes. Politicians like to sell legislation as a marvelous societal improvement. However, all they're really doing is taking something from someone who had it or will soon have it and giving it to someone (or someones) else.

Vast amounts of academic research proves humans hate losses more than twice as much as they like gains; i.e., a 25% gain feels as good as a 10% loss feels bad.[9] That's true for Americans. For Europeans, it's even higher. So when the risk of legislation increases—as it typically does in the first two years of a president's term—those who lose out hate losing much more than those who benefit from it like benefiting. Because we do it openly and publicly, it feels like a mugging, and anyone not directly involved fears they'll get mugged next—leading to heightened risk aversion overall and more variable returns with worse averages—just as you see in Table 7.1. But when legislative risk aversion decreases—as it typically does in years three and four—stock returns historically have been more uniformly positive.

Playing Presidential Term Politics

What's behind the front half/back half legislative risk aversion divide? What Congress can and can't agree on.

The word *politics*, as you may know, comes from the Latin *poli* meaning *many*, and *tics*, meaning "small blood-sucking creatures." In my view, there are plenty of fine people involved in local government. But national politics—totally different ball game. From what I've seen, even the most rational, well-intentioned, mentally healthy civil servant goes to Washington and within five years becomes a poli-tic. And a poli-tic's sole purpose in life is to get re-elected—or elected to higher office. Anything they do or don't do is ultimately aimed at campaigning, popularity and raising money they can use to fund (what they hope are) endless election campaigns.

Why do they like being poli-tics so much? No idea. Maybe they were dropped on their heads as children. I can't explain it. Maybe some of these ladies and gentlemen do suffer some kind of delusion they're somehow "helping mankind." But mostly I think it's about their ego. There is something about the Beltway that infects people with beltwayitis and motivates poli-tics into the bizarre dance they do.

I digress. A poli-tic just wants to get re-elected or elected to higher office. The president is Head Tic. He can't get elected to any higher office, and he really, *really* wants to get re-elected (and is very tick-ish). His gig is only eight years long, max. He gets just one shot at re-election—he wants to make sure it happens. And it usually does, as we will see.

Head Tics may not understand how capital markets work at all (never seen one yet who did) but surprisingly, they know political history pretty darn well. They know in the history of modern presidents, the president almost always loses some relative power to the opposition party in mid-term elections. (George W. Bush was the first Republican president in 100 years to buck this trend in the 2002 mid-term, but his party lost badly in 2006—as history would suggest.)

Therefore, the president knows that whatever he would pass that is most monumental—the crown jewel of his administration—must be passed in the first two years of his term (I say *his* because they've all been male so far), because he'll likely face a bigger uphill battle in the back half when he loses relative power.

Then, too, a president knows that "doing stuff" annoys somebody—like valuable independent voters. These folks aren't elected off their base—can't be. They're elected by making independents show up and think they are less reprehensible than the other option. So, after a flurry of activity in his first two years and with little prospect of getting much done in a hostile Congress in years three and four, the Head Tic typically sits back and tries to annoy as few folks as possible. (Sometimes, this backfires—if the world isn't going well, he can't do much about it with a hostile Congress.) Instead, he spends his time blaming the opposition party for his inaction. (E.g., "I would have gotten you all free ponies, but my opponents wouldn't let me. So re-elect me and elect more of my compatriots, and boot these pony-hating losers, and next time more free ponies!")

This isn't mere theory—it holds up in history. Most material legislation gets passed in the first two years of any president's term, whereas the back halves have much quieter legislative calendars. And as the Head Tic loses relative power and can pass less, we move from the highest level of political risk aversion in the front half to the lowest in the back half. Stocks overall like that—which is why market returns historically are nearly uniformly positive year three with the best averages, and very good averages in year four.

Year four, you get some politicking from the elections (more on this in a bit)—poli-tics start yammering on what they *plan* to do if elected. That can spook stocks a bit. But overall, with so many poli-tics on the road poli-ticking, there's not much going on in Washington—a material positive.

Think just recently. In the first year of Obama's presidency, we undertook national health care and all the controversy that went with that. In year two, we did so-called financial services regulatory reform (aka Dodd-Frank). In year three they haven't passed anything very significant (other than raising the debt ceiling—which is always contentious but always passes). That's because after the 2010 mid-terms, Congress can't agree on much. So not much gets passed and political risk aversion falls.

Political risk aversion shifting higher and lower can be a significant driver—for good or bad. But other drivers can and do matter, so this should never be your sole reason for bullishness or bearishness. But the pattern is pervasive enough to make you want to be more bullish otherwise than not in years three and four and be cognizant of increased political risk aversion in years one and two.

Look Beneath the Averages   Look within the first two years. Yes, the first two years have lower average returns, but that's tied more to variability than uniformly lackluster returns. Look back at Table 7.1. In years one and two, when returns aren't negative they're very frequently huge, double-digit positive. Not always, but enough to show you can't just assume years one and two must be bad.

What's going on in those years? If political risk aversion decreases for some reason in a year the market generally expects it to increase—for example, a heavily gridlocked Congress or some other set of events making poli-tics less enthusiastic about redistributing your money—that unexpected positive surprise can lead to better returns. Again, always look beneath averages to what comprise them.

Remember, too, the power of this pattern is that it's typically so little regarded and often ignored. If you suddenly hear a lot of people talking about it, that's a sign it likely has less oomph—for now. That has happened occasionally in the past. But because our memories are so short, it takes just a year, typically, for people to become disenchanted with it and forget. And as soon as that happens, you know it's useful again.

Perverse Inverse—It's Four and One

Ideology is dangerous in investing, and party doesn't matter, overall—but at certain points it can. Not because one party is inherently better or worse, but because capital markets are nothing more than people making decisions—hundreds of millions of people making billions and billions of decisions.

And people are naturally biased—as we have seen repeatedly in this book. But if you are free from bias and can tell when other investors' biases might influence their decision-making (and therefore, the market) you may see the world more clearly and potentially profit.

Biases play a particular role in year one and four of the cycle—the inaugural and election year. As mentioned earlier, in my experience and in countless polls, the investing class tends to be more Republican than not. (I don't say that to make you happy if you're Republican or angry if you're a Democrat. That's just an observation—and remember, in investing you're supposed to drop your ideology, anyway.)

Republican politicians see themselves as more pro-business. When they campaign, they say business-friendly things and promise business-friendly reforms—and markets typically like that. Democrats are seen as less business friendly, more interested in non-market-oriented social causes. Markets like that less. So election years (year four) when we elect a Republican, stocks rise 15.6% on average, but only 6.7% when we elect a Democrat.[10] (See Table 7.2.) Simple fact—other things being equal—if you knew in advance we would elect a Republican president, that might be extra motivation to be more bullish election year than if you knew in advance we would elect a Democrat.

Aha! Evidence Republicans are better?

No. The facts are simple. When we elect a Republican, the market does great in the election year but not so well in the inaugural year. And just the reverse—when we elect a Democrat, the market does less well in the election year but pretty darned well in the inaugural year. What's going on?

The moment a Republican gets elected, he's no longer a candidate, but president, and he starts thinking about re-election. He needs independent voters and marginal Democrats to get re-elected—he knows his Republican base has nowhere to go. A Republican president can't ride on a wave of deregulation, lower taxes or whatever it

Table 7.2   Perverse Inverse

	Election Year (Year 4)	Inaugural Year (Year 1)
Democrat wins	6.7%	14.9%
Republican wins	15.6%	0.8%

Source: Global Financial Data, Inc., S&P 500 Total Return Index from 12/31/1925 to 12/31/2010.

was he promised. He has to fight with his own party just as President Obama has had to fight with the liberal end of the Democratic party in 2011! Markets discover he's not as pro-business as they hoped. He isn't their pro-business champion. No, he is, rather, just a politician, so a Republican's inauguration year is more variable, averaging just 0.8%.[11] Look at those numbers in Table 7.1 again. The only Republican with a positive inaugural year was George H.W. Bush—the rest have all been negative—100%!

But the Democrat! He's just a politician, too. He came in vowing to go after Wall Street fat cats and to fight for the little guy—which scared the dickens out of markets in the election year—contributing to lower election year market averages. But he wants to get re-elected, too, and doesn't want to annoy Wall Street fat cats (who make a lot of campaign contributions). He, too, must move to the middle if he is to have a hair of a chance at re-election. It's the middle that makes the decisions. Markets then are pleasantly surprised the Democrat isn't quite so business-unfriendly as they feared, and the first year of a Democrat's term, they average 14.9%.[12] Returns are less variable, too. Outside of FDR's second and third terms (during the Great Depression), Carter is the only Democrat with a negative first year (and that was down only –7.2%)[13]—and he lost re-election.

Think about President Obama for a moment. He fits the pattern pretty perfectly. If you're a Republican, you don't like him, surely. But note that his health care bill is a lot less than he originally promoted. Ditto for financial services regulatory reform. In fact, his Democratic base isn't too happy with him today (as I write in 2011). That's pretty normal. The same thing happened to Bill Clinton in his first term. But, in characteristic form, President Obama's election year saw bad stock market returns and his inaugural year saw great stock market returns. Normal pattern.

So, you have reason to be more bullish than not in an election year if you think a Republican will win, and reason to be somewhat cautious if you think a Democrat will win. (Again, always taking into account other economic and sentiment drivers.) Then that flip-flops in the inaugural year. A key takeaway if you're a Republican: Don't make the mistake I saw so many make in 2009 and assume that because you so disliked this new Democrat president that the market couldn't go up big time. It can and usually does, because the fear is front-end loaded into the election year. As we said in Chapter 1, markets move in advance of things, not after them.

The Devil You Know

Reading this in 2011 and 2012, some may panic—thinking if President Obama is re-elected, that could be bad for stocks in 2012. But history is a good guide here, too, and that is not the case at all.

I have no idea if he wins or not—too early to have a clue as I write. I can say incumbents are devilishly hard to beat. In the history of the S&P 500, 14 incumbents have tried for re-election. Only three failed—Ford, Carter, and G.H.W. Bush. Ford never previously won anything outside of his House seat—and that in a district where if you got the Republican nomination, the congressional seat was yours because the district leaned so heavily Republican. He was a weak national candidate with no prior experience in big races. (More on him in a bit.)

That's how we got Carter—he ran against a very weak candidate in Ford. That was Carter's good luck. Carter's bad luck was to run for re-election against both the misery index and, much more importantly, one of the Republican party's all-time very best campaigners, Ronald Reagan—dubbed after the fact, "The Great Communicator."

G.H.W. Bush was fighting a recession that started on his watch that he did little to ameliorate. It ended on his watch, too, but it wasn't widely sensed or accepted that the corner had been turned (see Chapter 1 on how this is true after all recessions end). In fact, Bush was ridiculed for saying the recession ended—though he was right and the public was wrong, but that doesn't matter when it comes to voting. Plus, President Bush was up against someone who is generally considered one of the Democratic party's best all-time campaigners, Bill "I feel your pain" Clinton. Clinton very well took advantage of the public's disbelief that the recession was over despite Bush's protestations—remember his campaign's slogan, "It's the economy, stupid." Bush wasn't stupid at all, but Clinton very successfully made him seem so.

Incumbents are tough to beat. People often point to Obama's low approval rating—just 39% in August 2011 (according to Gallup). Many say that dooms him—no one has been re-elected on approval below 44% (or some such number). Fine, except that matters only if election day were tomorrow. As I write, there's over a year to election day—a lot can happen—approval rates are notoriously volatile. Today's approval rate is meaningless. This is just another example of how memories fail us—people don't remember how much presidential approval ratings can move.

At this point in his first term, Bill Clinton had a lower approval rate. So did Ronald Reagan. They both won re-election handily. Harry Truman's rate was higher at this point, but had been much lower at points throughout his first term—as low as 33%—and he was re-elected.[14] You know whose rates were higher at this point? One-termers G.H.W. Bush and Lyndon Johnson (who opted not to run for re-election on his own).

But what does that mean for markets? As I write in 2011, I'm not ready to make a stock market forecast for 2012, but there is one positive driver in its favor that you almost certainly haven't heard about: We will either re-elect a Democrat or newly elect a Republican—and that trade-off is a particular sweet spot for stocks.

Go back to what I said earlier about stocks' reactions to Democrats and Republicans in election years: Markets typically do well when we elect a Republican in the election year and fear a Democrat. But that effect is magnified in first-term elections and diminished in second term re-elections. When we *newly* elect a Republican, markets have especially high hopes—stocks have averaged 18.8% in those years (see Table 7.3). And a *newly* elected Democrat is even spookier—stocks average –2.7%.

But that Democrat that markets so feared in his initial election year isn't so darned scary anymore when he's an incumbent seeking re-election. We know him. We may like him or not, but we already know him. And if we re-elect him, that's because we collectively decided he wasn't so darned bad after all—like when we re-elected Bill Clinton in 1996 and stocks rose 23.0%.[15]

Years we have *re-elected* Democrats, stocks historically averaged 14.5%.[16] (See Table 7.3.) Not as good as when we first elect a Republican in the election year, but better than when we re-elect Republicans—when the average is 10.6%.[17] Markets are less impressed by the incumbent Republican's pro-business schtick his second time around in the election year. They already know at heart he's just another politician. So whether we re-elect a Democrat or newly elect a Republican—we will do one or the other in 2012—that's a powerful positive driver.

This pattern underscores the fundamentals driving the one in Table 7.3. And Table 7.4 shows the same inauguration year pattern holds, too. Markets are *really* relieved the newly elected Democrat isn't an out-and-out socialist—rising an average 22.1% his inaugural year.[18] Whereas the not-so-business-friendly-as-hyped newly elected Republican sees stocks fall an average –0.6% his inaugural year. And those impacts are all muted in second terms. Stock averages are fine but not great in the inauguration year for a re-elected Democrat—rising 8.9%.[19] And the Republican's second inaugural year averages a lackluster but not negative 2.7%[20]—obviously still with plenty of variability within these averages. Take these summary statements and go back to Table 7.3. You will see consistency within this trend. Yes, obviously some Democrats had a better and worse inaugural year than others. And, yes, George H.W. Bush's inaugural year is a singular exception to Republicans' inaugural years being below average. But you will see high consistency and that consistency is a reason to be doubly mindful of this fundamental force.

Nowhere in these data—actual history—do you see Republicans being overall better than Democrats or the reverse. You do get a sense that the market's expectations matters, and ideological biases can play a role—but those effects are short-lived (and, at times,

Table 7.3   Election Versus Re-Election—The Election Year Sweet Spot

	Democrat	Republican
Newly Elected	–02.7%	**18.8%**
Re-Elected	**14.5%**	10.6%

Source: Global Financial Data, Inc., S&P 500 Total Return Index.

Table 7.4   Perverse Inverse—Election Versus Re-Election

	Election Year (Year 4)	Inaugural Year (Year 1)
Democrat Newly Elected	–2.7%	22.1%
Republican Newly Elected	18.8%	–0.6%
Democrat Re-Elected	14.5%	8.9%
Republican Re-Elected	10.6%	2.7%

Source: Global Financial Data, Inc., S&P 500 Total Return Index.

useful in shaping forward-looking expectations for the next 12 to 24 months or so).

Many of us are very prone to politics and have watched the arena avidly for a long time. But we miss the messages politics sends us because our memories fail us. We miss the most basic patterns— that first and second years of presidents' terms are hugely variable—big ups or negative—and that third and fourth years are a very bullish factor. We miss that electing a Republican is good for markets in the election year but more bearish in the inaugural year—and a lesser but similar factor if we re-elect him. We miss that electing a Democrat is bearish in the election year and bullish in the inaugural year but also bullish for both when re-elected. All these basic patterns have danced in front of our eyes for decades, don't change much and have a lot of consistency—and yet we miss them. We miss them partly because of the same memory issues that plague us otherwise in elections and partly because we so strongly believe our political views that we're blind to when our politics works against us.

History on presidents and the stock market is easy to get and compile. Yet my guess is most investors don't even try because they made up their minds about politics a long time ago. And since they don't study history, they have to rely on their Swiss cheese–like memory—and we know what that does to their analytical capability. As much as you like or hate the guy or gal likely to be the next Head Tic—remember, overall there's not much evidence supporting any view he is inherently more disastrous for stocks overall.

Can certain policies be damaging to economic growth, corporate profitability, incentives to start and/or expand a business? Sure. I would never argue against that. But I see no evidence that either party has a monopoly on economic stupidity. (And keep in mind, this is all reason to invest globally.)

Let's look at some examples of political stupidity briefly. In July 2002, a Republican president and Congress signed the Sarbanes-Oxley bill into law—one of the stupidest and most anti-market bills to become law in the last decade and still a blight on our country. Dodd-Frank—a similarly stupid law with similar but lesser effects (so far) passed into law in 2010 by a Democratic president and Congress. Two parties in complete control—two bills similarly stupid. Similar outcomes from different parties. I could go on and on but there is no monopoly on stupidity by either party.

Two More Biases Most Miss

As I write in 2011, the 2012 presidential campaign is heating up. I don't know who the Republican nominee will be and don't have any prediction on the outcome of the election. While I have some formal training in political science, I don't consider myself expert at predicting election outcomes. On the other hand, knowing what has happened after the fact is pretty easy.

Or is it? Let me show you a form of after-the-fact phenomenon you likely don't know about at all. It's not meant as a prediction about 2012's election, but to show again how we often miss consistent patterns made up of things we know even very well—because our failing memories don't connect the dots. On this pattern, there are four exceptions and they are exceptions that truly help justify the rule.

The Republican Western Nominee Effect   First, since Thomas E. Dewey in 1948, every Republican presidential nominee—but for one—has had significant, bona fide Western roots.

That singular exception was Gerald Ford—who was born in Nebraska, but was a long-time Michigan congressman—not seen as Western at all. He became president through the very unusual route of being appointed, not elected, vice president—and *then* having the president resign, not die in office. As mentioned earlier, Ford was a weak national candidate. As a sitting president in 1976, Ford almost lost his party's nomination to Ronald Reagan—an unheard-of event in modern politics. That's how much Republicans dislike going with a nominee who isn't a Westerner. (And, naturally, he then lost.) Exception proving the rule.

All other Republican presidential nominees have had solid Western roots—ever since the legendary fight between Thomas Dewey from New York and his arch-rival, Robert Taft. Dewey was the Northeastern liberal Republican. Taft from the Midwest represented the conservative and more religious wing of the party. Dewey won the battle in the 1940s, but the Taft forces ultimately won the war. While Dewey was instrumental in the selection of Dwight Eisenhower as nominee in 1952, Ike—a Texas-born, Kansas-bred Westerner—had the Western orientation. (Or, perhaps better stated, the anti-Northeastern-liberal-Republican qualifications to be acceptable to the Taft followers.)

Nixon, from southern California, was seen as a hard-right candidate. He really wasn't that; politics is mostly illusion, anyway. Talk about illusion—even in 1968 and 1972 when he was effectively a New Yorker, he ran as a Californian. Nixon understood the split in the party and knew that he had to be seen as a Westerner because the party's spiritual core is there. Goldwater, Reagan, both Bushes, Dole, McCain—Westerners all! Yes, George H.W. Bush was born in the Northeast and arguably was a moderate Republican. But long before being Reagan's vice president for eight years—and longer before his nomination—he built permanent, solid roots in Texas (and felt comfortable in boots).

Interestingly, none of these Western nominees come from the Northwest, Rocky Mountain or Plains states—except Kansas. But Kansas has its own, quite unique political import in American history that is little appreciated. (See the Appendix.)

Republicans have been inherently distrustful of the Northern, liberal wing of Republican politics epitomized by Dewey, Nelson Rockefeller, Bill Scranton, John Lindsey and, most recently, 2011's front-runner (thus far—things can change fast as this goes to print) Mitt Romney. All this goes back to the Dewey-Taft fight, linking to whom Southern Republicans will support at the end. Southern Republicans are ultimately the party's swing votes—and they mostly distrust Northeastern moderates. Who will they nominate? I don't know and that isn't my point.

What's more, there is always a first time to do something different and it might be now. And exceptions to every rule can come along. If the Republicans do what they've always done, they will pick someone like Rick Perry with Western roots—a guy who knows how to wear boots and instantly knows a rattlesnake from any other. But perhaps not. Politics can change over time, too, and long-held patterns may no longer be valid—morphing now or in the years ahead.

I believe I understand why Republicans have settled so consistently on Westerners, but I'm not sure I'm right. And regardless if I'm right or not, it can't be proved, and my superficial political views don't really matter, either. If I can't prove it pretty conclusively, there's no reason to push the theory.

What we can say with certainty is that this pattern exists, not why. We can also say with certainty that no one notices! This pattern has gone on for more than 60 years—yet you never read about it. It is right before our faces and has happened repeatedly and our memories and analytics have been inadequate to notice it. It is a sign that people forget and can't process—even what they know and follow pretty well.

The Democratic Eastern Nominee Effect   By contrast—and another hugely obvious pattern most hugely miss—the Democrats do something quite different when nominating their presidential candidates. With three exceptions, for over 100 years, they've never nominated anyone who wasn't basically from a political base east of the Mississippi. They don't do Westerners. Ever notice that? Ever! Southerners? Yes—which the Republicans don't (unless you want to include Texas in the South—but I count it as part of the Southwest). Northeasterners? Yes. The Midwest? Yes. But never the true West. Not that Westerners haven't run—they have—they just don't get far. And my guess is most don't notice, even though these patterns are right in front of our faces. But our failing memories keep us from seeing them. And on a topic so many of us pay so much attention to!

The three exceptions are, again, ones tending to prove the rule. Harry Truman is one. He got there as Franklin D. Roosevelt's third vice-president—in office when FDR died. And a bit like Republican Gerald Ford, he was seen as a very weak candidate. Though elected vice president, he had been in office only 82 days when FDR died—not a lot of on-the-job experience to get prepared for the top job just at a time during World War II when America had a lot on the line. So he is an exception to the east of Mississippi rule. But, he got there unusually, and as a Kansas City–based politician, didn't come from far west of the Mississippi. He almost certainly never would have gotten the nomination the natural way at a later time had he not become president as he did.

Lyndon Johnson is a bigger exception, but not much bigger. A true Westerner from Texas! He evidenced all the hard-earned, up-from-the-bootstraps, rough-and-tumble, fiercely independent qualities Westerners pride themselves in. (That I pride myself in!) He, like Truman and Ford, got there by the vice presidential route. He got the nomination in 1964 as a sitting president—like Truman and Ford. But it isn't clear he ever would have been the nominee otherwise.

And the third exception is Hubert Humphrey, who as sitting vice president got the 1968 nomination when Johnson withdrew. Johnson realized—after Eugene McCarthy had an unexpectedly strong showing against him in the New Hampshire primary—that his base was not strong enough to get the nomination and win the general election. Again, very unusual! Adding to the unusual quality was that, in those days, the California primary was very much more important than it is now. After winning it, Robert Kennedy became the front-runner for the nomination on the night he was assassinated.

It isn't at all clear Humphrey would have secured the nomination had Robert Kennedy not been killed. He probably wouldn't have and was lagging markedly in the polls at the time. A minor but interesting point: Humphrey's political base in Minnesota was exactly two miles west of the Mississippi—an exception, but a minor one, to the rule. (And mind you, Humphrey lost the general.)

Otherwise the Democrats have picked folks only from east of the Mississippi. The most recent exception, who got the nomination the natural way, was William Jennings Bryan from Nebraska—and that was a long, long time ago—and not very far west, either. (Again, on Bryan, see the Appendix for his role in the legendary Wizard of Oz).

Again, these are just my theories—not provable in a scientific way and hence don't really matter much. And like with the Republicans, fundamentals may change in the future and we may see this phenomenon fade.

But here are two pretty compelling patterns right in front of you—you've seen politics forever and know the outcomes of elections. But most don't see the clear pattern. Our modern minds just aren't great at recognizing simple patterns sometimes because our memory and our analytics don't sync well. History is a great way to get past our failed memories—and start seeing more meaningful patterns, like the presidential term analysis, which can be explained by more fundamental factors.

Poli-Tics Go Global

Despite having shown the impact political risk aversion can have on markets, you may still think, "Well, that's interesting, but it may still be a quirk." True—except there's credible evidence elsewhere poli-tics can and do impact capital markets and economies.

If you think US poli-tics are poli-tickish, they can't hold a candle to some other parts of the world. For example, we may grump about our rotten political leaders in the US, but China is actually still communist. They have one political party—the Communist party. It's them or . . . well, no one. By definition!

And Communist party poli-tics really, *really* want to keep their jobs. It's not like in the US, where if a president or congressperson annoys a big swath of people, they get booted out of office and then go on to garner huge fees on the speakers' circuit or by lobbying. In communist nations, when folks get thrown out, they often end up in prison or dead.

China, although making some free market reforms in recent years, is still a top-down, command economy. Whereas US poli-tics (and others in other developed nations) fancy themselves able to control the economy, the Chinese government actually can— quite a bit. (Before you think that sounds grand, remember . . . commies.)

China has a five-year election cycle for its National People's Congress (NPC)—the single-house, legislative wing of the Chinese government. The president of China is selected by the congress, although it's not very transparent—lots of closed-door haggling goes on over who becomes the next president. Other than that, the local elections of NPC members aren't too different from that for US House and Senate members—though naturally the only party represented is the Communist party. If you don't like their platform, well, you best keep it to yourself.

To keep civil unrest to a minimum and keep people generally docile, the government uses all the throttles it can to juice economic growth in election years. This little-known fact drives an economic cycle that is useful to the politicians. They cause it and they benefit from it. To play this game, they always pull down growth and inflation in the year prior so they can add very heavy stimulus in election years without spiking inflation. It's a little like them inducing a big party with a lot of alcohol and taking the vote just before people get too drunk or start to get hung over.

Figure 7.1 shows this effect. Over the past 30 years, China's compound average growth rate (CAGR) is pretty darn fast—averaging about 10%. But election year averages an additional 0.9% over that, whereas the slowest growth year—the year prior—averages 1.1% under that average. They slam on the brakes, then ram the gas. Personally, I think this is a stupid thing to do but they've been doing it a long time and their culture motivates them to keep doing it.

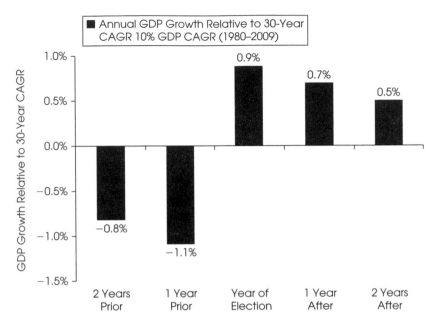

Figure 7.1   China's Term Cycle and Economic Growth

Source: Thomson Reuters.

Poli-Tics Versus Entrepreneurs

I don't see politicians as misguided out of ill intent. (At least not in democratic nations. In communistic and socialistic ones, there could be malice aforethought. Just my opinion.) This is where I differ from many ideological folks who think the guy (or gal) they hate is out to get them and the guy (or gal) they like is a sainted genius. Rather, I think most politicians are economically illiterate, politically savvy and completely ego-centric and self-centered narcissists.

Most folks who are career politicians (and most in national office generally are careerists) don't make decisions day to day that impact the profitability of a private venture. Their employees' livelihoods aren't in their very hands. They aren't held accountable by a board of directors who want to see increasing profits, shareholder value, etc. They don't get fired if they fail to produce profits over a reasonable period of time. Yes, they are held accountable by constituents (sort of). But pleasing constituents and running a profitable business venture aren't remotely comparable. (And just think of the many, many, many politicians who've done even terribly bad things and haven't gotten booted and have, in fact, had long careers.)

Because most career politicians haven't run a business and haven't been in the private sector in some time (if ever), they don't get in their bones the myriad, wild, near-incomprehensible number of drivers impacting the global economy. I can't see into any politicians' brains (nor want to—creepy), but they seem to overwhelmingly believe the economy is something that can easily be pushed and pulled one direction or another. Or controlled somehow. That they can regulate away most risk. They want you to believe this so you vote for them again. "Vote for me and I'll protect you. That other guy wants to steal your money and kick your dog!"

And for those poli-tics who did at one point run a business— good for them. But my guess is by their fifth year in Washington, they've forgotten those lessons. (Poli-tics have shorter memories than most investors.) Their memories seem overwhelmed by the whim of the public at the moment since everything comes back to winning just over half of a 33% voter turnout. They no longer think like a CEO trying to increase shareholder value and employ more people. They think like a career poli-tic, "Who can I dole out favors to so they'll give me campaign contributions to keep me in this nice, cushy office?"

You may think some politicians are bad, yes. But overall, aren't they just civil servants trying to help society? Maybe—that could be the motivation for some (at least initially). But if you want to help society, why not start a business that employs a bunch of people, paying them really well? And/or manufactures something use- ful much cheaper than a competitor—saving people a bunch of money? Or researches life-saving vaccines, cancer treatments, dia- betes cures, medical devices? Or provides a valuable service— managing money or lending money to other people who want to start businesses that manufacture vaccines, cheaper sneakers, safer cars, cool software, money-saving gizmos? Vastly more societal good has been done by the private sector than has ever been done or will be done by the government—in terms of increasing societal wealth, quality of life, etc.

I'm beyond proud of my grandfather, Arthur L. Fisher, MD (1875–1958). He was in the fourth graduating class of the Johns Hopkins School of Medicine (class of 1900). Johns Hopkins, the man, came from a family of means (they owned plantations and some other businesses) and increased that wealth exponentially through entrepreneurship and wise investing. He left a vast fortune at his death in 1873 and made many bequests—including one to start a hospital. He had a few directives—the hospital should seek out the best possible talent and serve as a platform for ongoing research. And the hospital would serve the poor, all races, free of charge—quite an amazing thing at the time. From that grew what is Johns Hopkins today—a world-class institution doing ground-breaking research—saving and improving lives globally for folks from all walks of life. It is almost every year and for many years now in a row, ranked as the top hospital in the world. It is in the top-10 ranked hospitals in almost every category. Its medical school is also similarly top tier.

No one made Johns Hopkins take advantage of a decent start in life and build a network of private businesses. No government mandate made him hand over, basically, all his wealth to private, phil-anthropic causes. He did it because that's who he was. You couldn't quantify the impact he's had on the world if you wanted to. And fond as I am of Johns Hopkins (the institution and the man), I realize there are countless other examples. To me, Johns Hopkins did more enduring good out of what was initially just a desire to get rich than any 10,000 politicians combined. You don't get charity without rich people. The overwhelming bulk of the charity in the world comes from America's rich.

Forget about Hopkins's philanthropy—or any philanthropy. Just think about the world of good done by successful entre-preneurs running their businesses. For a start, look just at the founder-CEOs on the *Forbes* 400. Try to tally up: How many employ-ees they have, how much they pay them, and what they pay them in benefits. Then think about their shareholders—how much have they been enriched overall by their sliver of ownership. Then think about all the businesses those businesses interact with—how they have benefited by selling intermediate goods *to* them or buying critical software (or desk chairs, or accounting services, or, or, or) *from* them. (And think of those businesses' employees and their shareholders and, and, and.) Then try to tally how much better, faster, cheaper, cooler, healthier and more entertaining the world is as a result of whatever it is their firms produce. You can't. It's mind-boggling and beyond comprehension.

A simple example: I couldn't run my firm were it not for Microsoft. Couldn't do it. Then, too, I'm typing looking into a Dell screen sitting next to a Cisco IP phone while getting a call on my BlackBerry. Don't get me started, but isn't the world vastly better off from those private citizens starting and running private firms than from any politician confiscating their (and your) earnings and using it to lecture us on what kinds of light bulbs to use?

Maybe you disagree. Fine! You can think I'm too cynical about politicians by half. Or more. Again, I don't much care what people think of me when I say some of these things. And, yes, I can accept that maybe I'm dead wrong. I'm expressing some views that can't really be proved quantitatively. Still, I hope that this chapter has convinced you that if you can stop thinking ideologically when it comes to markets—just when making investing decisions—you can start to see history's lessons, which may prove more profitable to you in the future than wearing a campaign button.

In politics, like in all other market-related phenomena, I hope I've gotten you to be good with the notion that money doesn't forget, but people do, and it's likely not that different this time.

It's (Always Been) a Global World, After All

Y ou frequently hear from the media things like, "The world is more interconnected than ever!" or ". . . in this increasingly global world . . ."

Almost always true—the world is more interconnected now than 10 years before that than 10 years before that than 10 years before that. What's strange is how agog folks get over how interconnected the world is "now." It's like when folks say "now" is a more volatile time (Chapter 3). Are they just noticing how global the world is? It takes a very short-term memory and a total disregard of non-US data and history to think this is a new phenomenon. Fact is, the world has always been pretty darn global—more global than most think and for much longer than most fathom.

And failing to remember that can cause major investing errors. US stocks are just 43% of the world market.[1] Yet, your run-of-the-mill US investor invests only about 14.4% of their portfolio, on average, overseas.[2] And that's an improvement. As recently as 1990, there were just 122 mutual funds considered *global* available in the US.[3] Forget about ETFs—they didn't exist until the mid-1990s. Now there are 2,758 global funds,[4] yet still investors aren't nearly as global as they could (or should) be.

And, of course, whose was the first mutual fund to invest on a truly global basis? Sir John Templeton, whose legend was built not only on his vision, his certainty that progress was ahead, and his ability to think outside the box without being compromised by the crowd—but heavily and also by his global vision. He saw clearly it was a global investing world with huge opportunities Americans underappreciated and missed out on completely (when he started doing it).

Not only do many Americans avoid foreign stocks—they don't even much think about it except when there's some major story like the PIIGS in 2010 and 2011. Or after some category has been hot like Emerging Markets were in 2009 and 2010.

It's not just US investors. At least the US is a huge chunk of the world. Brits tend to invest in Britain only (just 8.3% of world market cap!)[5] Germans in Germany only (3.5% of the world), Japanese *definitely* invest Japan only (7.8%) of the world,[6] Bhutanese in Bhutan only. You get the point.

Many fear foreign as being, well, foreign. And not just individuals—many professionals treat foreign stocks as a separate asset class—stocks, bonds, cash, *foreign!* Many, if they recommend foreign at all, recommend small allocations (10% maybe—20% tops). But non-US stocks make up 57% of the world![7]

What many investors (hopefully not you) fail to see is foreign economies and capital markets aren't so foreign. The world isn't just more closely linked today—it's always been that way—and always getting increasingly more linked in irregular fits and starts. People just forget that—or they just don't know to look. And if you aren't comfortable with that now, it only gets worse because the world will just get more interlinked from here. But we've been interlinked for far longer than we recognize—over 150 years. That's 150 years of not having our memories serve us well.

It may seem like semantics, but I don't like using the word *foreign* in investing. I prefer *global. Foreign* implies us versus them. Whereas *global* is a more holistic, top-down, fluid approach. It's not a choice of "foreign versus domestic" investing—one versus the other. Instead, you should think globally in every possible way. Why?

- Global forces have been at work for longer than most folks can fathom—we have evidence of that.
- Ignoring global can mean ignoring important factors influencing investment performance—*even if* you're a single-country investor.
- Going global means increasing opportunities to manage risk and enhance performance—history teaches us that.

It's Always Been a Small World

I study a lot of history. I hope you've appreciated that throughout this book and particularly toward the end of the previous chapter. And it always amazes me how even very good historians tend to think of globalization as starting after World War II. And that's historically ridiculous. Part of that could be because starting with World War I, we did get a short-term, *global* trend to extreme protectionism that culminated in my view with the disaster that was the Smoot-Hawley Tariff Act (more on that in a bit). But even though individual nations tried to build theoretical (and in some cases, actual) barriers in an attempt to halt globalization, they couldn't stop global macro forces from crossing borders. The world was intensely global well before World War I—a point most miss. (But not the always excellent Dr. Donald Boudreaux, who's 2008 book, *Globalization*, is a quick, easy read necessary for anyone interested in how today's global economy works.)

Exhibit 8.1 is another chart from my 1987 book, *The Wall Street Waltz*. It comes from a book by Wesley C. Mitchell—who in 1920 founded the National Bureau of Economic Research (NBER), the national scorekeeper of recessions, expansions and a slew of other economic data (plenty of which is used in this book). Mitchell also ran the NBER for 25 years and founded the American Statistical Association. He, along with Roger Babson, is credited for first standardizing economic statistics. In prior periods, economic analysis was a lot of holding-your-finger-to-the-wind and guessing (which I guess it still is to a large extent—and particularly for most folks who aren't more formally trained).

The graph shows economic cycles in major developed countries back to 1790, starting first with the US and UK—because the two Uniteds have the best data back the furthest in time. In 1840, we add France, then Germany in 1853. Cast your eye down. The black bars (recessions or depressions) mostly stack up. So do the light gray bars (expansion). Yes, someone went first, and some countries had longer expansions or lingered longer in recession. And you would expect someone to lead and someone to lag—as still happens now. But when the rest of the world was growing, that dragged individual nations along. Same with the reverse—if a few nations had the flu, others at least got the sniffles. It's largely the same today—although, admittedly, a bit more so. (This was printed in 1927—if

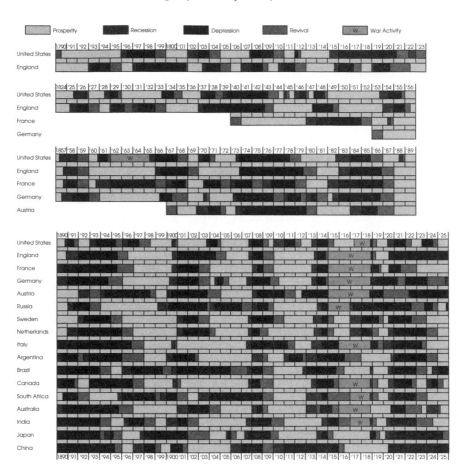

Figure 8.1   Business Cycles in Various Countries, 1790 to 1925—The World Moves in Sync

Source: Wesley C. Mitchell, *Business Cycles, The Problem and its Setting* (Cambridge, MA: National Bureau of Economic Research, 1927).

people can't get today how interconnected we are, imagine how this looked to folks way back then.)

A few additional points from Figure 8.1: A major country can't buck this trend. Unless you live on a desert island and trade with no one—not even Cuba is like that—you can't much buck global trends. And like Cuba, attempts to isolate yourself lead only to disaster. The Chinese learned this lesson during Mao's "Great Leap Forward" (which was neither great nor a leap nor forward). He mandated collectivism and self-sufficiency. Instead of importing steel from countries doing it better and cheaper, Mao forced citizens to build backyard furnaces and smelt scrap metal. The result? Tens of millions dead from starvation. You don't want to live in a non-interconnected world. And in America, you can't.

Another takeaway: Politicians love taking credit for growth and blaming downturns on opponents. Nice try. Look at that graph. If a recession is rolling globally, they can't stop it. All a politician in a major nation can do is take actions that might make domestic results a bit better relative to the rest of the world than otherwise; but the cycle will still roll with the world. Recessions are global; expansions, too.

Don't take this to mean if you see one nation falling into recession, you should automatically get defensive. The world tends to go in one direction—but not perfectly in lockstep and not at the same speed. And one country can do itself in and implode while the world is marching happily along—particularly smaller countries. Always, in every economic cycle, nations move at different speeds. There will be trouble spots in every expansion and some spots that fare relatively better in global contraction. But if the world is heading heavily one way, that's a sign of major global drivers impacting everyone to some degree. And if the world is going up or down, most major nations will be headed that way too—to a greater or lesser extent.

Capital Markets—Global for Centuries

Economies are strongly linked but so are capital markets—and it's been that way longer than we can measure very well. Figure 8.1 shows over four decades of US and non-US developed world annual stock market returns. Return magnitude can differ, but direction rarely does. And when there is divergence, it snaps back fast.

People often think foreign stocks are riskier. But if that were true, US and non-US stocks wouldn't behave so similarly. Were that so, when US stocks were up, foreign would be down, or sideways, or at least not so very tightly linked.

Another interesting point linking to Chapter 6: As far back as we have good non-US data, foreign stocks have annualized 9.4% and US 10.0%—pretty darn close.[8] Why? Though taking differing paths, finance theory says well-constructed categories should net pretty similar returns over time—just as these have.

Figure 8.2 shows over 40 years of stock history—a pretty long time. But how can I be so sure factors impacting stocks were global long before? Figure 8.3 shows a great, earlier example—the London, New York, Berlin and Paris stock exchanges leading up to and after the 1929 crash.

Again, I used this chart in my 1987 book, *The Wall Street Waltz*—and in 1987, few were banging the "global first" mantra. But this chart and its history speak heavily to the need to think globally even if you only invest domestically. Most of what you commonly read about the 1929 crash and the Great Depression usually focuses on US stocks and the US economy—as if we were an island and bad things happened only here in America. Total fiction. It was a fully global phenomenon—stock exchanges globally fell hard and huge—and it started outside of America first, a part of history almost never taught inside America.

Look at Figure 8.3. Note London and Berlin peaked first, way back in 1928! Paris traded choppily sideways for much of 1929 while New York was still rising. The markets in these other countries were warning us and yet an insular American wouldn't much notice. It pays to think globally and think about what is

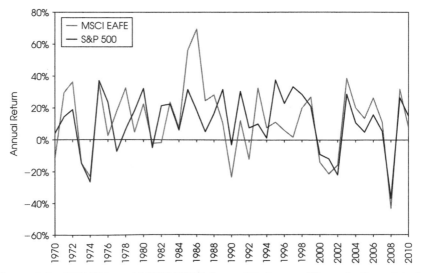

Figure 8.2   S&P 500 and MSCI EAFE Annual Returns—Strongly Correlated

Sources: Thomson Reuters, S&P 500 total return, MSCI EAFE net return, from 12/31/1969 to 12/31/2010.

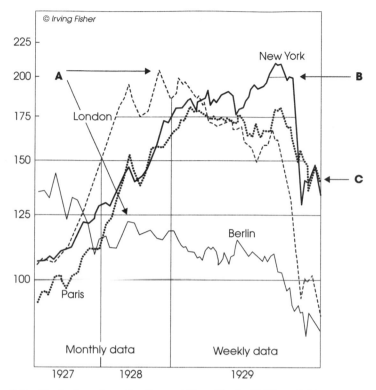

Figure 8.3   Paris, London, Berlin and New York, 1927 to 1929

Source: Irving Fisher, *The Stock Market Crash and After* (New York: The MacMillan Company, 1930).

happening overseas that may come to America soon—even if you will never, ever, own anything overseas.

This chart comes originally from a book by Irving Fisher (1867–1947). Many folks (incorrectly) presume we're related. Not so. He was the most famous and respected American economist of the 1920s. He was perhaps the foremost of what has come to be called the neo-classical economists who believed purely in free markets. His ilk was later replaced in primacy by the Keynesian school of economics for decades.

He's often credited with formalizing the *quantity theory* of money, an important cornerstone of twentieth-century economics. Inflation wonks and economists know this as MV = PQ. M is money supply, V is velocity (how quickly money moves through the economy—said alternatively, how many times it turns in a year), P is the price level (what you could think of as inflation), and Q, the number of transactions. Don't try inputting actual values—it's pure theory, but a good one and one Milton Friedman ascribed to—the impetus for his statement that "inflation is always and everywhere a monetary phenomenon." All that means is inflation is caused by too much money supply or too fast velocity or a combination.

People like to say inflation is caused by any number of weird things. Oil prices. Trade deficits. Budget deficits. None of those things have a direct link to money supply or velocity. When you boil it down, inflation is caused by excess money sloshing around not getting sopped up by economic activity. What most monetarists would say is that if you create more money than goods, velocity eventually normalizes and you get higher inflation. (Then there is a lot of debate about how fast, how fast under varying circumstances, effects of foreign trade and a lot more—but we don't need to go there now because it isn't central to our thesis of how memory works relative to market phenomena.)

But Irving Fisher's book, *The Stock Market Crash and After*, constitutes about the worst market call in history. Published in 1930, it contained Fisher's view stock prices would soon rise. Oops! Thereafter, the public was not kind to him and ridiculed him mightily. Even 40-plus years ago when I was a young economics student, people paid him a limited grudging respect for his earlier contributions while shredding his reputation in all other ways.

But fact is he was never a great forecaster—academic economists rarely are. He was also a bit creepy. As a result of a battle with tuberculosis, he was a health nut with a little goatee. An active vegetarian (that's not the creepy part), he wrote a national bestseller on health, diet and exercise: *How to Live: Rules for Healthful Living Based on Modern Science*.

That was all before 1929. But he believed all kinds of wing-nutty things like *focal sepsis*—the nonsense view that mental illness comes from infectious material in the roots of our teeth, among other places. And he was a eugenicist. Part of the reason he got so heavily ridiculed as the 1930s evolved was for reasons other than the 1929 crash. As Hitler emerged, eugenicists got very unpopular in America and around most of the world.

One irony of his focal sepsis fantasy is that when his daughter was diagnosed with schizophrenia, he had a focal sepsis doctor start taking parts of internal organs out of her until she ultimately died.

Wing-nut time and thank God for modern medicine. Couldn't do that today. Oh, and one final point that didn't help his popularity in the 1930s—he remained an ardent prohibitionist.

Anyway, despite his wing-nutty ways, he did make the excellent observation that overseas markets fell first, and stocks on New York's exchange may have been pressured by overseas liquidations. Probably so! Had you been watching overseas markets, you might have seen it coming—look at Figure 8.3 again. Point A shows where UK and German stocks peaked. New York and Paris peaked at about the same time at point B, then crashed hard into point C.

The crash was fully global, as was the Great Depression that ensued—a point most economists and historians rarely mention (if they even know). The same drivers were present globally—with local flavors.

Getting Cause and Effect Backward   For example, now it's widely recognized the disastrous Smoot-Hawley Tariff Act—which created new tariffs and raised existing ones on hundreds of goods—was one major driver of the Depression. Lots of people believe the 1929 crash *caused* the Great Depression. Nah—they forget. Markets then were no different from markets now. They move ahead of the economy and were pricing in a series of pretty disastrous policies they saw coming. Smoot-Hawley didn't pass until 1930, but Hoover campaigned on increasing tariffs on agricultural goods to "protect" US farmers. Congress was debating it long before it passed—the House passed its version in mid-May 1929! Global markets saw it coming.

Stupid protectionist policies breed more stupid protectionist policies—always. Smoot-Hawley spawned retaliatory tariffs globally. If people forget fast, politicians forget really fast. What happens when you make something more expensive? People want less of it! Politicians made trade more expensive globally with silly arbitrary tariffs, and the world got less trade—global trade fell by fully two-thirds between 1929 and 1934.[9] That dinged global growth hard. But simply said, you can't have an American trade barrier war that isn't at least two-sided. We raised tariffs, and they did. They raised tariffs, and we did.

Then too, the Fed rather bizarrely sucked a third of money supply out of the economy between 1928 and 1933. Most folks today understand that one way to counteract slowing economic activity and stave off deflation and the worst impacts of a recession is to *increase* money supply. Think of Fisher's equation—if *V* is slowing because the economy is slowing, you can balance the equation some (and perhaps prevent a deflationary death spiral) by increasing *M*—money supply. It's a far-from-perfect science—but you definitely don't want to suck money out while velocity is slowing.

Disastrous monetary policy combined with nincompoop, protectionist politicians effectively badly exacerbated what might have been a normal recession into the Great Depression. And that's what global stocks saw coming. (If you're interested in more on how monetary policy impacted not only the Great Depression, but economic policy for the US in the modern era, you must read Milton Friedman's *A Monetary History of the United States, 1867–1960.*)

Many also believe war-related production for World War II ended the Great Depression. If so, why, when the war ended, did the US and global economy not slip back into Depression? In reality, a mega-major contributing factor for the return to long-term economic vitality was the global community, quietly, agreeing Smoot-Hawley was nonsense. Starting with the Bretton Woods agreement in 1944, overall and on average, the world began reducing tariffs. There have been flare-ups of localized stupidity since, but overall, world trade has trended steadily more free since the end of World War II, and globalization—already long in place—has continued unabated. Interestingly, Smoot-Hawley is still technically on the books in the US. Politicians have a hard time admitting they were wrong.

Seeing the World Right

So, many think about the world wrong and can't see (or forget) how global it has been for so long. So what? It can lead to serious investing errors and lost opportunities to manage risk and enhance performance.

While many think foreign is risky, the real risk may be not investing there. Particularly if for any reason America's future is not so good. But even if you're a single-country investor, ignoring global means ignoring factors heavily impacting your home country stocks—whether US, UK, Germany, Japan or Bhutan.

Global Drivers Can Swamp

Suppose you decide to invest US-only. You're American. You live here, work here. You "get" here. Doesn't that mean home matters most? Not necessarily. Most macro-drivers are fully global. What happens abroad can matter here and vice versa. If the rest of the world is growing strongly, it's very hard for the US to go the opposite direction—regardless of whatever bad things you see at home, stupid politicians (sorry for being redundant), a myriad of social problems, bad education, broken families and all the rest. This is true when it comes to economies, capital markets, corporate earnings, etc. Likewise, if the rest of the world is headed into recession, America won't avoid it even if it's doing what you see as all the right things—maybe it will just get hit a little less than overseas.

Yes, there are drivers that uniquely impact individual nations—tax rates, regulation, monetary policy (to a degree), etc. Very frequently, country-specific drivers can leach out to impact other nations—like regulatory or tax changes causing multinational firms to shift how and where they do business, or the US presidential term anomaly, which seems to have global impact. But the more country-specific a driver is, the less it matters on a global scale. Maybe a negative country-specific driver is a reason to underweight that country (*if* you're a global investor). But you must always think world first, individual country a distant second. *Even if you are a single-country investor*—which I don't recommend—what happens globally can and will impact how stocks behave locally.

Overemphasizing the Local Which means: Beware how much weight you give to local matters over global. One good example—tax rate moves. Politicians love debating taxes, thundering away about how their proposals are smart and make them sainted, whereas their opponents are horrible people who want to destroy jobs or hate the poor or hate children or hate *you*.

Nearly every time we get tax policy debates, folks yammer about the supposed foregone conclusion result: Overwhelmingly, the investing class believes higher taxes hurt stocks and lower taxes are a magical market panacea. Not so—actually the history of tax rate moves and the market aftermath is mixed. And the basic reason, I believe, is because global comes first. Local comes second. And America can't buck the global trend even if it doesn't do something stupid or brilliant.

Figures 8.4, 8.5, 8.6 and 8.7 show the history of some major capital gains tax rate moves. In 1981 (Figure 8.4), the capital gains tax rate was cut from 28% to 20%. One would think stocks would rise markedly—they didn't. They fell 22% over the 12 months after the bill became law.[10] In 1987 (Figure 8.5), the cap gains rate moved

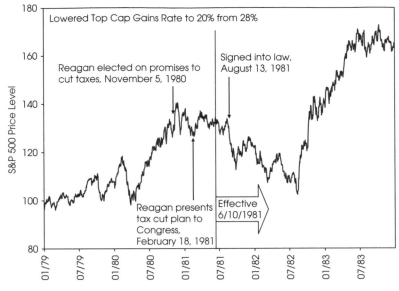

Figure 8.4   Economic Recovery Act of 1981 — Cap Gains Cut

Source: Global Financial Data, Inc. S&P 500 price return from 12/31/1978 to 12/31/1983.

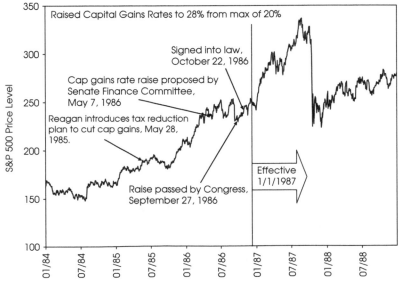

Figure 8.5   Tax Reform Act of 1986 — Cap Gains Hike

Source: Global Financial Data, Inc. S&P 500 price return from 12/31/1983 to 12/31/1988.

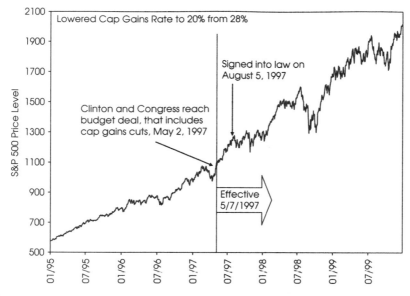

Figure 8.6   Taxpayer Relief Act of 1997—Cap Gains Cut

Source: Global Financial Data, Inc. S&P 500 price return from 12/31/1994 to 12/31/1999.

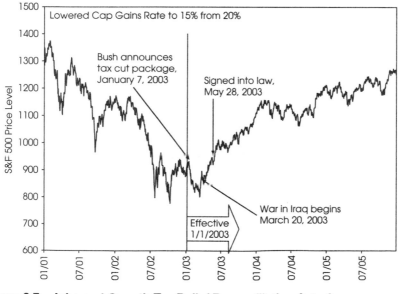

Figure 8.7   Jobs and Growth Tax Relief Reconciliation Act of 2003—Cap Gains Cut

Source: Global Financial Data, Inc. S&P 500 price return from 12/31/2000 to 12/31/2005.

back to 28%. The S&P 500 soared until the 1987 crash—which had nothing to do with the rate move.

In 1997 (Figure 8.6), the cap gains rate was cut again from 28% to 20%—and stocks continued on their bull market climb. And in 2003 (Figure 8.7), cap gains were cut to 15%. Stocks fell sharply initially before beginning a five-year bull market—which also had little to do with the rate move.

So stocks dropped big after a rate cut, rose hugely after a hike, and continued what they were doing anyway after two more cuts. All that tells you is, though politicians, pundits, your neighbor and your brother-in-law want you to think tax policy changes are paramount and hugely correlated to market health, they're generally an incremental change with a heavily isolated impact. And what's going on globally likely matters more for stocks. In each of these instances, America just kept going the direction of the global stock market—with truly hugely and tightly correlated numbers. The correlation coefficient on a weekly basis for these time periods between US stocks and non-US stocks was never less than 98%. Simple fact.

Personally, I think lower taxes are grand and an incremental *economic* positive almost always wherever implemented. (There are some minor exceptions like lowering an extant negative tax rate—or when a lowered tax rate promotes what economists would call an uneconomic substitution effect—but none of that is central to this book's thesis so I won't go there.) But history shows the market impact is inconclusive at best. Perhaps more important, there's little about US (or UK or German or Japanese or Bhutanese) tax policy that seeps out to impact other nations. Maybe aggressive tax policy changes make firms re-domicile in a business-friendlier place—but one nation's loss is another's gain, and there's not much material difference at a global level.

Tax changes can make differences to narrow categories like specific business industries—again, creating winners and losers—and perhaps creating inefficiencies. For example, if the UK is hammering banks with punitive taxes, that could make non-UK banks relatively more attractive. But it doesn't change the overall need for or role of banking in the world. These are nitpicky details. For broader markets, more macro, global drivers typically swamp single-country tax policy, particularly since tax changes are fairly marginal.

For example, even massive reductions in corporate and personal taxes likely don't help much if corporate profitability is cratering globally, if money velocity suddenly slows causing deflation or if a global recession is on the way. Conversely, you may hate proposed tax hikes, but if corporate profitability is growing nicely globally and the world economy ticking along—that likely means, tax hikes or no, your country gets dragged along for the ride.

So when headlines bemoan a tax policy—or any other uniquely local issue—is the end of the world (or, conversely, something insanely positive), know it won't likely have the impact many fear (or hope for). It's too small and local. Don't forget—global swamps. Ignore global at your peril.

Manage Risk, Enhance Performance

More importantly, investors who fail to see the world correctly miss opportunities to better manage risk and enhance performance. As I write in 2011, foreign investing has been somewhat more popular, thanks to a terrific run Emerging Markets stocks had in 2009 and 2010. My guess is when EM start lagging broader markets (which will happen eventually—leadership rotates, always), a big swath of investors who were new to non-US investing will revert. They'll again see foreign as "too risky."

And too bad! Most investors get that investing in even a random basket of stocks is less risky than investing in one stock. That one stock could rise 1,000%! It happens. But the downside risk is total. Heaps of academia prove the benefits of diversification as well as millennia of experiential evidence. And people tend to understand diversification as it applies to sectors. So why can't people see that investing globally is a logical next step? And not just after some non-US category like EM has been hot for some time, but always? What you really want to buy are the categories (as Sir John would) that haven't gotten hot yet.

In my 2006 book, *The Only Three Questions That Count*, and in my 2010 book, *Debunkery*, I detailed the myriad benefits of investing globally. Also, my colleague Aaron Anderson wrote a terrific 2009 book called *Own the World* on the why and how of global investing. If you're new to global, I recommend those three books and needn't retread that information here—outside the scope of this book.

But briefly, academics and professionals all agree, the more broadly you invest, the more opportunities you have to diversify away stock-specific risk. And nothing's broader than global. You can't quite do intergalactic. So, go global and you can add another risk management layer—diversifying away country-specific risk. If you're among the many who fear America's future is not as good as its past, going global is logical. And yet many of those same folks are the ones least prone to invest overseas because they've got the wrong-headed view that if America does poorly so must the rest of the world.

But think of the benefits shy of Armageddon. If there *is* disastrous tax policy locally, you aren't hurt too badly. And if a future President picks Charlie Sheen as head of the Fed, you can underweight America and still benefit in the long term from owning stocks. Or if some other country appoints Charlie Sheen, you can underweight that country.

Going global doesn't protect you from systemic risk—when the market falls dramatically as happens. But it does present an opportunity to spread risk on an even broader scale.

That's the risk management side in a nutshell. On the performance side, the broader you go, the more opportunities you get to make potentially performance-enhancing market bets. If you think German Industrials are likely to outperform, invest more heavily there. If you like Brazilian banks, put a bit more weight there. You needn't get all of your bets right—such a thing is impossible. And you don't have to make any bets at all if you lack conviction and can simply be largely neutral to the global index you manage against and remain passive but with global equity exposure (and probably still do better than most investors over time, as discussed in Chapter 2).

But if, over time, you get more market bets right than wrong, you can start adding value relative to your benchmark. A difficult thing, to be sure! But going global gives you more opportunities than a narrower category like a single country. Even a single country as big as the US!

I like showing investors Table 8.1 because as much as I talk about global, very single-country-focused folks sometimes don't get this—performance leadership changes. A lot, and always. You get the same basic story in Figure 6.1 in Chapter 6. It's the same with individual countries and a reason to never forget to think global, always.

Table 8.1 Top Five Performing Stock Markets Over the Past 20 Years

Year	#1		#2		#3		#4		#5		US Return
2010	Greece	90.4%	UK	10.3%	Hong Kong	9.2%	Austria	6.7%	Norway	1.1%	−2.1%
2009	Hong Kong	49.5%	Australia	35.6%	USA	**31.3%**	Singapore	25.0%	New Zealand	20.8%	31.3%
2008	Hong Kong	32.3%	Switzerland	18.1%	USA	**7.4%**	Singapore	6.3%	Netherlands	3.4%	7.4%
2007	Hong Kong	116.7%	Finland	83.2%	New Zealand	70.0%	Singapore	68.0%	Switzerland	46.7%	10.1%
2006	Finland	52.5%	Norway	24.1%	Japan	21.6%	Sweden	18.8%	Ireland	14.5%	2.0%
2005	Switzerland	45.0%	USA	**38.2%**	Sweden	34.1%	Spain	31.2%	Netherlands	28.9%	38.2%
2004	Spain	41.3%	Sweden	38.0%	Portugal	36.4%	Finland	34.7%	Hong Kong	33.1%	24.1%
2003	Portugal	47.4%	Switzerland	44.8%	Italy	36.4%	Greece	36.2%	Denmark	35.0%	34.1%
2002	Finland	122.6%	Greece	78.1%	Belgium	68.7%	Italy	53.2%	Spain	50.6%	30.7%
2001	Finland	153.3%	Singapore	99.4%	Sweden	80.6%	Japan	61.8%	Hong Kong	59.5%	22.4%
2000	Switzerland	6.4%	Canada	5.6%	Denmark	3.7%	Norway	−0.4%	Italy	−0.8%	−12.5%
1999	New Zealand	9.5%	Australia	2.7%	Ireland	−2.7%	Austria	−5.0%	Belgium	−10.2%	−12.0%
1998	New Zealand	26.1%	Austria	17.3%	Australia	−0.3%	Italy	−6.3%	Norway	−6.7%	−22.7%
1997	Greece	69.5%	Sweden	66.1%	Germany	64.8%	Spain	59.2%	Austria	57.8%	29.1%
1996	Austria	72.3%	Norway	54.5%	Greece	46.1%	Belgium	44.9%	Ireland	43.1%	10.7%
1995	Canada	28.9%	Norway	25.7%	Japan	25.6%	Denmark	25.3%	Austria	25.2%	5.7%
1994	Spain	50.2%	Portugal	48.4%	Ireland	47.6%	Singapore	46.7%	Norway	46.3%	15.3%
1993	Finland	50.1%	Hong Kong	41.2%	Germany	35.9%	Greece	32.9%	Norway	32.4%	6.0%
1992	Japan	−29.1%	Switzerland	−29.9%	USA	**−37.1%**	Spain	−40.1%	France	−42.7%	−37.1%
1991	Norway	88.6%	Australia	76.8%	Singapore	74.0%	Sweden	65.9%	Hong Kong	60.2%	27.1%
1990	Sweden	34.8%	Denmark	31.1%	Hong Kong	23.2%	Singapore	22.2%	Canada	21.2%	15.4%

Source: Thomson Reuters, individual country returns from 12/31/1989 to 12/31/2010.[11]

Global first, local a distant second. The table shows the top five performing countries over the past 20 years. The top five are almost always very different. The US is infrequently in the top five. There's a world of risk management and performance enhancement opportunity—if you choose it.

Conclusion

With that, reader, I bid you farewell for now. I hope this book was just a bit entertaining for you, but also educational and hopefully profitable. I hope, too, that you see that *the past is never predictive.*

Having read the book, you get that. Still, I could print a 10,000-page book that just repeats the phrase "the past is never predictive" over and over again and go door to door paying people $1 million to read it and commit it to memory—and *still* some blogger will say, "Fisher's nuts and thinks market history is all it takes to forecast stocks!"

So I say again, the past isn't predictive. That something happened a certain way in the past doesn't mean it must happen that way in the future. If you rely solely on history (and, I might add, charts) to navigate markets, you can get pretty darn lost—pretty often.

Instead, market history is a lab. A testing ground for your hypothesis. If the whole world says, "Well, X is happening, and we all know that means Y must occur next," you needn't take it on faith! You can check and see if X and Y correlate well in history. If they haven't, they aren't very likely to now—not unless you find a good, fundamental reason for something to strongly buck the odds. Sometimes, all the world is right and X does sometimes lead to Y. But in my long career, more often, what people expect doesn't happen. Or if it does, it happens for a different reason from what's commonly believed. Or maybe it's pure coincidence and not something you want to bet on!

Plus, if all the world sees X and expects Y, but you know from testing history that Y doesn't happen all that frequently (or maybe ever) after X, you can bet against them and win—more often than not. You could take that one step further and discover what *does* come after X! Or what actually causes Y. But to do that, you must first learn to use history as a lab. Use history to shape reasonable expectations, and from that, use your understanding of current economic, political and sentiment drivers to decide what you think is likeliest.

Then, too, remember that just because something seems reasonably likely to happen doesn't mean it must happen that way. Capital markets are incredibly complex. Sometimes, some intensely unexpected thing or things happen. And sometimes your reading of history will be wrong! But since investing is a probabilities game, not a certainties game, you must start somewhere in framing reasonable probabilities.

Another key item to remember: No matter how good your analysis and how sound your understanding of history—*you will be wrong* from time to time. Maybe a lot. That's ok. As I've said repeatedly in this book, 100% accuracy isn't possible and shouldn't be expected. If your investment goals require 100% accuracy, you will be disappointed and should perhaps adjust your expectations. But if you can make a regular study of relevant market history part of your analysis, you can start seeing the world more clearly and start improving your error rate. That's what history teaches us.

And my final words to you in this book are to remember that your memory is lousy for all these kinds of phenomena—but you're not alone. Everyone's memory is lousy. While I've shown you repeatedly that people frequently can't recall or see patterns in things they've seen many times—and now know that—when you put this book down, there is a tremendous human tendency to forget that, too. Don't let that happen. Build into your daily life the reality that your market memory is likely terrible and you need to study history to know what happened despite having lived through a pretty good swath of it. Money and markets may never forget, but surely people do. And *that* will not be different this time, next time, or any time in your life.

Happy investing.

Appendix

There's No Place Like Kansas

Politics are an important driver of capital markets, and Kansas is politically important to American politics, not the least because it's produced two Republican presidential nominees.

Kansas has long been the archetypal representation of American populism, via the home of Dorothy from the *Wizard of Oz*. Most Americans today believe this story is a children's fairy tale. It was actually written as a heavy, symbolic, populist monetary allegory of the political conflict over the gold standard versus the free silver movement. The following is an excerpt from my 2006 book, *The Only Three Questions That Count*, which details the deeper side of Oz. Most certainly, L. Frank Baum, in writing the original story, carefully picked Kansas as the center of American populism.

The Wizard of Oz and an Oz of Gold

Did you know when L. Frank Baum put pen to paper to write *The Wonderful World of Oz* (published in 1900 and later immortalized in the film starring, among others, Judy Garland, Ray Bolger, and Bert Lahr), he didn't intend to write a magical children's story? No. He meant it as sharp political satire and monetary allegory, involving the economic debates and political players of the 1890s.

Don't scour the movie for hidden meaning. The 1939 film was indeed intended as light-hearted fare during dark times. Instead, go back to the original text, where no one in 1900 could miss the meaning behind Dorothy's silver shoes. (Red looked better in Technicolor.) It should grab you instantly that "Oz" is an ounce of gold. Here is the story as Baum meant it.

(Continued)

In the 1890s and into the early part of the twentieth century, debate raged between those who supported the gold standard for our currency and those who would abandon it in favor of a bimetallic or even silver standard. After America returned to the gold standard in 1879, a period of ravaging deflation followed—prices and wages fell nationwide. A variety of policy mishaps, domestic and foreign, culminated in the Panic of 1893 and a subsequent global depression. This wasn't one of our very biggest depressions, but it wasn't insignificant, either. Though we now know there wasn't a single culprit, and American economic woes were part of a larger global trend, in America, the gold standard got its share of the blame.

Fervent support to lift the restriction on minting silver gained sudden popularity. William Jennings Bryan and his booming voice played front and center in the "free silver" movement. Critics saw this as inherently grossly inflationary. Supporters felt some inflation was in order. In popular press, the struggle was frequently framed (and greatly simplified) as a struggle between the "people" (who would benefit from a silver standard and increased inflation) and Eastern banking interests with the politicians in their pockets (who would benefit from the status quo). Incidentally, the "Common Man" versus "Big Business" is a story that still plays today. Funny how some things never change.

Baum crafted his tale against this backdrop, showing his support for the silver movement and Populist disgust for Grover Cleveland, William McKinley, and their gold-standard buddies. All the characters he created would have been familiar to his turn-of-the-century audience.

Dorothy, an impoverished yet dauntless farm girl from barren Kansas (where the Populist movement began) is our Everyman. She is plucky and represents the center of America—innocent, good of heart, young, energetic and hopeful. The City of Oz signifies America itself, particularly the East and specifically Manhattan—a land blinded by and wedded to gold and the gold standard. And, of course, the Yellow Brick Road! Yellow meaning gold!

The Witch of the East was pro-gold former Democratic president Grover Cleveland, an apt villain in the Populist view because he was elected president in 1892 (the second time—remember, he was also president from 1885 to 1889, and lost to Benjamin Harrison in 1888) and was in office when the Panic of 1893 unfurled. He was also a villain because he was a Democrat supporting the gold standard, abandoning the Populists, when in the Populist view, a Democrat should oppose the Republicans who supported the gold standard. Just as Cleveland got politically wiped out, the twister (the silver movement) drops Dorothy's house on top of the Witch of the East, leaving only the treasured silver shoes behind. Naturally, the

Munchkins, living in mindless deference in an Eastern suburb of Oz, didn't understand the power of the silver shoes. The Munchkins couldn't even find Kansas on a map, provincial Easterners they were, so they sent Dorothy to see the Wizard.

She is joined first by the Scarecrow—the underestimated Western farmer who in reality is quite astute. He is kept in blissful ignorance about the silver debate because the folks from Oz think he is too simple to understand such a complex topic—that is, until Dorothy and her silver shoes liberate him. Next up is the Tin Woodsman. Cruel Eastern interests have mechanized the common workingman and stolen his craft, and therefore his heart. Like so many in the 1890s, this once hearty and hale laborer is unemployed (rusted and unable to lift his axe). Finally, the Cowardly Lion joins the movement. The Lion is none other than William Jennings Bryan himself, the Democratic presidential candidate in 1896 and 1900—losing both times to William McKinley.

Bryan indeed had a commanding roar, but he was ultimately a loser and didn't have a lion's capability or courage. As the economy improved in the later 1890s, his supporters splintered. Some felt he should focus on other pressing political concerns of the day. Others preferred he continue to be the standard-bearer of the silver fight, and anything less was cowing to Eastern interests. He lost courage. He didn't have a lion's heart.

The Emerald Palace, where the Wizard resides, is of course, the White House—filled with acquiescing bureaucrats. The Wizard seems friendly and wants to help, yet he sends the four friends into the very den of the Witch of the West, who is no friend to their cause. The Wizard himself is in reality Marcus Alonzo Hanna, whom many saw as the "man behind the curtain" of McKinley's presidency. Hanna, from Ohio, was the ultimate backroom political boss of American history. He very much controlled Republican politics and, to a large extent, McKinley in the 1890s. The role of the Wizard having no real power but illusion is allegorical to politics being all about illusion.

The Wicked Witch of the West is President William McKinley, also from Ohio. How can someone from Ohio be the Wicked Witch of the West? Easy, if you're writing from Baum's point of view that everything was controlled by wicked New York City-based banking interests—then anything west of New York's Hudson River is "West." In those days, it was very common to refer to Minnesota and Wisconsin as part of the "Northwest." This is still why Northwest Airlines is based in Minnesota—same evolution of the word. We still refer to Ohio today as the Midwest. By contrast in the vernacular, the "mid-east" doesn't exist in America.

McKinley was staunchly pro-gold, pro-tariff and worse than Cleveland in the Populist view. (His annexation of Puerto Rico, Guam, the Philippines,

(Continued)

and Hawaii did little to endear him to his foes, who saw him as a greedy imperialist.) This Witch is anxious to get the silver shoes from Dorothy before she learns their true power, and tries to kill her (and the silver movement) off through a series of trials (the aforementioned annexations and Spanish-American War) meant to separate the four friends and the power they have as a united group. Glinda, the Good Witch of the South, waves her wand and resolves the foursome's problems, just as support from the South bolstered the Populist movement, before it ultimately died out, and Dorothy returned to Kansas, without her silver shoes.

The story is filled with more political and monetary allegory. The flying monkeys, the enslaved Winkies (nowhere to be found in MGM's version), the poppy field (golden), even the gifts the Wizard bestows on our heroes (a little liquid "courage" for the teetotaling lion—Bryan was a well-known Prohibitionist) didn't escape Baum's audience—they knew the meanings.

Don't believe me? There is a wonderful 1990 paper by Hugh Rockoff, "The 'Wizard of Oz' as a Monetary Allegory," which is available online or in your local library. Rockoff delves into more detail about the economic, monetary and political climate, along with the characters and narrative itself. Read that, and then re-read Baum's classic. It will be eye-opening for you. Sometimes even your favorite childhood stories aren't what they seem to be.

Source: Hugh Rockoff, "The 'Wizard of Oz' as a Monetary Allegory," *Journal of Political Economy* 98 (August 1990): 739–760.

Notes

Preface

1. CXO Advisory Group, "Guru Grades as of 06/30/2011." www.cxoadvisory
.com/gurus/.

Chapter 1—The Plain-Old Normal

1. Bloomberg Finance, L.P., as of 12/31/2010.
2. International Monetary Fund, *World Economic Outlook Database*, April 2011.
3. Ibid.
4. See note 2.
5. Bill Gross, "On the 'Course' to a New Normal," *Pimco Investment Outlook*
(September 2009), www.pimco.com/EN/Insights/Pages/Gross%20
Sept%20On%20the%20Course%20to%20a%20New%20Normal.aspx
(accessed 08/08/2011).
6. "Tech Turnaround Energizes Volunteers," *Charlotte Observer*, 12/13/2003.
7. "Welcome to the New Normal," *Fast Company* (04/30/2003), www.fastcompany
.com/magazine/70/3dlet.html (accessed 08/08/2011).
8. *Time* magazine cover (11/02/1987), www.time.com/time/covers/0,16641,
19871102,00.html (accessed 08/08/2011).
9. "Measuring the Economy by Realism, Not Pessimism," *Calgary Herald*
(01/07/1978).
10. "How Economies Grow," *New York Times* (06/15/1959).
11. US Bureau of Economic Analysis, "Gross Domestic Product Percent Change
From Preceding Period in Chained 2005 Dollars" (as of 05/26/2011).
12. "Produce More or Use Less," *Wall Street Journal* (10/20/1030).
13. US Bureau of Economic Analysis, "Gross Domestic Product Percent Change
From Preceding Period in Chained 2005 Dollars" (as of 05/26/2011).
14. Dakin Campbell, "Pimco's El Erian Says 'New Normal' Means Muted
Growth," *Bloomberg* (05/12/2009), www.bloomberg.com/apps/news?pid=
newsarchive&sid=abR5NmnjbwCQ&refer=home (accessed 08/08/2011);
Jennifer Ablan, "Pimco Says Slow Global Growth the 'New Normal,'" *Reuters*
(05/12/2009), www.reuters.com/article/2009/05/12/businesspro-us-pimco-
outlook-idUSTRE54B3UA20090512 (accessed 08/08/2011); Sam Mamudi,
"Boom Times Are Over," *MarketWatch* (05/28/2009), www.marketwatch.com/
story/pimcos-gross-boom-times-are-over (accessed 08/08/2011); Mohammed

El-Erian, "Life After the Financial Crisis," *BusinessWeek* (05/21/2009), www
.businessweek.com/magazine/content/09_22/b4133073646280.htm (accessed
08/08/2011).

15. US Bureau of Economic Analysis, as of 07/29/2011.
16. Thomson Reuters, MSCI World Index net returns from 03/09/2009 to
    06/09/2009; S&P 500 total returns from 03/09/2009 to 06/09/2009.
17. Thomson Reuters, MSCI World Index net returns from 03/09/2009 to
    03/09/2010; S&P 500 total returns from 03/09/2009 to 03/09/2010.
18. Thomson Reuters, MSCI Word Index net returns, S&P 500 total returns from
    03/09/2009 to 12/31/2010.
19. Alison Fitzgerald, "Obama Fears 'New Normal' of High Profits Without Job Growth,"
    Bloomberg (11/07/2010), www.businessweek.com/news/2010-11-07/obama-fears-
    new-normal-of-high-profits-without-job-growth.html (accessed 08/08/2011).
20. Tom Raum, "Higher Jobless Rate Could Be New Normal," *Press-Enterprise*
    (11/07/2009), www.pe.com/business/local/stories/PE_Biz_S_vanish08.3362a99
    .html (accessed 08/08/2011).
21. Joshua Zumbrun, "Strong Growth Could Come With High Unemployment,"
    Forbes (07/15/2009), www.forbes.com/2009/07/15/federal-reserve-economy-
    business-washington-unemployment.html (accessed 08/08/2011).
22. Stephen Gandel, "Is Inflation Causing Americans to Stop Spending?"
    Time (03/28/2011), http://curiouscapitalist.blogs.time.com/2011/03/28/
    is-inflation-causing-americans-to-stop-spending/ (accessed 08/08/2011).
23. Ken Fisher, "Don't Be Distracted by Monkey Business," *Forbes* (11/04/2010),
    www.forbes.com/forbes/2010/1122/investing-portfolio-strategy-ken-fisher-
    monkey-business.html (accessed 08/08/2011).
24. Michael J. Mandel, "The New Economy: It Works in America. Will It Go
    Global?" *BusinessWeek* (01/31/2000), http://nybw.businessweek.com/bwplus/
    icstory00.htm (accessed 08/08/2011).
25. "Analyst: 'This Is What We Call a Jobless Recovery,'" *Dallas Business Journal*,
    02/05/2010 www.bizjournals.com/dallas/stories/2010/02/01/daily35.html (accessed
    08/16/2011).
26. "Jobless Claims Fall Slightly, Trade Gap Widens," *Reuters* (06/10/2010),
    www.reuters.com/article/2010/06/10/us-usa-economy-joblessclaims-view-
    idUSTRE6592R120100610 (accessed 08/16/2011).
27. David Leonhardt, "US Jobless Rate at 5.9% in June; A Slight Increase," *New York
    Times* (07/06/2002), www.nytimes.com/2002/07/06/business/us-jobless-rate-at-
    5.9-in-june-a-slight-increase.html?scp=6&sq=david+leonhardt&st=nyt (accessed
    08/16/2011).
28. Sue Kirchoff, "Economic Reports Suggest Recovery Faltering," *Boston Globe*
    (11/02/2002).
29. "CFO Survey: Economic Recovery Accelerating," SmartPros.com (10/01/2003),
    http://accounting.smartpros.com/x40789.xml (accessed 08/16/2011).
30. Robert A. Rosenblatt and Stuart Silverstein, "State's December Jobless Rate
    Dips 0.4%; Analyst Says Picture Is Bleak," *Los Angeles Times* (01/19/1993),
    http://articles.latimes.com/1993-01-09/news/mn-1034_1_jobless-rate
    (accessed 08/16/2011).

31. Associated Press, "Jobless Rate Holding Fast at 7 Percent," *Times-News* (05/08/1993), http://news.google.com/newspapers?id=n90iAAAAIBAJ&sjid=0yQEAAAAIBAJ&pg=6312,1930260&dq=jobless+recovery+robert+reich+clear+evidence&hl=en (accessed 08/16/2011).

32. Julia Lawlor, "More Jobs, But Not Good Ones," *USA Today* (09/07/1993).

33. US Bureau of Labor Statistics.

34. Kathy Partin, "Cooper Says Program Cutbacks Hurt, But Economy Is the Real Problem," *Daily News* (06/04/1983), http://news.google.com/newspapers?id=0SNCAAAAIBAJ&sjid=qaoMAAAAIBAJ&pg=3632,3820285&dq=economy+is+the+real+problem&hl=en (accessed 08/16/2011).

35. "Jobless Recovery?" *New York Times* (11/27/1938), http://query.nytimes.com/mem/archive/pdf?res=F30713FF3A581A7A93C5AB178AD95F4C8385F9 (accessed 08/16/2011).

36. Global Financial Data, Inc., S&P 500 total return from 12/31/2009 to 12/31/2010; Thomson Reuters, MSCI World net return from 12/31/2009 to 12/31/2010; US Bureau of Economic Analysis; International Monetary Fund.

37. "Stock Market's Nose Dive Fuels Fears of 'Double-Dip' Recession," *Washington Times* (07/13/2002).

38. Sue Kirchoff, "GDP Grew a Weak 1.1% in Quarter Anemic Showing Stirs Worries of Double-Dip Recession," *Boston Globe* (08/01/2002).

39. Associated Press, "Markets Spooked by Possibility of Double-Dip," *USA Today* (08/02/2001).

40. David Leonhardt, "Recession, Then a Boom? Maybe Not This Time," *New York Times* (12/30/2001) http://select.nytimes.com/gst/abstract.html?res=F50C1FFE34550C738FDDAB0994D9404482 (accessed 08/16/2011).

41. Ibid.

42. Associated Press, "Double Dip Recession Is Feared," *Tuscaloosa News* (07/26/1991), http://news.google.com/newspapers?id=PDgdAAAAIBAJ&sjid=xKUEAAAAIBAJ&pg=5012,6049403&dq=double+dip+recession&hl=en (accessed 08/16/2011).

43. Ibid.

44. See note 42.

45. Anne Swardsen, "Fed Fears Double-Dip Recession," *The Bulletin* (08/11/1991), http://news.google.com/newspapers?id=v45TAAAAIBAJ&sjid=loYDAAAAIBAJ&pg=1409,5328108&dq=double+dip+recession&hl=en (accessed 08/16/2011).

46. John D. McClain, "Retail Sales Bounce Back," *The Telegraph* (08/13/1991), http://news.google.com/newspapers?id=NxJgAAAAIBAJ&sjid=MZQMAAAAIBAJ&pg=6473,2393112&dq=double+dip+recession&hl=en (accessed 08/16/2011).

47. Associated Press, "National Economy Stalled on Brink of Double-Dip Recession," *Lodi News-Sentinel* (12/04/1991), http://news.google.com/newspapers?id=U5czAAAAIBAJ&sjid=HTIHAAAAIBAJ&pg=6556,4195055&dq=double+dip+recession&hl=en (accessed 08/16/2011).

48. Associated Press, "Economists Backing Off on Recession Predictions," *Youngstown Vindicator* (02/16/1981), http://news.google.com/newspapers?id=NxdcAAAAIBAJ&sjid=JIUNAAAAIBAJ&pg=3817,83991&dq=double+dip+recession&hl=en (accessed 08/16/2011).

49. Louis Rukeyser, "Whatever Happened to the Double-Dip Recession?" *Milwaukee Journal* (03/22/1981), http://news.google.com/newspapers?id=62caAAA AIBAJ&sjid=yCsEAAAAIBAJ&pg=6890,1651394&dq=whatever+happened+ to+the+double+dip+recession&hl=en (accessed 08/16/2011).

50. The National Bureau of Economic Research.

51. Through 12/31/2010. Performance is hypothetical and reflects *Forbes* magazine's calculation of simulated trades based on Ken Fisher's *Forbes* picks in *Forbes* magazine versus the S&P 500 Index during the same period. The hypothetical performance is based on transactions not made and is not an indication of actual performance by Ken Fisher or Fisher Investments. *Forbes'* calculation methodology is based solely on calendar years and assumes readers buy $10,000 of each of Ken Fisher's stock picks published in *Forbes* and immediately subtracts a 1 percent hypothetical brokerage commission. That is compared to putting $10,000 into an S&P 500 Index fund at the same date with no hypothetical commission and no other fees. Hypothetical performance does not include the impact of taxes or any other costs, if any.

For example, in 2004, Ken Fisher recommended 51 stocks in *Forbes* throughout the year. If $10,000 had been put into each stock, the total invested would have been $510,000, which would have appreciated by year-end 2004 to $574,000, a 12.6 percent appreciation. The same amount of money invested in the S&P 500 Index at those various times without a hypothetical commission would have totaled $548,000 for a return of 7.6% at the end of 2004. Using this methodology, Ken Fisher's *Forbes* stock picks tied the S&P 500 in 1998; lagged it in 1997, 2002 and 2008; beat it in 1996, 1999 to 2001, 2003 to 2007, 2009 and 2010; and beat it overall by an average annualized 5.3% for calendar years 1996 through year-end 2010. Past performance is no assurance of future returns. Investing in securities involves the risk of loss.

52. "About Language: Double Dip or Dead-Cat Bounce?" *New York Times* (11/10/1991), www.nytimes.com/1991/11/10/magazine/about-language-double-dip-or-dead-cat-bounce.html?src=pm (accessed 08/16/2011).

53. The National Bureau of Economic Research.

Chapter 2—Fooled by Averages

1. Alexandra Twin, "Recharging the Rally," *CNN Money* (03/26/2009), http://money.cnn.com/2009/03/26/markets/markets_newyork/index.htm (accessed 08/10/2011).

2 Adam Shell, "Many Wonder If This Stock Market Rally Is Sustainable," *USA Today* (05/08/2003), http://www.usatoday.com/money/markets/us/2003-05-07-markets_x.htm (accessed 09/12/2011).

3. David Craig and Beth Belton, "As Economy Slows, Dow Jumps 245 in Four Days," *USA Today* (08/03/1996).

4. "Wall Street Runs Hot, Cold and Down," *Chicago Tribune* (12/28/1990).

5. Paul Jarvis, "Investors Ponder 'Peaking Pattern,'" *Bangor Daily News* (05/06/1985).

6. Jack Lefler, "Paramount Market Question: Upswing Real Thing, Is It a Buying Point?" *Daytona Beach Morning Journal* (11/01/1962).

7. Global Financial Data, Inc., S&P 500 total return, annualized, 12/31/1925 to 12/31/2010.

8. Global Financial Data, Inc., MSCI World Index total return, 12/31/1969 to 12/31/2010.

9. Thomson Reuters, MSCI World Index net return, 10/31/2007 to 09/09/2009.

10. Thomson Reuters, MSCI World Index net returns and S&P 500 Index total returns from 03/09/2009 to 03/09/2010.

11. Ken Fisher, "Anticipate the V," *Forbes* (02/16/2009).

12. Sterling F. Green, "Apprehension Over Business Outlook Gone," *Gettysburg Times* (10/18/1958).

13. Robert E. Bedingfield, "The Stock Market: How It Works," *New York Times* (04/19/1959).

14. "Stocks Post Rise Despite Late Selling," *Chicago Daily Tribune* (07/13/1962).

15. "Volume Is Second Heaviest in History of NY Exchange," *Pittsburgh Post-Gazette* (01/29/1975).

16. Global Financial Data, Inc., S&P 500 Index total return from 10/3/1974 to 11/28/1980.

17. Associated Press, "Market Posts Moderate Gains," *Sumter Daily Item* (04/14/1982).

18. Global Financial Data, Inc., S&P 500 Index total return from 8/12/1982 to 8/25/1987.

19. Associated Press, "Stock Market," *Argus-Press* (08/13/1984).

20. "Market Dips With New Year Profit Sales," *Union Democrat* (01/02/1986).

21. Thomson Reuters, MSCI World Index net returns from 12/31/1985 to 12/31/1986; MSCI World Index net returns from 12/31/1985 to 12/31/1986.

22. "A Closing High: Dow Rises 21.96 to 3,397.99," *New York Times* (05/20/1992), http://select.nytimes.com/gst/abstract.html?res=F10613FD3F5D0C738EDDA C0894DA494D81 (accessed 08/10/2011).

23. Global Financial Data, Inc., S&P 500 Index total return from 10/11/1990 to 03/27/2000; Thomson Reuters, MSCI World Index net return from 09/28/1990 to 03/27/2000.

24. Associated Press, "Stocks Withstand Bond Sell-Off," *Milwaukee Sentinel* (03/29/1995).

25. Art Pine, "Greenspan Warns of Market's Surge," *Los Angeles Times* (02/27/1997), http://articles.latimes.com/1997-02-27/business/fi-32822_1_ stock-market/2 (accessed 08/10/2011).

26. Thomson Reuters, MSCI World Index net return from 12/05/1996 to 03/03/27/2000; Global Financial Data, Inc., S&P 500 Index total return from 12/05/1996 to 03/24/2000.

27. "Experts' Outlook," *Dallas Morning News* (07/01/2003).

28. Thomson Reuters, MSCI World Index net returns from 12/31/2002 to 12/31/2003; MSCI World Index net returns from 10/09/2002 to 10/31/2007.

29. Jeff Sommer, "Is the Recent Rally Irrational Exuberance?" *New York Times* (09/19/2009), www.nytimes.com/2009/09/20/business/economy/20mark.html (accessed 08/10/2011).

30. Patrice Hill, "Dow Rages Over 10,000; Economy Struggles," *Washington Times* (10/15/2009), www.washingtontimes.com/news/2009/oct/15/dow-rages-back-over-10000/ (accessed 08/10/2011).

31. Global Financial Data, Inc., S&P 500 Total Return Index from 12/31/1925 to 12/31/2010.
32. Global Financial Data, Inc., MSCI World Index net return from 12/31/1969 to 12/31/2010.
33. "Quantitative Analysis of Investor Behavior," Dalbar Inc. (March 2011).
34. Global Financial Data, Inc., S&P 500 Index total returns annualized from 12/31/1990 to 12/31/2010.

Chapter 3—Volatility Is Normal—and Volatile

1. Global Financial Data, Inc., S&P 500 Total Return Index, Thomson Reuters, MSCI World Index net return from 12/31/2008 to 12/31/2009 and from 12/31/2009 to 12/31/2010.
2. Dave Carpenter, "Can Stocks Put Together a Fourth-Quarter Drive?" MSNBC .com (10/01/2010), www.msnbc.msn.com/id/39446887/ns/business-stocks_ and_economy/ (accessed 10/10/2011).
3. Steven Pearlstein, "The Dust Hasn't Settled on Wall Street, But History's Already Repeating Itself," *The Washington Post* (07/31/2009), www.washington post.com/wp-dyn/content/article/2009/07/30/AR2009073004115.html (accessed 08/10/2011).
4. Global Financial Data, Inc., S&P 500 Total Return Index.
5. Ibid.
6. See note 4.
7. See note 4.
8. Global Financial Data, Inc., S&P 500 Total Return Index from 12/31/2008 to 12/31/2009.
9. Global Financial Data, Inc., S&P 500 Total Return Index from 12/31/1997 to 12/31/1998.
10. Global Financial Data, Inc., S&P 500 Total Return Index from 12/31/2009 to 12/31/2010.
11. See note 4.
12. Global Financial Data, Inc., S&P 500 Total Return Index from 12/31/1952 to 12/31/1953.
13. Global Financial Data, Inc., S&P 500 Total Return Index from 12/31/2004 to 12/31/2005.
14. Global Financial Data, Inc., S&P 500 Total Return Index from 12/31/1950 to 12/31/1951.
15. Global Financial Data, Inc., S&P 500 Total Return Index from 12/31/1972 to 12/31/1973.
16. Global Financial Data, Inc., S&P 500 Total Return Index from 12/31/2007 to 12/31/2009.
17. Thomson Reuters, S&P 500 total return from 12/31/2008 to 12/31/2009 and from 03/09/2009 to 12/31/2009.
18. Matthew Philips, "Fast, Loose, and Out of Control," *Newsweek* (05/31/2010), www.newsweek.com/2010/06/01/fast-loose-and-out-of-control.html (accessed 08/10/2011).
19. See note 4.

20. See note 4.
21. Global Financial Data, Inc., West Texas Intermediate Oil Price (US$/Barrel) and Onions, Average Price to Farmers (US$/CWT) from 12/31/1999 to 04/30/2011.
22. Thomson Reuters, S&P 500 total return.
23. See note 4.
24. See note 4.
25. Global Financial Data, Inc., S&P 500 total return from 12/31/1962 to 12/31/1963.
26. Global Financial Data, Inc., S&P 500 total return from 12/31/1935 to 12/31/1936, from 12/31/1936 to 12/31/1937, and from 12/31/1937 to 12/31/1938.
27. US Bureau of Economic Analysis.
28. Ibid.
29. See note 27.
30. See note 27.

Chapter 4—Secular Bear? (Secular) Bull!

1. David Rosenberg, "No Free Lunches in Debt-Fuelled Bear Rally," *Financial Times* (02/14/2011), www.ft.com/intl/cms/s/0/6563dda4-3845-11e0-8257-00144feabdc0.html#axzz1Mk78n3Oc (accessed 08/10/2011).
2. Thomson Reuters, MSCI World net returns from 10/09/2002 to 10/31/2007.
3. Thomson Reuters, S&P 500 total returns from 10/09/2002 to 10/09/2007.
4. Global Financial Data, Inc., Dow Jones Industrials Average price return from 12/31/1964 to 12/31/1981.
5. Ibid.
6. Global Financial Data, Inc., S&P 500 total return from 12/31/1964 to 12/31/1981.
7. Thomson Reuters, MSCI World net return from 12/31/2009 to 12/31/2010.
8. Thomson Reuters, S&P 500 total return and MSCI World net return from 12/31/1999 to 12/31/2009.
9. Thomson Reuters, S&P 500 total return and MSCI ACWI total return from 12/31/1999 to 12/31/2009.
10. Thomson Reuters, MSCI World net returns from 10/09/2002 to 10/31/2007; S&P 500 total returns from 10/09/2002 to 10/09/2007.
11. Global Financial Data, Inc., S&P 500 total return from 12/31/1964 to 12/31/1984.
12. Global Financial Data, Inc., S&P 500 total return from 12/31/1964 to 12/31/1989.
13. Gregg S. Fisher (no relation), "Stocks Versus Bonds and the Absurdity of Static Benchmarking," *Investment News* (09/27/2009), www.investmentnews.com/apps/pbcs.dll/article?AID=/20090927/REG/309279981 (accessed 08/10/2011).
14. Stephen Foley, "It Won't Take Much for Fears of a Lost American Decade to Become Reality," *The Independent* (07/31/2010), www.independent.co.uk/news/business/comment/stephen-foley-it-wont-take-much-for-fears-of-a-lost-american-decade-to-become-reality-2040075.html (accessed 08/10/2011).

15. Simon Kennedy, "Pimco's El-Erian Says Industrial Economies Risk 'Lost Decade,'" *Bloomberg Businessweek* (10/11/2010), www.businessweek.com/news/2010-10-11/pimco-s-el-erian-says-industrial-economies-risk-lost-decade-.html (accessed 08/10/2011).
16. Michael J. Mandel, "The New Economy," *BusinessWeek* (01/31/2000), www.businessweek.com/careers/content/jan1990/b3666002.htm (accessed 08/10/2011).
17. Bloomberg Finance, L.P. as of 12/31/2010.
18. Global Financial Data, Inc., S&P 500 total return from 12/31/1925 to 12/31/2010.
19. Global Financial Data, Inc., S&P 500 total return from 08/31/1929 to 08/31/1939.
20. Global Financial Data, Inc., S&P 500 total return from 08/31/1939 to 08/31/1949.
21. Global Financial Data, Inc., S&P 500 total return from 12/31/1925 to 12/31/2010.
22. Global Financial Data, Inc., S&P 500 total return from 12/31/1938 to 12/31/1948.
23. Global Financial Data, Inc., S&P 500 total return from 12/31/1928 to 12/31/1938.

Chapter 5—Debt and Deficient Thinking

1. *The Daily Southern Cross* (09/15/1868), 2.
2. "Is the US Going Broke?" *Time* (03/12/1972), www.time.com/time/covers/0,16641,19720313,00.html (accessed 08/09/2011).
3. "The Debt Bomb: The Worldwide Peril of Go-Go Lending," *Time* (01/10/1983), www.time.com/time/covers/0,16641,19830110,00.html (accessed 08/09/2011).
4. "Value-Added Tax for US," *Los Angeles Times* (02/18/1988), http://articles.latimes.com/1988-02-18/local/me-43252_1_tax-increases-tax-reform-value-added-tax (accessed 08/09/2011).
5. McArthur, "Bush Wants US to Borrow Its Way to Prosperity," *Toronto Star* (11/22/1991).
6. Stephanie Anderson-Forest, Ann Therese Palmer, Douglas Robson and Laura Cohn, "Will Refis Help Refloat the Economy?" *BusinessWeek* (04/02/2001), www.businessweek.com/magazine/content/01_14/b3726009.htm (accessed 08/09/2011).
7. Ian Verrende, "Japan's Catastrophic Economic Aftershock," *The Age* (03/15/2011), www.theage.com.au/business/japans-catastrophic-economic-aftershock-20110314-1bugs.html?skin=text-only (accessed 08/09/2011).
8. US Federal Reserve, as of 01/01/2011.
9. George H. Hemple, "The Postwar Quality of State and Local Debt," (National Bureau of Economic Research, 1971), www.nber.org/books/hemp71-1 (accessed 08/09/2011).
10. Ibid.

Chapter 6—Long-Term Love and Other Investing Errors

1. Ibbotson Associates, Small Stock Total Return Index and S&P 500 total return from 02/01/1926 to 12/31/2010.
2. Russell 2000, Russell 2000 Value, Russell 2000 Growth, MSCI EAFE; Barclays Aggregate, S&P/Citigroup Primary Growth, S&P/Citigroup Primary Value, S&P 500 Value from 12/31/1990 to 12/31/2010. All returns total returns except MSCI EAFE, which is net. S&P/Citigroup Primary Value index measures the performance of the value style of investing in large cap US stocks. The index is constructed by dividing the top 80% of all US stocks in terms of market capitalization into a Value index, using style. S&P/Citigroup Primary Growth index measures the performance of the growth style of investing in large cap US stocks. The index is constructed by dividing the top 80% of all US stocks in terms of market capitalization into a Growth index, using style.
3. Jeremy Warner, "High Energy Prices Need Not Mean Doom," *Sydney Morning Herald* (01/21/2011), www.smh.com.au/business/high-energy-prices-need-not-mean-doom-20110120-19y2e.html (accessed 08/09/2011).
4. Global Financial Data, Inc., USA 10-Year Government Bond Total Return Index, S&P 500 total from 12/31/1925 to 12/31/2010.
5. Ibbotson & Associates, NCREIF Property Total Return Index from 12/31/1977 to 12/31/2010.
6. Thomson Reuters, MSCI World Index net return from 12/31/1977 to 12/31/2010; Global Financial Data, Inc., S&P 500 total return 12/31/1977 to 12/31/2010.
7. Federal Housing Finance Agency's FHFA Home Price Index (all transaction, quarterly data) from 12/31/1977 to 12/31/2010.
8. Global Financial Data, Inc., MSCI World Index net return, S&P 500 total return, Gold Bullion Price–New York (US$/Ounce) from 11/30/1973 to 6/30/2011.
9. Global Financial Data, Inc., USA 10-Year Government Bond Total Return Index from 11/30/1973 to 6/30/2011.

Chapter 7—Poli-Ticking

1. "Stock Report: Today's Stock Market Resides in the State of Indecision," *News Tribune* (09/10/1992).
2. "Parties Battle Over Best Wall Street Results," *Asbury Park Press* (08/16/2009).
3. Nick Poulos, "Does Stock Market Action Predict Presidential Vote?" *Chicago Tribune* (12/12/1971).
4. Richard Benedetto, "In Poll, Dems Score Better on Key Issues," *USA Today* (10/31/1996).
5. Danny King, "Would Higher Taxes for the Wealthy Help or Hurt the US Economy?" *Daily Finance* (09/21/2010), www.dailyfinance.com/2010/09/21/expiring-tax-cuts-for-wealthy-americans/?icid=sphere_copyright (accessed 08/09/2011).
6. Global Financial Data, Inc., S&P 500 Total Return Index from 12/31/1925 to 12/31/2010.
7. Ibid.

8. See note 6.
9. Daniel Kahneman and Amos Tversky, "Prospect Theory: An Analysis of Decision Under Risk," *Econometrica* 47(2) (March 1979): 263–292.
10. Global Financial Data, Inc., S&P 500 Total Return Index from 12/31/1925 to 12/31/2010.
11. Ibid.
12. See Note 10.
13. Global Financial Data Inc., S&P 500 Total Return Index from 12/31/1976 to 12/31/1977.
14. "Presidential Approval Tracker," *USA Today*, www.usatoday.com/news/washington/presidential-approval-tracker.htm (accessed 08/30/2011).
15. Global Financial Data Inc., S&P 500 Total Return Index from 12/31/1995 to 12/31/1996.
16. See note 10.
17. See note 10.
18. See note 10.
19. See note 10.
20. See note 10.

Chapter 8—It's (Always Been) a Global World, After All

1. Thomson Reuters, *MSCI All Country World Index*, as of 06/30/2011.
2. The Investment Company Institute, as of 12/31/2010.
3. Thomson Reuters.
4. Morningstar, as of 08/01/2011.
5. Thomson Reuters, MSCI All Country World Index, as of 06/30/2011.
6. Thomson Reuters, MSCI All Country World Index, as of 06/30/2011.
7. Thomson Reuters, MSCI All Country World Index, as of 06/30/2011.
8. Thomson Reuters, MSCI EAFE Index net return, S&P 500 Index total return from 12/31/1969 to 12/31/2010.
9. US Department of State.
10. Global Financial Data, Inc., S&P 500 Index price return from 08/13/1981 to 08/13/1992.
11. Thomson Reuters, MSCI Australia, MSCI Austria, MSCI Belgium, MSCI Canada, MSCI Denmark, MSCI Finland, MSCI France, MSCI Germany, MSCI Greece, MSCI Hong Kong, MSCI Ireland, MSCI Italy, MSCI Japan, MSCI Netherlands, MSCI New Zealand, MSCI Norway, MSCI Portugal, MSCI Singapore, MSCI Spain, MSCI Sweden, MSCI Switzerland, MSCI UK, MSCI USA, all total return indexes from 12/31/1989 to 12/31/2010.

Index

211